ASIAN POLITICAL, ECONOMIC AND SOCIAL ISSUES

SOUTHEAST ASIA

EXAMINATIONS OF U.S. AND CHINESE ECONOMIC ENGAGEMENT

ASIAN POLITICAL, ECONOMIC AND SOCIAL ISSUES

Additional books in this series can be found on Nova's website under the Series tab.

Additional e-books in this series can be found on Nova's website under the e-book tab.

ASIAN POLITICAL, ECONOMIC AND SOCIAL ISSUES

SOUTHEAST ASIA

EXAMINATIONS OF U.S. AND CHINESE ECONOMIC ENGAGEMENT

PAULINE NELSON
EDITOR

nova publishers
New York

NOTICE TO THE READER

Library of Congress Cataloging-in-Publication Data

ISBN: 978-1-63484-696-7

Published by Nova Science Publishers, Inc. † New York

CONTENTS

PREFACE

Both the United States and China seek to deepen their economic engagement with the 10 Association of Southeast Asian Nations (ASEAN) members: Brunei Darussalam, Burma, Cambodia, Indonesia, Laos, Malaysia, the Philippines, Singapore, Thailand, and Vietnam. ASEAN countries are seeking to further integrate their economies and create an economic community by the end of 2015. According to International Monetary Fund data, if ASEAN countries were a single nation, their collective 2014 GDP would represent the seventh largest economy in the world. In 2011, the President announced a renewed focus—known as the rebalance—on the Asia-Pacific region. The U.S. Department of State and U.S. Agency for International Development prepared a 5-year strategy for the rebalance. This book examines what available data indicate about U.S. and Chinese trade and investment with ASEAN countries and what actions the U.S. and Chinese governments have taken to further economic engagement with these countries.

In: Southeast Asia
Editor: Pauline Nelson

ISBN: 978-1-63484-696-7

Chapter 1

SOUTHEAST ASIA: TRENDS IN U.S. AND CHINESE ECONOMIC ENGAGEMENT*

United States Government Accountability Office

WHY GAO DID THIS STUDY

Both the United States and China seek to deepen their economic engagement with the 10 ASEAN members: Brunei Darussalam, Burma, Cambodia, Indonesia, Laos, Malaysia, the Philippines, Singapore, Thailand, and Vietnam. ASEAN countries are seeking to further integrate their economies and create an economic community by the end of 2015. According to International Monetary Fund data, if ASEAN countries were a single nation, their collective 2014 GDP would represent the seventh largest economy in the world. In 2011, the President announced a renewed focus—known as the rebalance—on the Asia-Pacific region. The U.S. Department of State and U.S. Agency for International Development prepared a 5-year strategy for the rebalance.

GAO was asked to examine the United States' and China's economic engagement in the region. This report examines (1) what available data indicate about U.S. and Chinese trade and investment with ASEAN countries and (2) what actions the U.S. and Chinese governments have taken to further

* This is an edited, reformatted and augmented version of a United States Government Accountability Office publication, No. GAO-15-724, dated August 2015.

economic engagement with these countries. GAO analyzed publicly available economic data and Chinese government documents and reviewed documentation from 10 U.S. agencies. GAO also interviewed U.S. officials and private sector representatives.

Technical comments on a draft of this report from several agencies were incorporated by GAO where appropriate. GAO is not making any recommendations in this report.

WHAT GAO FOUND

China has surpassed the United States in goods trade with Association of Southeast Asian Nations (ASEAN) countries and trades a similar amount of services, but U.S. investment exceeds reported Chinese investment. China surpassed the United States in goods trade with ASEAN countries in 2007. In 2014, China's total goods trade of $480 billion was more than twice the U.S. total goods trade of $220 billion. Although China is their largest outside trading partner, ASEAN countries trade more with each other. Limited available data indicate that in 2011, the United States and China each traded about $37 billion in services with ASEAN countries. From 2007 through 2012, U.S. foreign direct investment flows to ASEAN countries of $96 billion exceeded China's reported $23 billion.

The United States and China are furthering economic engagement with ASEAN countries in several ways.

- **Trade agreements.** The United States has a free trade agreement (FTA) with one ASEAN country, Singapore, while China has an FTA with all 10 ASEAN countries. The United States and China are each party to separate regional trade agreement negotiations—the United States through the Trans-Pacific Partnership and China through the Regional Comprehensive Economic Partnership. China's existing FTAs do not address aspects of trade addressed in the U.S.-Singapore FTA, such as intellectual property, the environment, and labor rights.
- **Support for firms.** From 2009 through 2014, U.S. agencies provided approximately $6 billion in financing for U.S. firms in ASEAN countries. China reports billions of dollars more in financing than the United States worldwide, but data on China's financing in Southeast Asia are unavailable.

- **Support for regional integration.** In fiscal years 2009 through 2013, U.S. agencies provided $536 million in trade capacity building assistance to ASEAN countries. China has promised tens of billions of dollars for infrastructure development through new funds and multilateral institutions like the Asian Infrastructure Investment Bank, expected to begin operations in 2015.

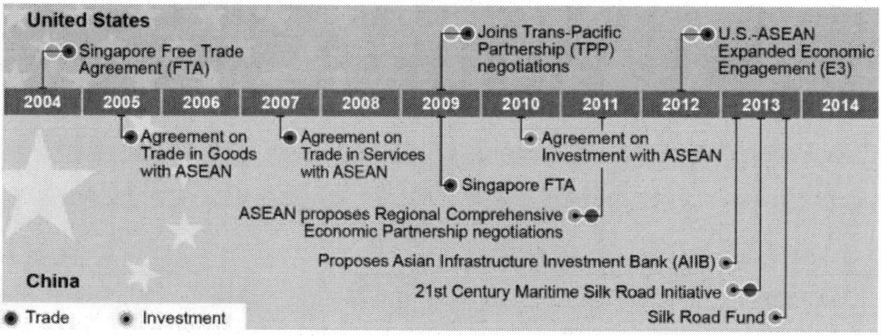

Source: GAO analysis of Chinese and U.S. documents. | GAO-15-724.

Key U.S. and Chinese Trade and Investment Initiatives with Association of Southeast Asian Nations (ASEAN) Countries, 2004 to 2014.

ABBREVIATIONS

ADB	Asian Development Bank
AIIB	Asian Infrastructure Investment Bank
APEC	Asia-Pacific Economic Cooperation
ASEAN	Association of Southeast Asian Nations
BEA	U.S. Bureau of Economic Analysis
China Ex-Im	Export-Import Bank of China
CLMV	Cambodia, Laos, Burma (Myanmar), and Vietnam
Commerce	U.S. Department of Commerce
DAC	Development Assistance Committee
EU	European Union
Ex-Im	U.S. Export-Import Bank
FDI	foreign direct investment
FSO	foreign service officer
FTA	free trade agreement
FTAAP	Free Trade Area of the Asia-Pacific

GDP	gross domestic product
IMF	International Monetary Fund
LES	locally employed staff
MCC	Millennium Challenge Corporation
ODA	official development assistance
OECD	Organisation for Economic Co-operation and Development
OPIC	Overseas Private Investment Corporation
RCEP	Regional Comprehensive Economic Partnership
Sinosure	China Export & Credit Insurance Corporation
State	U.S. Department of State
TCB	trade capacity building
TIFA	Trade and Investment Framework Agreement
TPP	Trans-Pacific Partnership
UN	United Nations
USAID	U.S. Agency for International Development
USDA	U.S. Department of Agriculture
USTDA	U.S. Trade and Development Agency
USTR	Office of the United States Trade Representative
WTO	World Trade Organization

* * *

August 13, 2015

The Honorable Steve Chabot
Chairman
Committee on Small Business
House of Representatives
The Honorable Matt Salmon
Chairman
The Honorable Brad Sherman
Ranking Member
Subcommittee on Asia and the Pacific
Committee on Foreign Affairs
House of Representatives

Southeast Asia is a growing economic power. The 10 members of the Association of Southeast Asian Nations (ASEAN) have a combined gross domestic product (GDP) of about $2.5 trillion and population of about 620 million.[1] Through ASEAN, these countries are seeking to further integrate their economies and create an economic community by the end of 2015.

Both the United States and China have signaled a greater interest in expanding their economic engagement in Southeast Asia through, for example, proposed and expanded free trade agreements (FTA).[2] In 2011, the President announced a renewed focus, known as the rebalance, on the Asia-Pacific region, including Southeast Asia. In 2014, in response to a congressional mandate,[3] the U.S. Department of State (State) and U.S. Agency for International Development (USAID) issued a 5-year strategy for the rebalance. The strategy seeks, among other things, to increase economic growth and trade in the Asia-Pacific and to strengthen regional organizations such as ASEAN. In 2013, China proposed an ASEAN-China cooperation framework designed to build political consensus on deepening their relationship and focused on economic development and mutual benefits.

You asked us to review the nature of the United States' and China's economic engagement in Southeast Asia. This report examines (1) what available data indicate about U.S. and Chinese trade and investment with ASEAN countries and (2) what actions the U.S. and Chinese governments have taken to further economic engagement with these countries.[4]

To examine the United States' and China's engagement with ASEAN countries, we analyzed publicly available data on U.S. and Chinese trade in goods, trade in services, and foreign direct investment. All dollar figures in this report are in nominal terms unless otherwise specified. To determine the extent to which U.S. and Chinese firms compete in ASEAN countries, we analyzed data from the U.S. Department of Commerce (Commerce), the World Bank, and the Asian Development Bank (ADB). To identify actions that the U.S. and Chinese governments have taken to further economic engagement, we reviewed U.S., Chinese, and ASEAN trade agreements and documents and official Chinese statements. We conducted fieldwork in two ASEAN countries, Indonesia and Vietnam, and interviewed officials from U.S. and third-country agencies and private sector representatives.[5] We tried to arrange visits with Chinese government officials in the ASEAN countries we visited and in Washington, D.C.; however, they were unable to accommodate our requests for a meeting. To assess the reliability of data, where possible, we cross-checked the data with other sources, evaluated the data for internal consistency, and consulted with U.S. officials. We consider the data we present to be reliable for our purposes and have noted caveats as appropriate regarding the limitations in some data. See appendix I for additional information about our scope and methodology.

We conducted this performance audit from April 2014 to August 2015 in accordance with generally accepted government auditing standards. Those standards require that we plan and perform the audit to obtain sufficient, appropriate evidence to provide a reasonable basis for our findings and conclusions based on our audit objectives. We believe that the evidence obtained provides a reasonable basis for our findings and conclusions based on our audit objectives.

BACKGROUND

Southeast Asian nations have growing populations and economies. According to a 2014 study by the Asian Development Bank Institute, the combined populations of ASEAN countries are projected to reach 700 million by 2030.[6] This study also found that ASEAN countries' collective nominal GDP increased by an average of 5.7 percent annually from 1992 to 2013, despite the Asian financial crisis in 1997 and 1998 and the global financial slowdown in 2008 and 2009. According to International Monetary Fund (IMF) data, if ASEAN countries were a single nation, their collective 2014 GDP would represent the seventh largest economy in the world. However, a study by the Economic Research Institute for ASEAN and East Asia found that while the average poverty level in ASEAN countries declined from about 45 percent in 1990 to about 16 percent in 2010, about 95 million people in these countries in 2010 lived in poverty.[7] In addition, a study by the Institute of Southeast Asian Studies has estimated that ASEAN countries would need about $600 billion from 2010 to 2020 to meet their infrastructure investment needs.[8]

ASEAN countries are located astride key sea lanes between the Persian Gulf and the economic centers of East Asia. The U.S. Energy Information Administration, based on a 2011 United Nations (UN) Conference on Trade and Development Review of Maritime Transport, estimated that more than half of the world's annual merchant fleet tonnage passed through the Straits of Malacca, Sunda, and Lombok on to the South China Sea in 2010 and that about 15 million barrels of oil passed through the Strait of Malacca between Singapore and Indonesia each day in 2013.[9] The South China Sea also has important fishing areas and is thought to be rich in oil and natural gas reserves. Figure 1 shows the names and locations of the ASEAN countries.

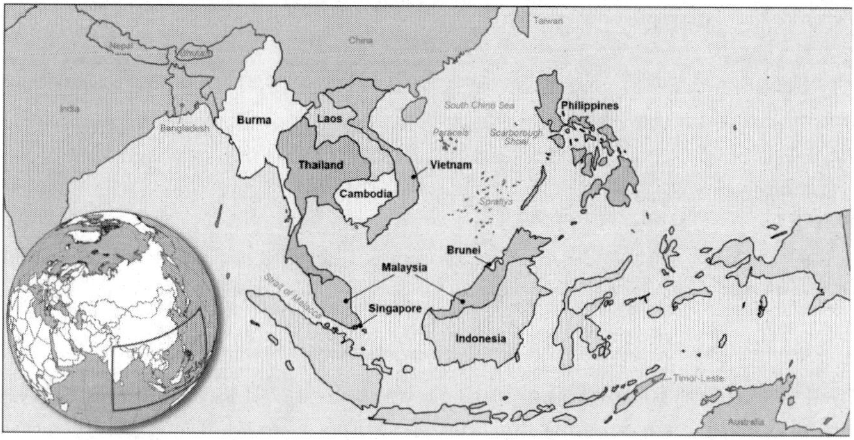

Source: Map Resources (maps). | GAO-15-724.

Figure 1. Countries in the Association of Southeast Asian Nations (ASEAN).

History of ASEAN

The leaders of Indonesia, Malaysia, the Philippines, Singapore, and Thailand founded ASEAN in 1967 to accelerate economic growth, social progress, and cultural development in the region through joint projects and cooperation. In 1976, ASEAN countries agreed to the Treaty of Amity and Cooperation in Southeast Asia, which called for peaceful resolution of disputes and mutual respect for the independence, sovereignty, equality, territorial integrity, and national identity of all nations. Also in 1976, ASEAN established the ASEAN Secretariat, an administrative body with representatives from each member nation, in Jakarta, Indonesia, to provide greater efficiency in the coordination of ASEAN organizations and more effective implementation of projects and activities. ASEAN's membership expanded to include Brunei in 1984, Vietnam in 1995, Laos and Burma in 1997, and Cambodia in 1999.

ASEAN amended the Treaty of Amity and Cooperation in 1998 to permit states outside Southeast Asia to accede to the treaty with the approval of all 10 members. China acceded to the treaty in 2003. The United States acceded to the treaty in July 2009 and the following year became the first non-ASEAN country to establish a dedicated mission to ASEAN. In 2011, the United States appointed its first resident Ambassador to ASEAN. China established a mission to ASEAN in October 2012.

ASEAN Country Economies

Economic development in the first six ASEAN members—Brunei, Indonesia, Malaysia, the Philippines, Singapore, and Thailand, known as the ASEAN 6—is generally more advanced than in the newer members—Cambodia, Laos, Burma (Myanmar), and Vietnam, known as the CLMV countries (see table 1). The business environment also varies significantly across ASEAN countries. In Transparency International's 2014 Corruption Perceptions Index, which measures perceived levels of public sector corruption among 175 countries and territories, ASEAN countries' rankings ranged from 7 for Singapore to 156 for Cambodia and Burma.[10] The World Bank's 2014 ease of doing business ranking of 189 economies ranked Singapore at 1, as having the most business-friendly regulations, and Burma at 177, the lowest ranked ASEAN country.[11]

Governance of ASEAN

As stated in ASEAN's Charter, ASEAN emphasizes noninterference in the domestic matters of its members and respect for their sovereignty and territorial integrity.[12] According to U.S. officials, as well as officials at the ASEAN missions of other countries, the primary mode of decision making in ASEAN is consensus. Further, according to an ADB study, the Secretariat does not direct ASEAN but instead plays a coordinating and facilitating role.[13] The Chair of ASEAN rotates annually among members; Burma served as the 2014 Chair and Malaysia as the 2015 Chair. Biannual ASEAN summit meetings are used to make decisions on key issues, provide policy guidance, and set the objectives of ASEAN.

ASEAN Economic and Connectivity Initiatives

In 2003, ASEAN leaders adopted a plan to create an ASEAN Community by 2015, comprising security, sociocultural, and economic communities. According to the ASEAN Economic Community Blueprint (the Blueprint), the ASEAN Economic Community will be a

- single market and production base that includes the free flow of goods, services, investment, capital, and skilled labor;

Table 1. Selected Economic Indicators for ASEAN Countries, 2014

Country	GDP per capita	GDP[a] (dollars in billions)	Population (millions)	Ranking in Transparency International's 2014 Corruption Perceptions Index of 175 countries/territories[b]	Ranking in World Bank's Ease of Doing Business Index of 189 economies[c]
ASEAN-6 countries					
Singapore	$56,319	$308	5.5	7	1
Brunei	36,607	15	0.4	Not ranked[d]	101
Malaysia	10,804	327	30.3	50	18
Thailand	5,445	374	68.7	85 (tie)	26
Indonesia	3,534	889	251.5	107	114
Philippines	2,865	285	99.4	85 (tie)	95
CLMV countries					
Vietnam	2,053	186	90.6	119	78
Laos	1,693	12	6.9	145	148
Burma	1,221	63	51.4	156 (tie)	177
Cambodia	1,081	17	15.3	156 (tie)	135
Total	$3,991	$2,475	620		

Legend: ASEAN = Association of Southeast Asian Nations. CLMV = Cambodia, Laos, Burma (Myanmar), and Vietnam. GDP = gross domestic product.

Source: GAO analysis of data from the International Monetary Fund's World Economic Outlook; Transparency International's Corruptions Perceptions Index, 2013 and 2014; and the World Bank's Doing Business 2015. | GAO-15-724.

Note: Some values shown represent estimates by the International Monetary Fund (IMF).

[a]Values are based on GDP in national currency converted to U.S. dollars using market exchange rates (yearly average). Exchange rate projections are provided by country economists for the group of other emerging market and developing countries.

[b]Transparency International is a global organization that publishes a corruption perceptions index based on expert opinion from around the world. The index measures the perceived level of public sector corruption, where a ranking of 1 indicates the lowest level of perceived corruption relative to other countries included in the index.

[c]The World Bank publishes an annual report that investigates each country's regulations that enhance or constrain business activity. The report attempts to track and measure the ease of doing business, trade, or exchange in each country.

[d]Brunei was not ranked in 2014 but was ranked 38 of 177 countries and territories in 2013.

- highly competitive economic region that includes consumer protection and regional cooperation for intellectual property rights;
- region of equitable economic development based on inclusive growth and narrowing the development gap; and

- region fully integrated into the global economy that negotiates for FTAs and trade facilitation.

ASEAN established a monitoring mechanism called the ASEAN Economic Community scorecard to report the progress of implementing various measures and to identify implementation gaps and challenges. According to a 2013 ADB study of progress in achieving the ASEAN Economic Community, a significant milestone of economic integration has been the substantial progress in tariff liberalization, but removal of nontariff barriers, such as import bans and subsidies, new import procedures and requirements, and technical barriers, remain as major impediments.[14]

In 2010, ASEAN adopted the Master Plan on ASEAN Connectivity, which envisioned enhancing intraregional connectivity to encourage trade, investment, tourism, people-to-people exchanges, and development. The plan identifies needed improvements to physical connectivity (e.g., roads, rail, power supply, and port facilities); institutional connectivity (e.g., mutual recognition arrangements for movement of skilled labor in the region and harmonization of rules, regulations, procedures, and standards); and people-to-people connectivity (e.g., reducing visa requirements and enhancing training opportunities and outreach).

U.S. Goals for Southeast Asia

In late 2011, the President announced that the United States would rebalance its worldwide engagement to include a greater focus on the Asia-Pacific region. In April 2014, pursuant to a mandate in the Department of State, Foreign Operations and Related Programs Appropriations Act, 2014,[15] State and USAID provided Congress with a strategy for the rebalance that states the following goals for the region:

- Deepen U.S. security ties and alliances in the region to, among other things, deter and defend against threats to the region and the United States and resolve disputes peacefully.
- Advance U.S. prosperity and inclusive economic growth in the region through the expansion of U.S. exports and investment, increased regional economic integration, and sustainable development.
- Strengthen partnerships with China and emerging partners to, among other things, promote trade and economic growth.

- Shape an effective regional architecture of robust regional institutions and multilateral agreements to strengthen regional stability and economic growth.
- Support sustainable development, democracy, and human rights by advancing regional commitment to democratic development and human rights and addressing health threats and climate change.

In addition, other U.S. agencies have stated goals specific to the region. USAID's Regional Development Mission for Asia seeks, for example, to increase regional institutions' ability to promote sustainable and inclusive regional growth. The Secretary of Commerce has stated that the economic dimension of the rebalance includes deepening trade and investment ties with existing partners; working multilaterally to build both the hard and soft infrastructure necessary for growth of emerging partners; and building new mechanisms to establish a level playing field for commerce across the region, such as the proposed Trans-Pacific Partnership (TPP) FTA. TPP is currently being negotiated by the Office of the United States Trade Representative (USTR). Other agencies also work to promote U.S. economic engagement in Southeast Asia. (See app. II for more information about selected U.S. entities' roles and responsibilities and areas of involvement in ASEAN countries.)

Chinese Goals for Southeast Asia

Chinese government leaders have stated goals regarding Southeast Asia that emphasize regional connectivity as well as mutual benefit and noninterference. For example, in 2013, Chinese President Xi Jinping spoke of increasing engagement and rapport with China's neighbors to foster China's development while benefitting countries on its periphery.[16] Chinese leaders also regularly refer to the Five Principles of Peaceful Coexistence, originally espoused in a 1954 agreement between China and India: mutual respect for sovereignty and territorial integrity, mutual nonaggression, noninterference, equality and mutual benefit, and peaceful coexistence. Moreover, at the 16th ASEAN-China Summit in 2013, Premier Li Keqiang proposed a framework for cooperation between China and ASEAN, known as the 2 + 7 cooperation framework, with a stated goal of deepening cooperation by focusing on economic development and expanding mutual benefit.[17]

China has also articulated policy regarding Southeast Asia in two documents. China's 2011-2015 Five Year Plan emphasizes developing infrastructure and other connections with neighboring countries, improving the quality of Chinese exports instead of export volume, increasing China's level of investment in other countries in mutually beneficial ways, and increasing its influence in international economic and financial institutions. A 2014 Chinese government white paper on foreign aid states that China actively promotes cooperation between developing nations while seeking mutually beneficial results and respecting other countries' development paths.[18] According to the paper, China's assistance to ASEAN countries has focused on narrowing development gaps within ASEAN by funding infrastructure construction, supporting agricultural development, and providing technical training. (App. II provides more information about selected Chinese agencies' roles and responsibilities and areas of involvement in Southeast Asia.)

China has claimed sovereignty over the islands of the South China Sea and has illustrated its claims by marking a "nine dash line" on its maps that encircles most of the South China Sea and its land features, including the Paracels and Spratlys. The ASEAN countries of Vietnam, Brunei, Malaysia, Indonesia, and the Philippines have competing claims with China and with each other. China has also conducted dredging operations to create new above-water features in the South China Sea, raising tensions between China and ASEAN countries with interests in the South China Sea.

China Has Surpassed the United States in Trade in Goods with ASEAN Countries and Trades a Similar Amount of Services, but U.S. Investment Exceeds China's

Chinese trade in goods with ASEAN countries has grown rapidly since 2001, surpassing U.S. trade in goods since 2007. Most of the goods that the United States and China trade with ASEAN countries are for industrial use. Although the United States and China are important trading partners of ASEAN countries, trade among ASEAN countries exceeds their trade with either the United States or China. Available data, though limited, indicate that the total value of U.S. trade in services with ASEAN countries is similar to the value of China's but U.S. foreign direct investment (FDI) in ASEAN countries has exceeded China's FDI. U.S. FDI was concentrated in four of the ASEAN 6 countries—Indonesia, Malaysia, Singapore, and Thailand—and more Chinese FDI was in the CLMV countries—Cambodia, Laos, Burma (Myanmar), and

Vietnam. While Chinese and U.S. firms compete in ASEAN countries, available data indicate that U.S. firms compete more directly with firms from Europe, South Korea, and Japan.

China's Total Trade in Goods with ASEAN Countries Surpassed the United States' in 2007, but Neither Predominates in the Region

Chinese trade in goods with ASEAN countries has surpassed U.S. trade in goods and has grown as a share of China's total trade in goods, while U.S. trade in goods with ASEAN countries has declined as a share of total U.S. trade in goods. Both U.S. and Chinese firms compete with many other countries for the ASEAN market. U.S. and Chinese trade in goods with ASEAN countries reflects these countries' inclusion in global supply chains.

Chinese Goods Trade with ASEAN Countries Has Grown More Rapidly Than U.S. Goods Trade

In 2014, China's total goods trade with ASEAN countries was more than double that of the United States: $480 billion for China and $220 billion for the United States. In 1994 through 2014, Chinese total trade in goods with ASEAN countries grew much more rapidly than U.S. total trade in goods with ASEAN countries.

- In 2007, China surpassed the United States in total goods trade with ASEAN countries, and the gap has continued to grow.
- Chinese imports from ASEAN countries surpassed U.S. imports from ASEAN countries in 2008. In 2014, China imported $208 billion of goods from ASEAN countries, and the United States imported $142 billion.
- Chinese exports to ASEAN countries surpassed U.S. exports in 2005. In 2014, China exported $272 billion of goods to ASEAN countries, and the United States exported $79 billion.

After China acceded to the World Trade Organization (WTO) in 2001, Chinese goods trade increased worldwide, and at a faster rate in ASEAN countries. Chinese goods trade in ASEAN countries increased in nominal terms every year except 2009. The United States has run a trade deficit with

ASEAN countries in every year from 1994 through 2014, while China had a trade deficit or slight surplus with ASEAN countries from 1994 through 2011 before running a growing surplus from 2012 through 2014. In 2014, China had a goods trade surplus of $64 billion with ASEAN countries, while the United States had a goods trade deficit of $63 billion.

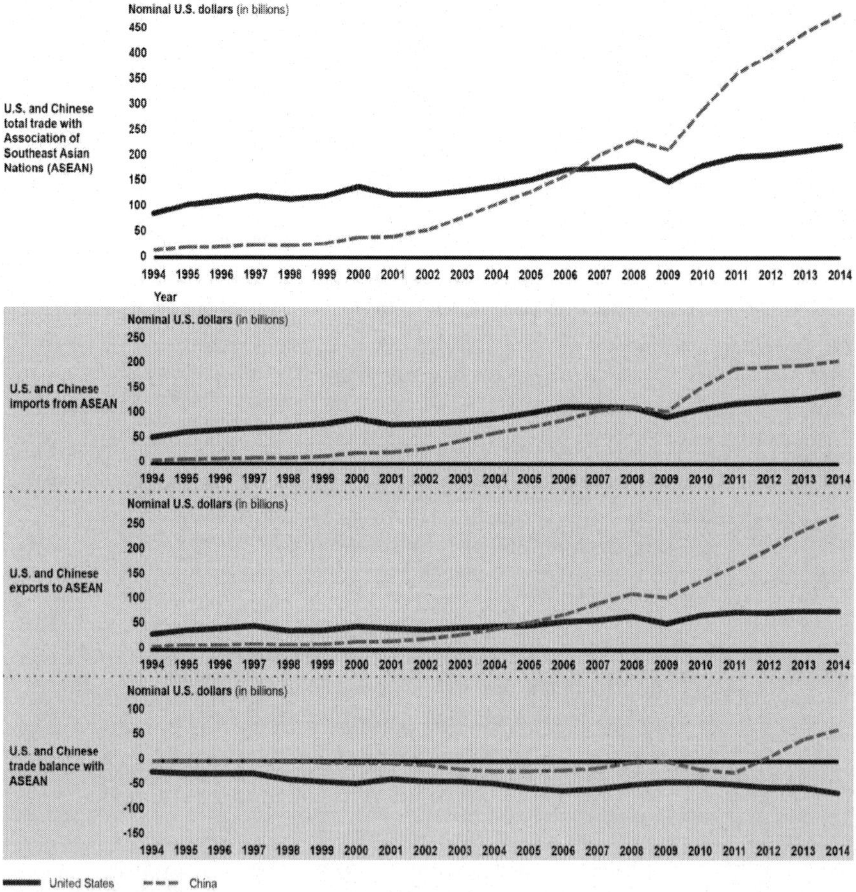

Source: GAO analysis of U.S. and Chinese data from the United Nations Commodity Trade database. | GAO-15-724.

Note: The trade values shown are nominal—that is, not adjusted for inflation. Changes in values over time are due in part to changes in the prices of traded goods.

Figure 2. U.S. and Chinese Trade in Goods with ASEAN Countries, 1994-2014.

Figure 2 shows the growth of U.S. and Chinese trade in goods with ASEAN countries from 1994 through 2014.

The relative importance of trade in goods with ASEAN countries since 1994 has increased for China but decreased for the United States. From 1994 through 2014, Chinese trade in goods with ASEAN countries rose from 6.1 percent to 11.2 percent of total Chinese trade in goods. In contrast, during the same period, U.S. trade in goods with ASEAN countries fell from 7.2 percent to 5.5 percent of total U.S. trade in goods.

Most Goods That the United States and China Trade with ASEAN Countries Are for Industrial Use

Most of the goods that the United States and China trade with ASEAN countries are goods for industrial use, reflecting ASEAN countries' integration into the U.S. and Chinese global supply chains.[19]

- **Total trade.** U.S. and Chinese trade in industrial goods (capital and intermediate goods) with ASEAN countries represented, respectively, about 62 percent and 80 percent of their total trade with ASEAN countries in 2014, down from 71 percent and 87 percent in 2007. In 2014, consumer goods represented 25 percent of the United States' total trade with ASEAN countries and 14 percent of China's. The remaining goods were not classified according to these categories.
- **Imports.** Goods for industrial use represented 59 percent of U.S. imports from ASEAN countries and 88 percent of Chinese imports in 2014. Among industrial goods, microchips were the top U.S. and Chinese import from ASEAN countries. Consumer goods represented 35 percent of U.S. imports from ASEAN countries and 7 percent of Chinese imports in 2014.[20]
- **Exports.** Goods for industrial use represented 67 percent of U.S. exports to ASEAN countries and 74 percent of Chinese exports to ASEAN countries in 2014. Among industrial goods, microchips were the top export to ASEAN countries from both the United States and China. Consumer goods represented 8 percent of U.S. exports to ASEAN countries and 20 percent of Chinese exports in 2014.[21]

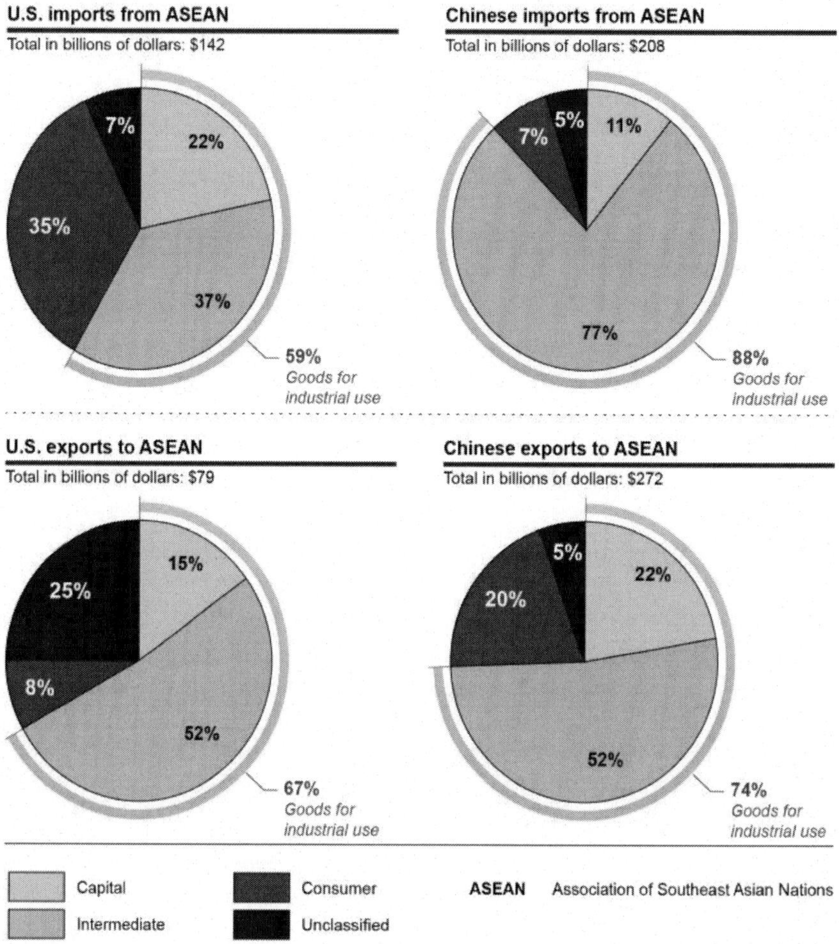

Source: GAO analysis of U.S. and Chinese data from the United Nations Commodity Trade database. | GAO-15-724.

Notes: We used the United Nations Statistics Division's Broad Economic Categories to classify U.S. and Chinese total trade in goods into these categories. We define goods for industrial use as capital and intermediate goods and consumer goods as consumption goods. According to the Organisation for Economic Co-operation and Development, an intermediate good can be defined as an input to the production process that has itself been produced and, unlike capital, is used up in production. Unclassified goods are goods that are not classified as capital, intermediate, or consumer goods. Some percentages do not sum to 100 due to rounding.

Figure 3. U.S. and Chinese Trade in Goods with ASEAN Countries by Use, 2014.

Figure 3 shows U.S. and Chinese trade in goods with ASEAN countries by use in 2014.

For more information about the composition of goods trade by ASEAN countries with the United States and China by type, see appendix III.

The United States and China Are Key Trading Partners of ASEAN Countries, but ASEAN Countries Trade Most among Themselves

ASEAN countries trade more with each other than with other trading partners.[22] China is the largest outside trading partner of ASEAN countries, followed by the European Union (EU), Japan, and the United States.

- **Exports.** In 2013, ASEAN countries exported $330 billion in goods to other ASEAN countries, $115 billion in goods to the United States, and $153 billion in goods to China. The United States is the fifth largest market for ASEAN countries' goods exports, behind other ASEAN countries, China, the EU, and Japan. From 2003 through 2013, the U.S. share of ASEAN exports fell from 15.4 percent to 9.1 percent, while China's share of ASEAN exports increased from 6.4 percent to 12.2 percent.
- **Imports.** In 2013, ASEAN countries imported $278 billion in goods from other ASEAN countries, $92 billion from the United States, and $198 billion from China. The United States is the fifth largest source of ASEAN goods imports, behind other ASEAN countries, China, the EU, and Japan. From 2003 through 2013, the United States' share of ASEAN imports fell from 13.0 percent to 7.6 percent, while China's share of ASEAN imports increased from 8.2 percent to 16.2 percent.

Figure 4 shows ASEAN countries' exports and imports of goods, by trading partner, in 2003, 2008, and 2013.

In 2011 through 2013, 7 of the 10 ASEAN countries exported more goods to China than to the United States: only Cambodia, the Philippines, and Vietnam exported more goods to the United States (see Figure 5). However, while most individual ASEAN countries traded more goods with China than with the United States, they exported the majority of their goods to many other countries.

In 2011 through 2013, 9 of the 10 ASEAN countries imported more goods from China than from the United States. Brunei was the only exception, importing slightly more goods from the United States (see Figure 6). Individual ASEAN countries imported goods from a diverse set of trading partners.

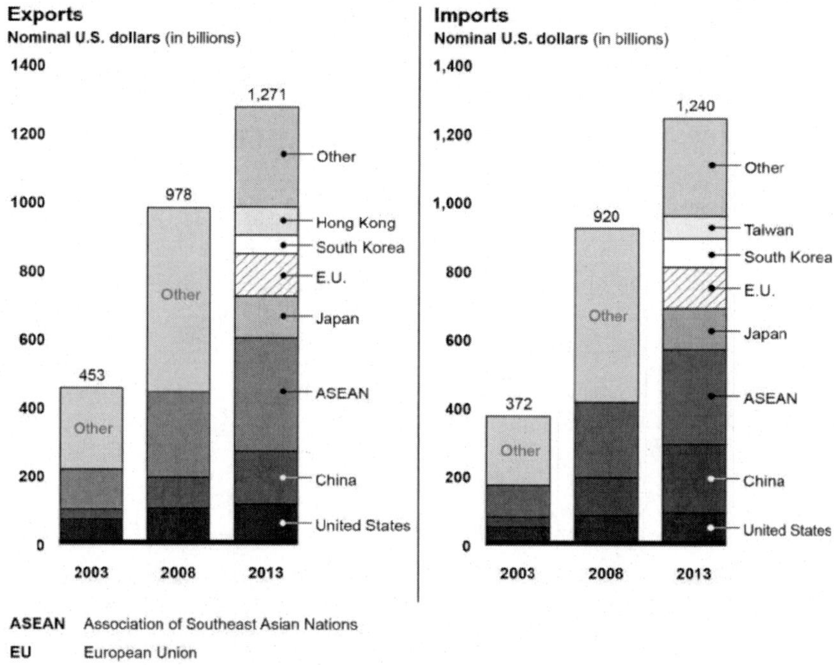

Source: GAO analysis of data from ASEANstats database. | GAO-15-724.

Notes: The trade values shown are nominal—that is, not adjusted for inflation. Changes in values over time are due in part to changes in the prices of traded goods. Hong Kong is a special administrative region of China, but we have included it in this report as a separate country because it is an economic entity separate from the rest of China and is able to enter into international agreements on its own behalf in commercial and economic matters. Although the United States does not have diplomatic relations with Taiwan, we have listed it as a separate country because whenever the laws of the United States refer or relate to foreign countries, nations, states, governments, or similar entities, such terms shall include and shall apply to Taiwan.

Figure 4. ASEAN Countries' Exports and Imports of Goods, by Trading Partner, 2003, 2008, and 2013.

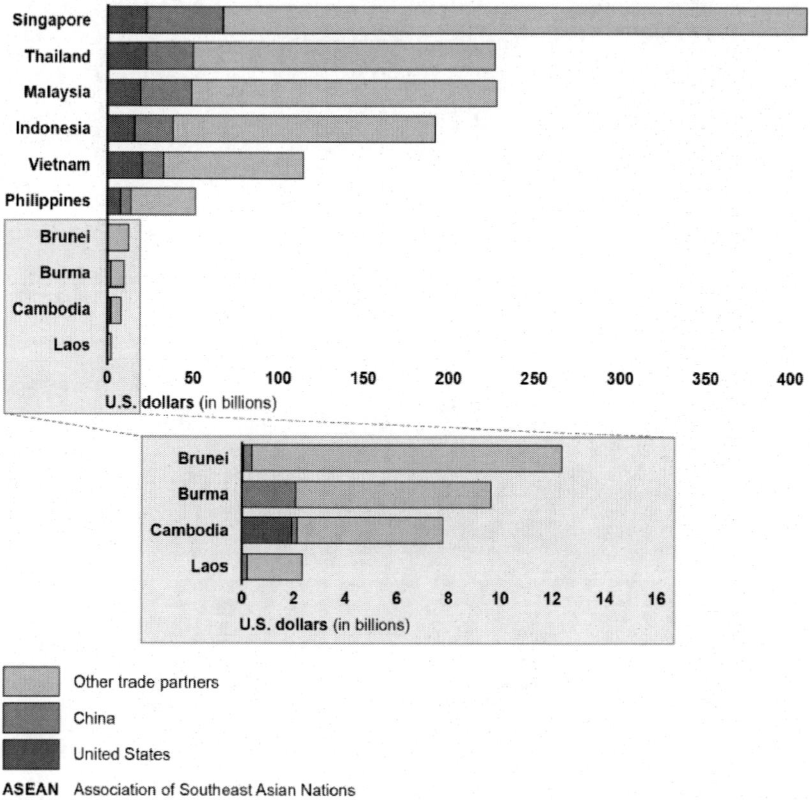

Source: GAO analysis of data from ASEANstats database. | GAO-15-724.

Notes: We report the average trade in goods between individual ASEAN countries and the United States and China for 2011 through 2013 because trade with some countries, such as Brunei, can fluctuate significantly across years.

According to data reported by the United States and China to the United Nations (UN) Commodity Trade Database, only Cambodia and Vietnam exported more goods to the United States than to China on average from 2011 through 2013. However, data from the ASEANstats database show that the Philippines, in addition to Cambodia and Vietnam, exported more goods to the United States than to China on average from 2011 through 2013. Reasons for the variation between the data from the UN Commodity Trade Database and the ASEANstats database include differences in the valuation of goods and in data quality.

Figure 5. Individual ASEAN Countries' Exports of Goods to the United States and China, Averaged for 2011-2013.

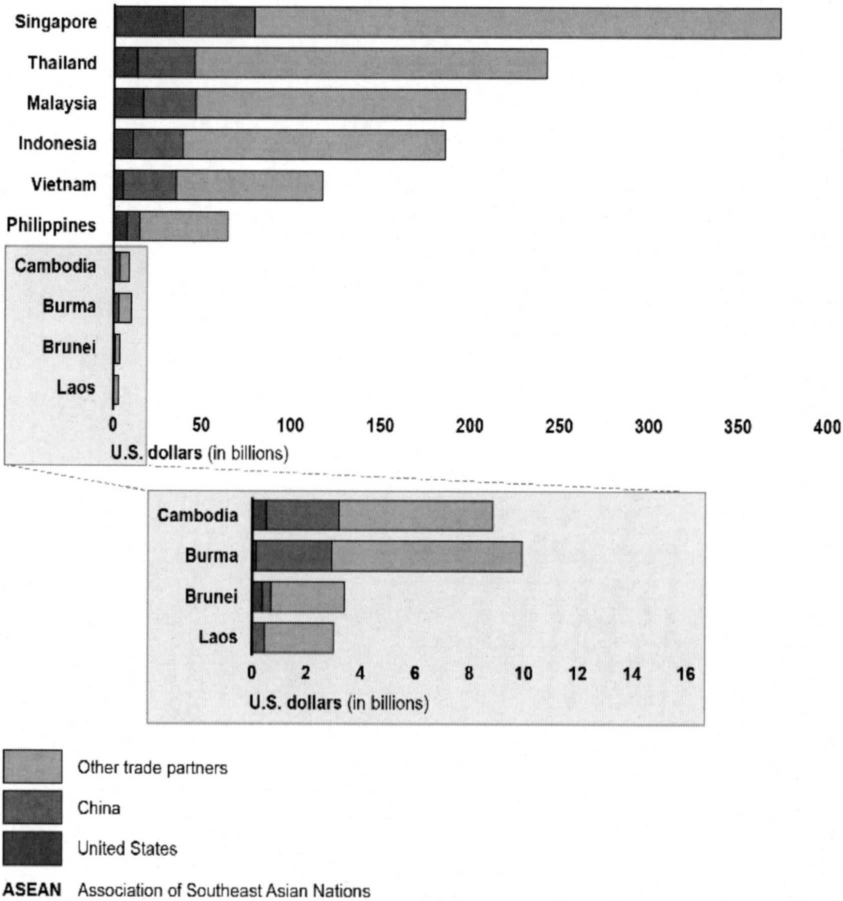

Source: GAO analysis of data from ASEANstats database. | GAO-15-724.

Notes: We report the average trade in goods between individual ASEAN countries and the United States and China for 2011 to 2013 because trade with some countries, such as Brunei, can fluctuate significantly across years.

According to data reported by the United States and China to the United Nations Commodity Trade Database, all ASEAN countries imported more goods from China than from the United States on average from 2011 through 2013. However, data from the ASEANstats database show that Brunei imported more goods from the United States than from China on average from 2011 through 2013. Reasons for the difference include differences in the valuation of goods and differences in data quality.

Figure 6. Individual ASEAN Countries' Imports of Goods from the United States and China, Averaged for 2011-2013.

The United States' role relative to China's in ASEAN countries' goods and services trade may be greater when the amount of intermediate inputs to the traded goods and services is taken into account. For example, because of the nature of global supply chains, a consumer phone from a U.S. company may be assembled in China but incorporate components from Germany, Japan, South Korea, and other countries.[23] Although components of a country's exports may originate in other countries, export data from the United Nations Commodity Trade database count the full value of the export for only the exporting country. Data from the Organisation of Economic Co-operation and Development (OECD) and the WTO attempt to account for the value added to a finished export by each contributing country. Data from the United Nations, WTO, and the International Trade Centre, as well as our estimates, showed that ASEAN countries imported more in total goods and services from China in 2009 than from the United States. However, OECD-WTO's data show that ASEAN countries imported $41 billion in value-added goods and services from China in 2009 and $52 billion from the United States. This suggests that Chinese exports contained a higher portion of components produced elsewhere than did U.S. exports. Similarly, some components of the goods and services that ASEAN countries exported to the United States and China were produced outside ASEAN countries. Data from the United Nations, WTO, and the International Trade Centre, as well as our estimates, showed that ASEAN countries exported more in total goods and services from China in 2009 than from the United States. However, according to OECD-WTO data, ASEAN countries exported $86 billion in value-added goods and services to the United States in 2009 and $47 billion to China.[24]

Total U.S. Trade in Services with ASEAN Countries Is Similar to China's, but Available Data Have Limitations

Although our analysis of U.S. and Chinese trade in services with ASEAN countries represents broad estimates rather than precise values, these data indicate that the United States and China traded approximately the same total value of services in 2011. Our calculations, based on data from the U.S. Bureau of Economic Analysis (BEA) and other sources,[25] indicate that the U.S. trade in services with ASEAN countries totaled approximately $37 billion in 2011.[26] According to UN, WTO, and International Trade Centre estimates of Chinese trade in services for 2011, China's trade in services with ASEAN countries also totaled approximately $37 billion. In 2011, the United States exported more services to ASEAN countries than it imported from them, and China imported more services from ASEAN countries than it exported to them.

- **U.S. and Chinese imports.** We calculated that the United States imported approximately $14 billion in services from ASEAN countries in 2011 and approximately $16 billion in 2012. 27 In 2012, the top categories for U.S. service imports from ASEAN countries were (1) business, professional, and technical services (approximately $6 billion) and (2) travel and passenger fares (approximately $5.7 billion). Estimates from the UN, the WTO, and the International Trade Centre on Chinese trade in services for 2011 indicated that China imported approximately $23 billion in services from ASEAN countries. China does not publish data on its service imports from ASEAN countries by category of service.
- **U.S. and Chinese exports.** We calculated that the United States exported approximately $23 billion in services to ASEAN countries in 2011 and approximately $25 billion in 2012.[28] In 2012, the top categories for U.S. service exports to ASEAN countries, totaling approximately $15 billion, were (1) business, professional, and technical services and (2) royalties and license fees. Estimates from the UN, the WTO, and the International Trade Centre on Chinese trade in services for 2011 indicated that China exported approximately $13 billion in services to ASEAN countries. China does not publish data on service exports to ASEAN countries by category of service.

Both U.S. and Chinese trade in services with ASEAN countries are small in value compared with their goods trade. In 2011, total U.S.-ASEAN services trade was 19 percent of the value of U.S.-ASEAN goods trade, while the estimated total China-ASEAN services trade was 10 percent of the value of China-ASEAN goods trade.

U.S. Investment in ASEAN Countries Exceeded Chinese Investment from 2007 through 2012, but Available Data Have Limitations

Data on FDI in ASEAN countries from the United States and China have limitations, in that U.S. and Chinese FDI data may not accurately reflect the countries to which U.S. and Chinese FDI ultimately flows.[29] However, available data show that from 2007 through 2012, U.S. FDI flows to ASEAN countries totaled about $96 billion, exceeding China's reported FDI of about $23 billion.[30] However, annual Chinese FDI flows increased each year during this period, from $1 billion in 2007 to $6 billion in 2012 in nominal terms (see Figure 7). According to BEA, U.S. FDI in ASEAN countries in 2003 through 2013 was concentrated in holding companies, which accounted for about half of total U.S. FDI.[31] Manufacturing, especially computer and electronic products manufacturing, was the second largest category of U.S. FDI.

From 2007 through 2012, U.S. investment was concentrated in several of the ASEAN 6 countries whereas a larger share of Chinese investment was in the CLMV countries (see Figure 8). Almost all U.S. FDI flows were to four of the ASEAN 6 countries—Indonesia, Malaysia, Singapore, and Thailand. U.S. FDI flows exceeded China's FDI flows in these countries. U.S. FDI flows in the four ASEAN 6 countries represented 99 percent of all U.S. FDI flows to ASEAN countries during this period.[32] However, Chinese FDI flows exceeded U.S. FDI flows for the four CLMV countries.

Chinese FDI flows to these four countries totaled $7.8 billion for 2007 through 2012, whereas U.S. FDI flows to those countries totaled around $0.5 billion. China's FDI in CLMV countries represented 35 percent of Chinese FDI in ASEAN countries in this time period. For both the United States and China, the largest FDI flows were to Singapore. Singapore is a regional financial hub; therefore, according to BEA, a portion of FDI in Singapore is likely to have been reinvested in other countries, which may include other ASEAN countries.

U.S. and Chinese Firms Often Compete in Different Sectors

Data on competition between U.S. and Chinese firms in ASEAN countries are limited but indicate that the United States competes more often with firms from Europe, South Korea, and Japan than with Chinese firms. In addition,

U.S. firms tend to obtain World Bank and ADB contracts in different sectors than Chinese firms.

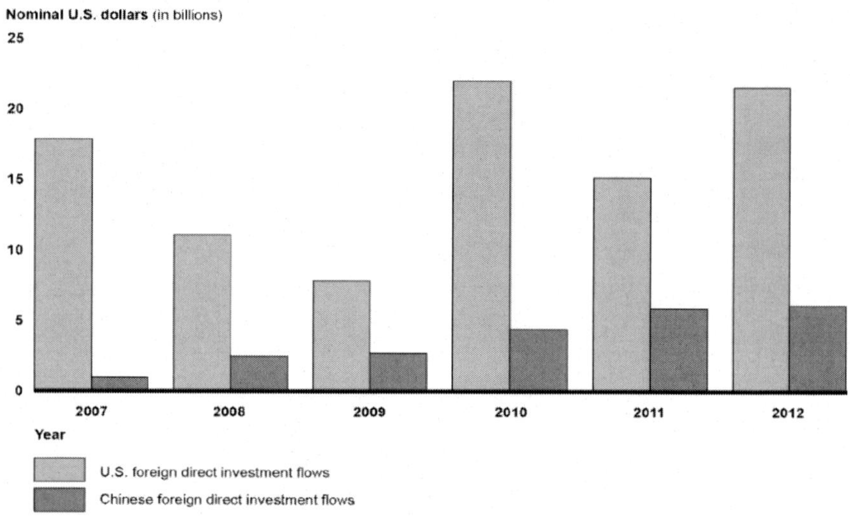

Source: GAO analysis of data from the U.S. Bureau of Economic Analysis and Chinese data from the United Nations Conference on Trade and Development. | GAO-15-724.

Notes: Foreign direct investment (FDI) flows to the Association of Southeast Asian Nations (ASEAN) countries represent FDI activities within a given period of time. Although China has reported investment data since 2003, it began including financial investment in its total investment data in 2007. Chinese FDI does not include Hong Kong. Investment data are reported in nominal values— that is, not adjusted for inflation. When using a U.S. gross domestic product deflator, we calculated that cumulative U.S. and Chinese FDI flows for 2007 through 2012 were $94 billion and $22 billion, respectively, in 2009 dollars. We rounded data reported by the U.S. Bureau of Economic Analysis to the nearest million dollars.

Figure 7. U.S. and Chinese FDI Flows to ASEAN Countries, 2007-2012.

Goods Export Data Indicate That U.S. Firms Exporting to ASEAN Countries Compete More with Japanese and European Firms Than with Chinese Firms

From 2001 through 2014, U.S. exports of goods to ASEAN countries were more similar to Japanese and EU exports than to Chinese exports, suggesting that U.S. firms are more likely to compete directly with Japanese and EU firms than with Chinese firms for exports to ASEAN countries.

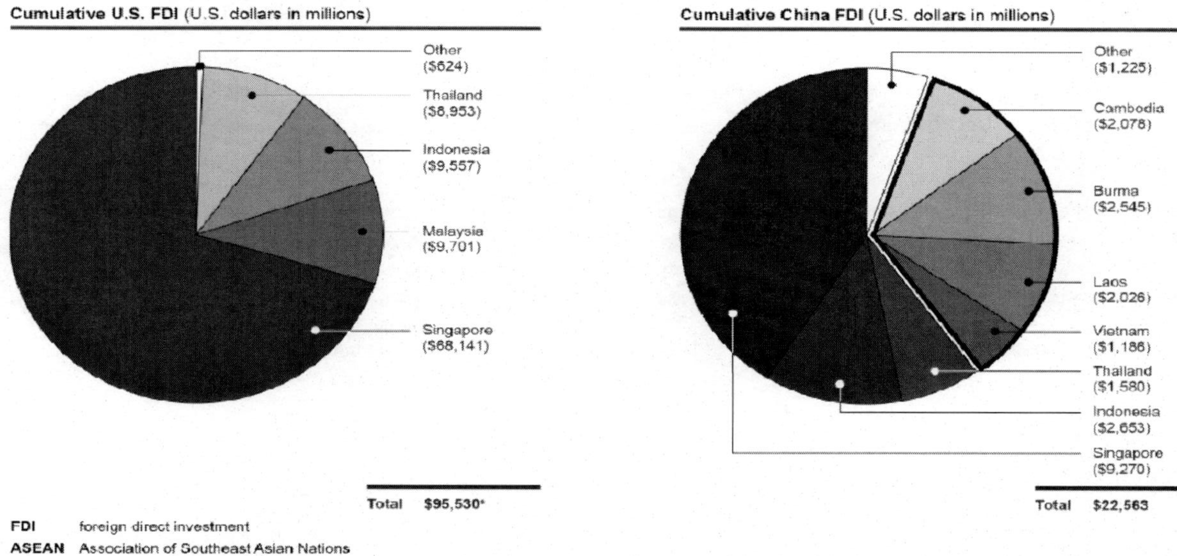

Source: GAO analysis of data from the U.S. Bureau of Economic Analysis and Chinese data from the United Nations Conference on Trade and Development. | GAO-15-724.

Note:

[a]Total U.S. cumulative FDI flows to ASEAN include U.S. cumulative FDI flows to the Philippines. U.S. cumulative FDI flows to the Philippines were negative (-$1.4 billion) from 2007 through 2012 and are not depicted in the figure. Flows from U.S. affiliates in the Philippines to the U.S. parent companies were larger than flows from the U.S. parent companies to U.S. affiliates in the Philippines.

Figure 8. U.S. and Chinese FDI Flows to ASEAN Countries by Country, 2007-2012.

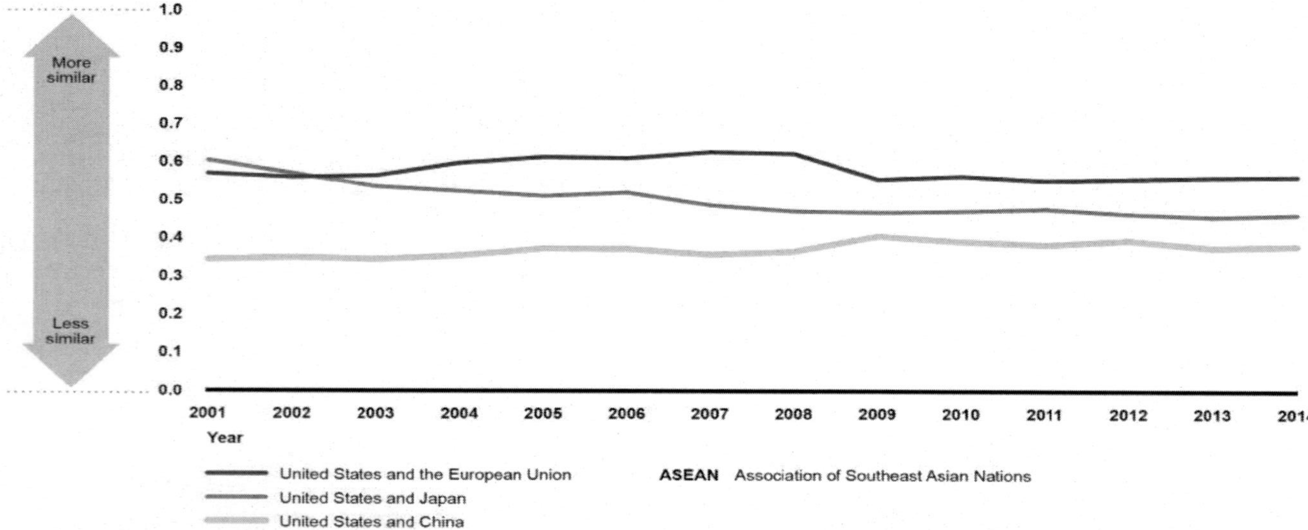

Source: GAO analysis of U.S., Chinese, European Union countries,' and Japanese data from UN Commodity Trade database. | GAO-15-724.

Note: An index value of 1 would mean that each good a country exported to ASEAN countries represented the same percentage of the country's total exports to ASEAN countries as that of the other country. A zero value would indicate no overlap—the countries export entirely different goods. Our analysis excludes exports of special transactions and commodities not classified by kind, because those exports include many different types of goods.

Figure 9. Export Similarity Index of U.S. Exports of Goods to ASEAN Countries and Chinese, European Union, and Japanese Exports of Goods to ASEAN Countries, 2001-2014.

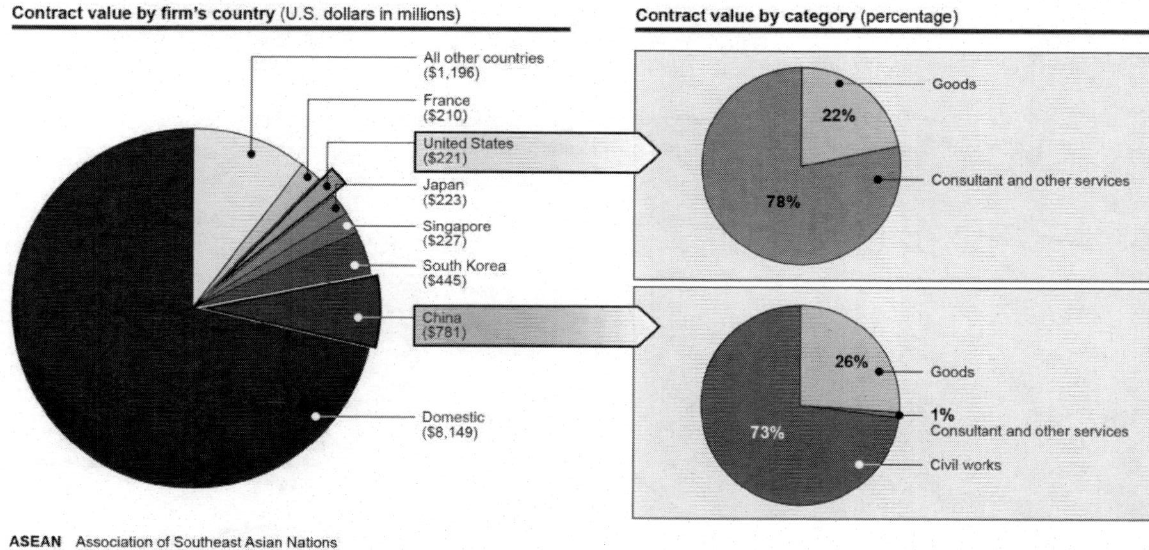

Source: GAO analysis of World Bank data. | GAO-15-724.

Notes: Civil works include construction and maintenance of all types of infrastructure, such as roads, dams, power plants, and buildings. The World Bank fiscal year is from July 1 to June 30.

Figure 10. World Bank-Financed Contracts Obtained by Firms from the United States, China, and Other Countries in ASEAN Countries, Fiscal Years 2000-2014.

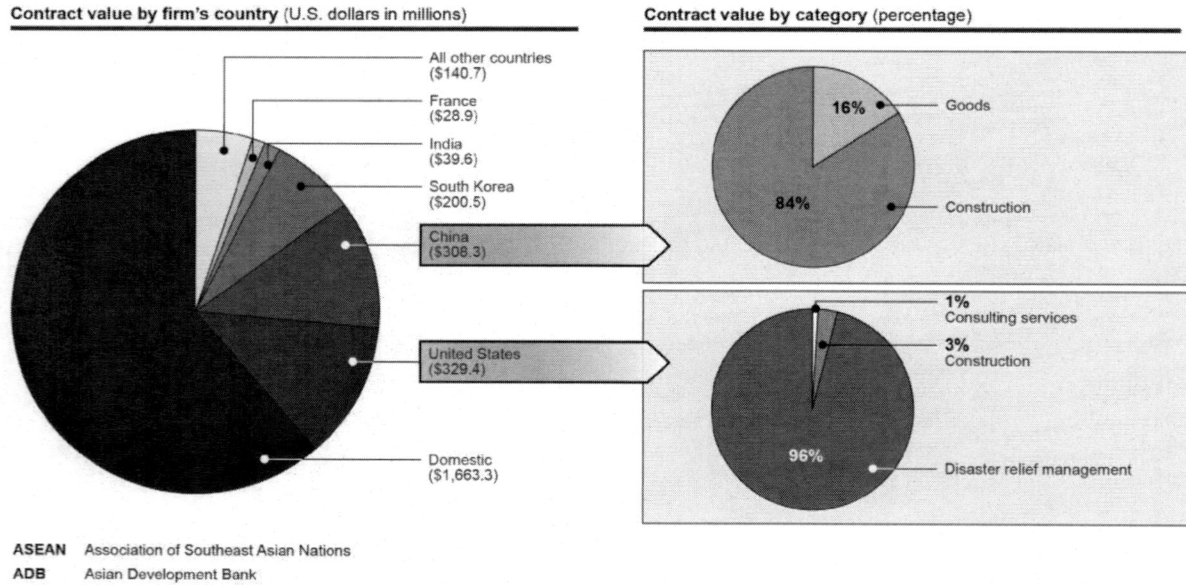

Source: GAO analysis of World Bank data. | GAO-15-724.

Note: ADB publishes data only for consulting contracts with a contract value above.

$0.1 million and for construction and goods contracts with a value above $1.0 million. We determined the country of a firm based on its address in ADB's data, although the firm's parent may be headquartered in another country.

Figure 11. ADB-Financed Contracts Obtained by Firms from the United States, China, and Other Countries in ASEAN Countries, 2013-2014.

To assess the extent of the similarity of exports, we calculated a commonly used index to compare U.S., Chinese, and other countries' exports to ASEAN countries.[33] From 2001 through 2014, U.S. exports to ASEAN countries have consistently been more similar to EU and Japanese exports than to Chinese exports (see Figure 9). However, during this period, Chinese exports to ASEAN countries have grown more similar to U.S. exports, while Japanese exports have grown less similar to U.S. exports.[34] This is consistent with the pattern for Chinese exports globally. According to an IMF study, China has traditionally competed with other Asian countries, and although large differences remain, China's exports are becoming more similar to those of advanced economies, such as Germany and the United States. China's export similarity index with the United States grew from 0.248 in 1995 to 0.333 in 2008, according to the IMF study.[35]

Available Data Suggest That U.S. and Chinese Firms Compete Most Often with Other Countries' Firms for Government Contracts in ASEAN Countries and Obtain Contracts in Different Sectors

We identified three data sources that provide some information on individual contracts competed for, or obtained by, U.S. and Chinese firms. These data indicate that in ASEAN countries, U.S. firms compete more often with firms from countries other than China and tend to be awarded contracts in different sectors. We analyzed data for contracts funded by the World Bank and ADB as well as data from Commerce's Advocacy Center on host-government contracts. The World Bank and ADB track the awardees of their contracts, as well as contract size and sector. The Advocacy Center tracks contract competitors and awardees for the U.S. firms that apply for and receive its support, as well as the size and sector of the contract. Although these data represent a small share of activity in the region, they provide insights into the degree of competition between U.S. and Chinese firms for the projects represented.

World Bank Contracts

From 2000 through 2014, both U.S. and Chinese firms were awarded hundreds of World Bank-financed contracts in ASEAN countries, but they tended to obtain contracts in different sectors (see Figure 10).[36] Excluding contracts that went to domestic firms, our analysis of World Bank data showed that Chinese firms were awarded a higher dollar value of World Bank contracts in ASEAN countries ($781 million) than firms from any other country.[37] Civil works projects accounted for about 73 percent of the value of

World Bank contracts that Chinese firms were awarded in ASEAN countries, and contracts for consulting services accounted for less than 1 percent. In contrast, U.S. firms did not obtain any World Bank contracts for civil works in ASEAN countries, and contracts for consulting services accounted for about 78 percent of the value of World Bank contracts obtained by U.S. firms. Contracts for goods accounted for about 22 percent of the value of the contracts that U.S. firms obtained in ASEAN countries and about 26 percent of the value of contracts obtained by Chinese firms.

ADB Contracts

ADB has also predominantly awarded contracts to U.S. and Chinese firms in different sectors in ASEAN countries (see Figure 11). Similar to World Bank contracts, most ADB contracts in 2013 and 2014 went to domestic firms in the project country. However, U.S. firms received the largest amount of contract value ($329 million) awarded to foreign firms and Chinese firms received the second largest ($308 million). Nearly all ADB contract value awarded to U.S. firms was for management of emergency assistance to typhoon-affected areas of the Philippines. In contrast, Chinese firms received 84 percent of their contract value for construction. Of Chinese construction contracts, the largest share, $242 million, was for road transportation projects in Vietnam, Cambodia, and Laos. Chinese firms received 16 percent of their contract value ($50 million) for goods to be used in the electricity and renewable energy sectors, such as transformers, wires, and hydraulic equipment. U.S. firms received one contract for a renewable energy construction project, a $9 million contract for a geothermal plant in Indonesia.

Commerce Advocacy Center Data

U.S. firms that received support from Commerce's Advocacy Center in fiscal years 2009 through 2014 competed less often with Chinese firms than with firms from other countries. The Commerce data cover those public sector contracts competed for by U.S. firms in ASEAN countries for which the Advocacy Center received an application by a U.S. firm for commercial advocacy.[38] Chinese firms competed for 30 out of these 172 contracts (see table 2). The value of the contracts for which Chinese firms competed was $6.8 billion—6 percent of the $112 billion in total contract value for which U.S. firms were competing and less than the total value competed for by nine other countries' firms. U.S. firms that applied for Advocacy Center support competed against firms from only China or from China and other developing countries in only five cases. U.S. firms were most likely to compete with

Chinese firms in the telecommunications sector, where U.S. and Chinese firms competed for 5 of 8 contracts; and the energy and power sector, where U.S. and Chinese firms competed for 7 of 19 contracts.

Table 2. Nationalities of Firms Competing with U.S. Firms That Applied for Advocacy Center Support for ASEAN Country Government Contracts, Fiscal Years 2009-2014

Nationalities of firms competing with U.S. firms	Contracts competed	
	Value (dollars in millions)	Number
France	$75,472	70
South Korea	25,483	24
Russia	22,066	11
Sweden	18,871	14
Japan	17,310	23
Switzerland	15,608	11
Germany	13,614	38
United Kingdom	9,829	27
Bulgaria	8,610	1
China	6,827	30
Spain	6,755	19
Italy	6,450	32
All contracts (U.S. total)	$112,473	172

Legend: ASEAN = Association of Southeast Asian Nations.

Source: U.S. Department of Commerce Advocacy Center. | GAO-15-724.

Notes: Firms from at least 25 other countries competed against U.S. firms for the contracts, but none of those countries' firms competed for more than $5 billion in contracts. For several contracts, the U.S. firm or firms that applied for Advocacy Center support were competing against a consortium of firms from more than one country; those contracts and their entire value is included in each known participating country's total.

THE UNITED STATES AND CHINA ENGAGE WITH ASEAN COUNTRIES THROUGH TRADE AGREEMENTS, SUPPORT FOR FIRMS, AND SUPPORT FOR REGIONAL INTEGRATION

To further economic engagement with ASEAN countries, the United States and China each have entered into existing trade agreements and are parties to ongoing negotiations. The two countries also support their domestic firms by providing export financing and other services. The United States supports regional economic development and integration as part of its trade capacity building (TCB) assistance to strengthen institutions and governance. China supports regional economic development and integration through capacity building and has provided billions of dollars for infrastructure development. China has also promised additional billions of dollars for future infrastructure construction in the region, including through the creation of the new multinational Asian Infrastructure Investment Bank, headquartered in Beijing.

The United States and China Have Existing and Proposed FTAs with ASEAN Countries

The United States has an FTA with Singapore, while China has free trade and investment agreements with all 10 ASEAN countries as well as a separate FTA with Singapore.[39] The United States is party to the ongoing TPP negotiations, which include 4 ASEAN countries. China is party to the Regional Comprehensive Economic Partnership negotiations, which include all ASEAN countries.

The United States Has an FTA with Singapore, while China Has Free Trade and Investment Agreements with All ASEAN Countries

U.S.-Singapore FTA

The January 2004 U.S.-Singapore FTA eliminated tariffs for U.S. exports to Singapore and phased out tariffs for Singapore's exports to the United States over a 10-year period. [40] As a result of the U.S.-Singapore FTA, goods from the United States and Singapore no longer face any tariffs in each other's markets. For example, Singapore faces no tariff on its exports to the United States of a type of medicine, a top Singapore export in 2014, for which other U.S. trading partners with normal trade relations face a tariff of 6.5 percent. In addition to eliminating tariffs, the U.S.-Singapore FTA provided greater access for U.S. service providers[41] and addressed trade issues, such as strengthening Singapore's intellectual property rights protection,[42] government procurement, protection of the environment, and protection of labor rights.[43] According to USTR, the U.S. goods trade surplus with Singapore was $14.1 billion in 2014; and the U.S. services trade surplus with Singapore was $5.8 billion in 2013, the latest data available.[44]

China-ASEAN Framework Agreement on Comprehensive Economic Cooperation

China's framework agreement with the ASEAN countries comprises a series of trade and investment agreements focused on expanding access to each other's markets. From 2004 through 2009, China and the ASEAN countries signed three agreements:

- The China-ASEAN Trade in Goods Agreement entered into force in July 2005. The agreement separates goods into different groups, each with different timelines for tariff reduction. For example, under the agreement the parties committed to reduce tariffs to zero for most goods traded between the ASEAN 6 and China by 2012; CLMV countries agreed to reduce most tariffs to zero by 2018. The parties also agreed to reduce tariffs for goods categorized by a country as sensitive or highly sensitive for its economy to no more than 5 percent by 2018 for ASEAN 6 countries and by 2020 for CLMV countries. CLMV countries may also designate more goods as sensitive or highly sensitive than China and the ASEAN 6 countries.[45] According to the WTO, the average Chinese tariff on imports from ASEAN countries in 2013 was 0.7 percent (0.8 percent for Laos and Cambodia), compared with an average of 9.4 percent for all of China's trading partners.[46] For example, according to WTO data, ASEAN countries face no tariff on a type of rubber, a key export from ASEAN countries to China in 2014, for which other Chinese trading partners with normal trade relations face a tariff of 8 percent.[47] Similarly, for example, according to WTO data, China faces a 10 percent tariff on women's cotton jackets and blazers, a top Chinese export to Vietnam in 2014, for which other Vietnamese trading partners with normal trade relations face a 20 percent tariff.
- The China-ASEAN Trade in Services Agreement entered into force in July 2007. The agreement provides market access for participant countries' companies and requires that firms located in participant countries be given treatment equal to domestic service providers in agreed-upon sectors. All countries signing the agreement agree to the specific service sectors to which the agreement applies in each country. The agreement permits CLMV countries to open fewer sectors and liberalize fewer types of transactions.
- The China-ASEAN Investment Agreement entered into force in February 2010. Under the agreement, China and ASEAN countries

commit to treat each other's investors as equal to domestic investors and investors from other countries with which China and ASEAN countries have signed investment agreements. The agreement also included a provision on how disputes between the investor and the invested country are to be settled.

In August 2014, China and ASEAN announced discussions to upgrade these agreements. The second round of discussions, held in February 2015, focused on investment, economic cooperation, and other areas.

China-Singapore FTA

The China-Singapore FTA, which entered into force in 2009, included tariff reductions for goods beyond those covered under the China-ASEAN Trade in Goods Agreement. All of China's exports to Singapore, and almost all of Singapore's exports to China, enter the respective countries tariff free.[48] As of 2014, Singapore generally did not apply any tariffs on any imports, including those from the United States and China. According to Singapore's Ministry of Trade and Industry, the FTA also included provisions to expand access for Singapore's and China's service providers beyond each country's WTO commitments for certain sectors such as business and hospital services.

Unlike the U.S.-Singapore FTA, China's FTAs with ASEAN and Singapore do not address issues such as protection of intellectual property rights and labor rights. For example, the China-ASEAN FTA does not address protection of the environment and labor rights and only reaffirms each country's commitments to WTO provisions on the protection of intellectual property rights. According to USTR, China's existing FTA covers only three areas—goods, services, and investment— while the U.S.-Singapore FTA has 21 chapters covering a wide range of areas, including intellectual property rights, government procurement, environment, and labor rights. In addition, according to USTR, China's FTA is significantly less ambitious in the areas of services and investment than the U.S.-Singapore FTA. USTR expects that, although negotiations are ongoing, TPP will be a more ambitious and comprehensive agreement than the proposed Regional Comprehensive Economic Partnership (RCEP).

The United States and China Are Each Party to Different Proposed Regional FTAs

The United States and China are actively engaged in ongoing negotiations for TPP and RCEP, respectively. Several countries in the Asia-Pacific region, including ASEAN countries, are parties to negotiations for both agreements (see Figure 12).

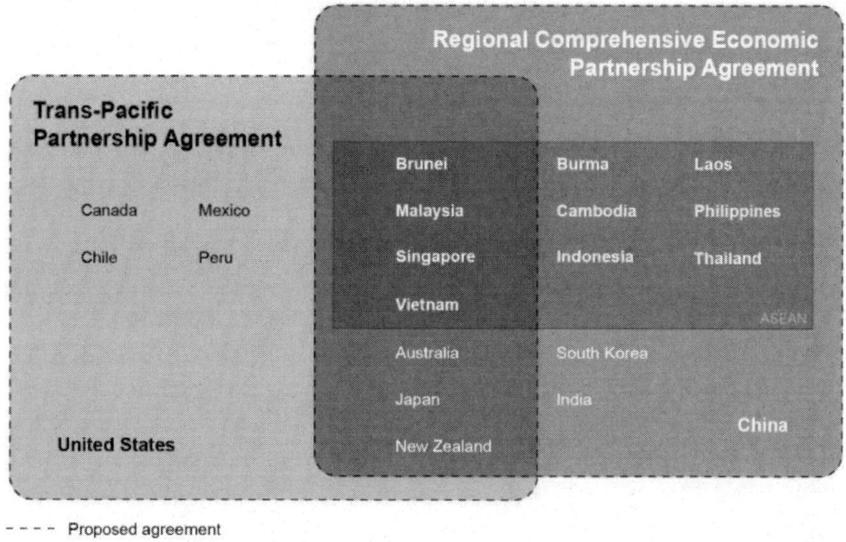

Source: GAO analysis of proposed free trade agreements. | GAO-15-724.

Figure 12. Participants in Proposed Regional Free Trade Agreements with Association of Southeast Asian Nations (ASEAN) Countries.

Trans-Pacific Partnership (TPP) Agreement Negotiations

As of August 2015, the United States Trade Representative is engaged in TPP negotiations with 11 other Asia-Pacific region countries, including 4 ASEAN countries—Brunei, Malaysia, Singapore, and Vietnam. According to our analysis of World Bank and UN data, in 2013, the 12 Asia-Pacific countries negotiating TPP had a combined population of approximately 800 million people; had a combined GDP of almost $28 trillion, about 37 percent of global GDP; and covered about 26 percent of world goods trade.[49] The four ASEAN countries that are engaged in TPP negotiations accounted for 58 percent of U.S. trade with ASEAN countries. Launched in 2002, with the United States joining in 2009, TPP has had several rounds of negotiation, the most recent in July 2015. Although TPP's text is not finalized, in 2011 negotiators agreed that it would address, for example, ensuring a competitive business environment; providing TCB in developing countries; improving customs procedures; addressing impediments to e-commerce; creating clear rules for addressing disputes; and protecting the environment, labor rights, and intellectual property rights, among other issues. USTR is seeking to finalize TPP in 2015.[50]

Regional Comprehensive Economic Partnership Agreement Negotiations

China, the 10 ASEAN countries, and five other countries are currently negotiating RCEP to expand trade and investment access. In 2011, ASEAN proposed establishing RCEP to broaden and deepen existing FTAs between the ASEAN countries and six others—Australia, China, India, Japan, New Zealand, and South Korea. According to our analysis of World Bank and UN data, RCEP negotiating partners have a combined population of more than 3.4 billion people, have a combined GDP of more than $21 trillion—more than 28 percent of global GDP—and account for about 29 percent of world goods trade.[51] According to U.S. officials we spoke with, RCEP will not greatly expand the six existing ASEAN agreements but will synthesize their provisions in a single comprehensive agreement. RCEP negotiation working groups include those for trade in goods, trade in services, investment, intellectual property, competition, and economic and technical cooperation. The eighth round of RCEP negotiations was held in Kyoto, Japan, in June 2015. Details of RCEP, like those of TPP, are not finalized, but the negotiating parties have stated that they hope to complete the agreement in 2015.

Existing FTA Relationships between FTA Negotiating Partners

China and the United States each have existing FTAs with a number of their negotiating partners in the proposed regional FTAs. The United States has existing FTAs with 6 of its 11 TPP negotiating partners (see Figure 13). Of the 66 possible FTA pairings among the 12 TPP participants, 42 FTAs are currently in place. China has FTAs with ASEAN and New Zealand and, in June 2015, signed FTAs with Australia and South Korea. The Australia and South Korea FTAs have not entered into force (see Figure 14). Counting ASEAN as a single negotiating partner, there are 21 possible FTA pairings among RCEP participants, 12 of which are currently in place.[52]

Both TPP and RCEP include major trading partners with which China and the United States do not currently have FTAs. According to our analysis of UN and BEA data, TPP negotiating partners with which the United States does not have an existing FTA represented approximately 7 percent of both U.S. goods trade and U.S. services trade in 2013 (see table 3). In 2013, bilateral goods trade between the United States and Japan, the largest U.S. trading partner engaged in TPP negotiations without a U.S. FTA, represented 5 percent of total U.S. goods trade and 7 percent of U.S. services trade. The six TPP negotiating partners with which the United States has an existing FTA constituted 33 percent of U.S. goods trade in 2013 and 16 percent of U.S. services trade. According to our analysis of data from the UN, the WTO, and the International Trade Centre, Chinese trade with India and Japan—the two countries in RCEP with which China has not negotiated an FTA— represented 9 percent of total Chinese goods trade in 2013 and more than 8 percent of Chinese services trade in 2011 (see table 4). Chinese trade with ASEAN, Australia, New Zealand, and South Korea represented 21 percent of total Chinese goods trade in 2013 and more than 18 percent of Chinese services trade in 2011.

In 2014, leaders of economies that belong to the Asia-Pacific Economic Cooperation (APEC) forum, which includes seven ASEAN economies, the United States, and China, among others, agreed to undertake a study of issues related to the realization of a Free Trade Area of the Asia-Pacific (FTAAP). 53 The study is to be completed by the end of 2016. According to a statement issued at APEC's 2014 meeting, FTAAP is not viewed as an alternative to TPP and RCEP but will build on current and developing regional architectures. APEC identified TPP and RCEP as possible steps toward eventual realization of FTAAP.

The United States and China Each Support Firms in ASEAN Countries

The United States and China provide support and financing to their firms that trade and invest in ASEAN countries. U.S. agencies provide financing and maintain overseas personnel to promote U.S. policies and support U.S. firms. While country-specific data on Chinese financing are unavailable, the Chinese government provides significantly greater financing than the United States worldwide and has taken steps to support Chinese investment in ASEAN countries.

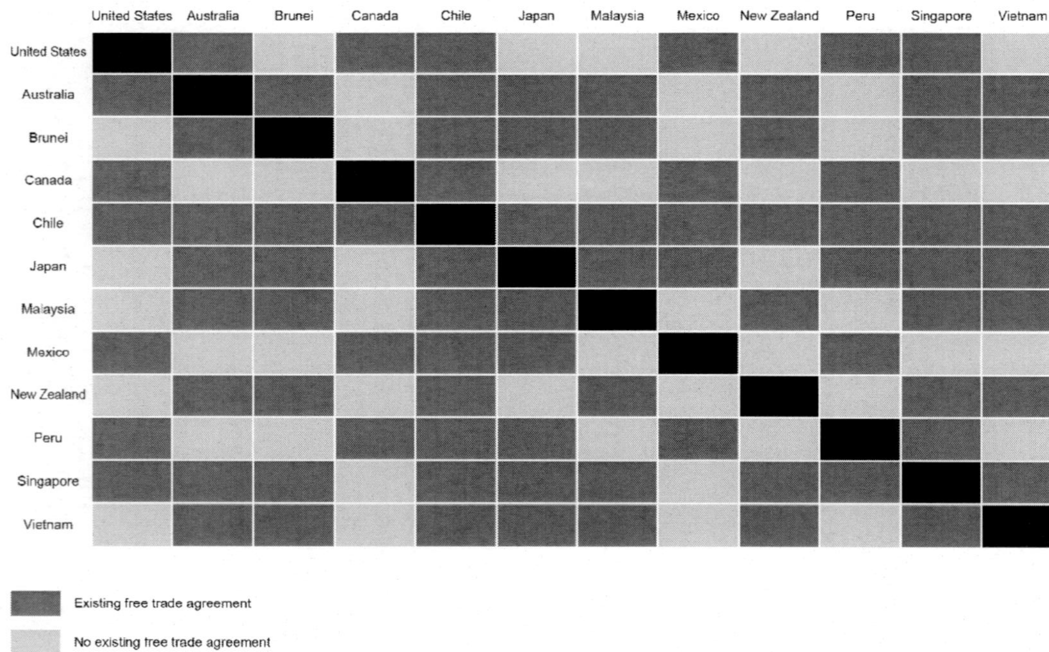

Source: GAO analysis of country documents. | GAO-15-724.

Figure 13. Existing Free Trade Agreements between the United States and Trans-Pacific Partnership Negotiating Partners.

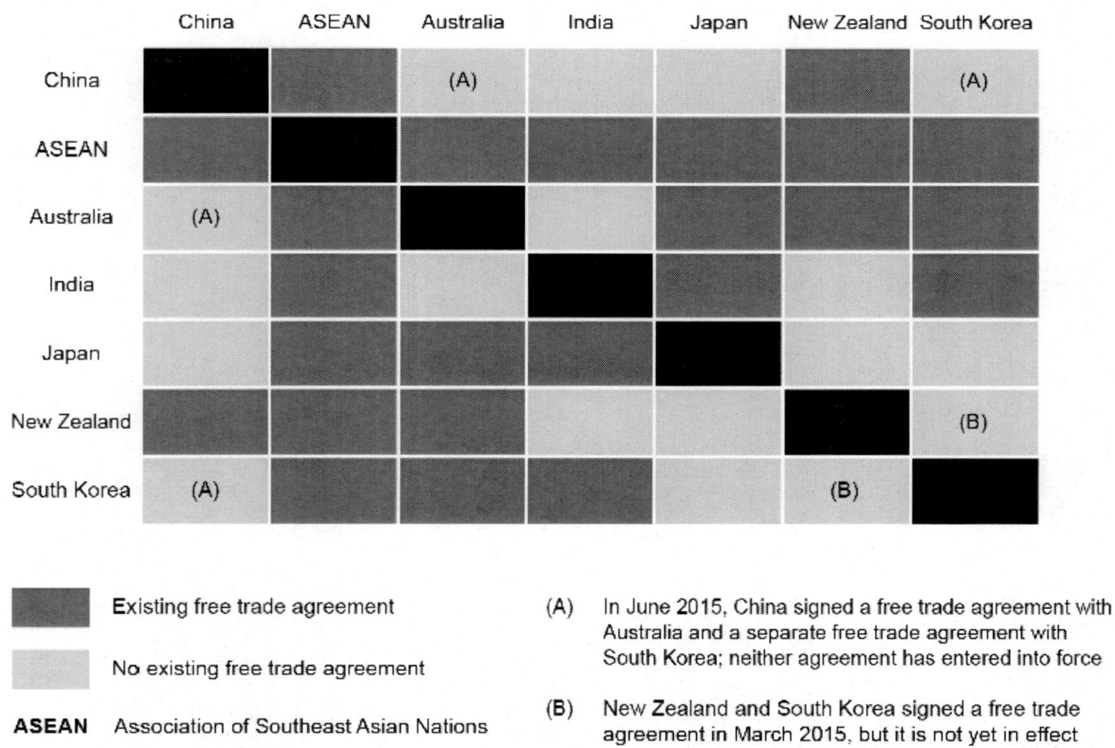

Source: GAO analysis of Asean and country documents. | GAO-15-724.

Figure 14. Existing Free Trade Agreements between China and Regional Comprehensive Economic Partnership Negotiating Partners, as of June 2015.

Table 3. Bilateral Goods and Services Trade between the United States and Trans-Pacific Partnership (TPP) Negotiating Partners, 2013

Nominal dollars in billions				
	Total goods trade with the United States	**Percentage of total U.S. goods trade**	**Total services trade with the United States**	**Percentage of total U.S. services trade**
TPP negotiating partners with existing U.S. free trade agreements				
Australia	$35.3	1	$26.1	2
Canada	637.4	16	93.7	8
Chile	28.7	1	4.8	0
Mexico	509.1	13	47.6	4
Peru	18.5	0	a	a
Singapore	48.7	1	17.0	1
Subtotal	**$1,277.8**	**33**	**$189.2**	**16**
TPP negotiating partners without existing U.S. free trade agreements				
Brunei	$0.6	0	a	a
Japan	207.4	5	$76.3	7
Malaysia	41.0	1	4.2	0
New Zealand	6.9	0	3.6	0
Vietnam	31.0	1	a	a
Subtotal	**$286.9**	**7**	**$84.1**	**7**
Total[b]	**$1,564.6**	**40**	**$273.3**	**24**

Source: GAO analysis of U.S. data on trade in goods from the United Nations Commodity Trade database and U.S. data on trade in services from the Bureau of Economic Analysis. | GAO-15-724.

Notes: U.S. 2014 trade in services data are not available. Some numbers do not sum to totals because of rounding.

[a]The Bureau of Economic Analysis has not released data on U.S. trade in services for these countries because of confidentiality and data limitations.

[b]Services trade totals do not include the countries with no reported data. These countries are likely to represent 1 percent or less of U.S. services trade.

Table 4. Bilateral Goods and Services Trade between China and Regional Comprehensive Economic Partnership (RCEP) Negotiating Partners, 2013

Nominal dollars in billions				
	Total goods trade with China, 2013	**Percentage of total China goods trade, 2013**	**Total services trade with China, 2011[b]**	**Percentage of total China services trade, 2011[b]**
RCEP negotiating partners with existing China free trade agreements				
ASEAN	$443.6	11	$36.9	9
Australia[a]	136.5	3	13.7	3
New Zealand	12.4	0	No data	No data
South Korea[a]	274.2	7	23.3	6
Subtotal	**$866.7**	**21**	**$73.9**	**18**
RCEP negotiating partners without existing China free trade agreements				
India	$65.4	2	No data	No data
Japan	312.4	8	33.8	8
Subtotal	**$377.8**	**9**	**$33.8**	**8**
Total	**$1,244.5**	**30**	**$107.7**	**26**

Source: GAO analysis of Chinese data from the United Nations Commodity Trade database and estimates from a United Nations Conference on Trade and Development, World Trade Organization, and International Trade Centre joint dataset. | GAO-15-724.

Notes: The latest data on Chinese trade in services are for 2011. Some numbers do not sum to totals because of rounding.

[a]In June 2015, China signed a free trade agreement with Australia, and a separate free trade agreement with South Korea; neither agreement has entered into force.

[b]Services trade totals do not include the countries with no reported data.

The United States Has Provided More Than $6 Billion in Financing for Exports to, and Investments in, ASEAN Countries since Fiscal Year 2009

According to our analysis of U.S. agency data, from fiscal years 2009 through 2014, the United States provided more than $6 billion in financing to support U.S. exports to, and investment in, ASEAN countries (see table 5). During that period:

- The U.S. Export-Import Bank (Ex-Im) authorized about $5.4 billion in loans, loan guarantees, and insurance to support U.S. exports to ASEAN countries.[54] Worldwide, Ex-Im authorizations were $27.3 billion in 2013 and $20.5 billion in 2014.

- The Overseas Private Investment Corporation (OPIC), the United States' development finance institution, committed about $664 million in financing to support U.S. investment projects in ASEAN countries.[55]

Table 5. Ex-Im Authorizations and OPIC Commitments in ASEAN countries, Fiscal Years 2009 to 2014

Nominal U.S. dollars (in millions)			
Fiscal year	Ex-Im authorizations in ASEAN countries[a]	OPIC commitments in ASEAN countries	Total[b]
2009	$551.0	$7.0	$558.0
2010	807.4	1.4	$808.8
2011	777.4	265.8	$1,043.2
2012	689.3	28.5	$717.8
2013	2,106.2	311.0	$2,417.3
2014	499.3	50.0	$549.3
Total	$5,430.7c	$663.8d	$6,094.5

Legend: ASEAN = Association of Southeast Asian Nations; Ex-Im = U.S. Export-Import Bank; OPIC = Overseas Private Investment Corporation.

Source: GAO analysis of OPIC data and Ex-Im annual reports and data. | GAO-15-724.

[a]Ex-Im generally provides financing to businesses when private financing is unavailable; therefore, fluctuations in its financing activity may reflect changes in the business and banking environment rather than Ex-Im's initiative.

[b]These data do not include Ex-Im multibuyer insurance, which may include multiple countries, or OPIC funds recorded as provided to the Asia and the Pacific Region, which have not been used in ASEAN countries.

[c]Worldwide, Ex-Im's authorizations totaled $161.8 billion in fiscal years 2009 through 2014 in nominal terms.

[d]Worldwide, OPIC's commitments totaled $19.7 billion in fiscal years 2009 through 2014 in nominal terms.

U.S. financing is provided under the OECD Arrangement on Officially Supported Export Credits, which governs the United States' and other member countries' official export financing. Under the arrangement, OECD countries transparently report their financing transactions and agree to notify, consult, and share information with other participants if they offer loan terms more generous than those the arrangement specifies.

According to our analysis of Ex-Im data, in fiscal years 2009 through 2014, Ex-Im's authorizations in ASEAN countries largely consisted of loan guarantees and were concentrated in Indonesia and Singapore. For example, about half of the $2.1 billion that Ex-Im authorized to support U.S. exporters in ASEAN countries in fiscal year 2013 was for a loan guarantee to a U.S. firm exporting commercial aircraft to Indonesia. According to our analysis of OPIC data, OPIC's two largest individual commitments in ASEAN countries from 2009 through 2014, each for $250 million, were for investment guarantees in fiscal year 2013 for a research center, medical school, and teaching hospital in Malaysia and in fiscal year 2011 for construction and development of solar power projects in Thailand.[56]

China Provides Competitive Financing but Does Not Publish Country-Specific Data

U.S. Ex-Im estimates and data from China's export credit agencies indicate that China provides significantly more financial support to its exporters worldwide than does the United States. In 2014, Ex-Im estimated in an annual report to Congress that China provided $111 billion worldwide in official export support in calendar year 2013, far more than Ex-Im's $15 billion in calendar year 2013. [57] Ex-Im's report noted that Chinese export credit agencies—along with those of Japan and South Korea—have multiple advantages, including greater funding capacity, the ability to lend in dollars at competitive rates, and lending programs that are not bound by OECD agreements. China is not a participant in the OECD Arrangement on Officially Supported Export Credits. The Ex-Im report also expressed concern that Chinese concessional loans provided to other governments as development assistance—including some loans with terms likely outside the range allowed by OECD agreements—may affect the competitiveness of U.S. exports.[58]

Three Chinese state-owned institutions offer various types of financing to support Chinese firms engaged in international business, including business in ASEAN countries. These three institutions do not publish data by country on their financing for exports, imports, and investment by private and state-owned enterprises.

- **Export-Import Bank of China (China Ex-Im).** China Ex-Im provides support for the import and export of goods and services, including Chinese companies' overseas construction and investment projects. China Ex-Im is also the conduit for China's official concessionary lending to developing countries. No data are publicly available on China Ex-Im financing for specific countries in Southeast Asia. According to its 2014 annual report, China Ex-Im provided a total of $70 billion in export and import credits worldwide that year.[59]
- **China Development Bank.** The China Development Bank supports state-backed projects, such as airports, railways, and bridges.

Although the bank does not publish country-specific data on its overseas lending, it reported that of its net loan balance of $1.24 trillion for 2014, 12.7 percent ($157 billion) was provided to recipients outside mainland China. The bank did not specify whether those recipients included foreign governments, Chinese companies operating overseas, or both.[60]

- **China Export & Credit Insurance Corporation (Sinosure)**. Sinosure provides credit insurance to protect against nonpayment of commercial debt, including by buyers of exports, and also provides investment insurance. Sinosure's most recent publicly available annual report from 2011 does not include country-specific data but states that Sinosure insured more than 11 percent of China's total exports that year. Also in 2011, Sinosure provided 36 percent of its short-term export credit insurance coverage—the type of insurance it most commonly provided—for exports in Asia, compared with 29 percent in Europe and 20 percent in North America. According to a report published by the OECD, Sinosure insured almost 15 percent of China's exports in 2013.[61]

U.S. and Chinese Entities Support Business and Investment in ASEAN Countries

Multiple U.S. entities, such as the U.S. Departments of State (State), Commerce, and Agriculture (USDA), provide export promotion services and other support to help U.S. firms enter ASEAN markets or expand their presence in ASEAN countries.[62] For example:

- **State.** State maintains economic officers in each of the 10 ASEAN countries. State supports U.S. export promotion efforts by engaging with foreign governments on policies that affect U.S. economic and commercial interests and by supporting other U.S. agencies' export promotion efforts, among other things.
- **Commerce.** Commerce maintains a presence in seven ASEAN countries and a regional office in Singapore.[63] Commerce provides export promotion services to U.S. firms, including advocacy and commercial diplomacy, market intelligence, matchmaking with local firms, trade counseling, and trade promotion programs. Commerce also leads or supports trade missions.[64] From 2009 through 2014, Commerce led 11 trade missions to ASEAN countries covering a range of industries, such as aerospace, education, energy, and textiles.

- **USDA.** USDA maintains a presence in seven ASEAN countries.[65] USDA provides export promotion services for U.S. agricultural exporters, such as market intelligence and international trade missions. USDA also offers multiple market development programs in partnership with U.S. food and agriculture industry groups.[66]

For information about State, Commerce, and USDA staffing in ASEAN countries, see appendix IV.

The Chinese government also pursues agreements with other countries to facilitate trade and investment by Chinese firms in other countries, including ASEAN countries. For example:

- **Special economic zones.** China's Ministry of Commerce has worked with some ASEAN countries to set up special economic cooperation zones to facilitate cross-border investment and trade. According to China's Ministry of Commerce, the Chinese government supports Chinese firms that establish and invest in the zones by offering financing, and facilitating movement of materials, equipment, labor, and foreign exchange between China and the zones. China also negotiates with the host government in the areas of tax, land, and labor policies to support firms that choose to invest in the zones. According to Chinese embassy websites, as of 2012, Chinese firms had set up five zones in four countries—Cambodia, Thailand, Vietnam, and Indonesia—91 enterprises had established businesses, and more than $930 million had been invested in the zones.
- **Currency swaps.** China also facilitates cross-border trade in local currencies with ASEAN countries.[67] Chinese agencies have publicly reported that China has currency swap agreements with the central banks of Indonesia, Malaysia, Thailand, and Singapore totaling 650 billion Chinese yuan.[68] Currency exchanges help to facilitate trade and investment between the countries by eliminating the cost of converting to a third currency, ensuring that sufficient amounts of foreign currency are available for transactions, and reducing the risk of exchange rate fluctuation. These agreements encourage trade between China and the countries involved in the agreements to be settled in those countries' currencies rather than in dollars. Chinese Premier Li Keqiang, the second-highest ranked Chinese Communist party official, has stated that China also plans a pilot program to allow currency swaps for cross-border transactions with other countries of

the Greater Mekong Subregion (Vietnam, Laos, Cambodia, and Burma).[69]

The United States Supports Capacity Building to Foster ASEAN Economic Development, while China Supports Infrastructure Development

The United States and China both provide assistance to ASEAN countries to support regional economic development and integration. U.S. initiatives have included enhancing governance and regional connectivity by, for example, efforts to improve customs procedures across ASEAN countries. Chinese initiatives have focused on infrastructure development. China has promised billions of dollars for infrastructure investment through new funds and multilateral institutions, such as the Asian Infrastructure Investment Bank.

The United States Has Supported Economic Development in ASEAN Countries by Enhancing Governance and Regional Connectivity

In fiscal years 2009 through 2013, the United States identified $536 million of its assistance to ASEAN countries and the ASEAN Secretariat as TCB assistance—that is, development assistance intended to improve a country's ability to benefit from international trade.[70] U.S. TCB assistance has supported initiatives aimed at, among other things, helping ASEAN countries draft laws and regulations, improve public financial management, train government officials, meet WTO commitments, and increase accountability and transparency. U.S. TCB assistance has supported multiple initiatives to advance ASEAN's goal of increased connectivity and integration throughout the region.[71] For example:

- **ASEAN Connectivity through Trade and Investment.** This 5-year, $16.2 million USAID program, begun in 2013, seeks to facilitate trade through improving standards and systems, boosting the capacity of small and medium-sized enterprises, accelerating the deployment of clean energy technologies, and expanding connectivity. One of the program's objectives is to provide support for the ASEAN Single Window, which will integrate ASEAN's 10 national single customs windows to enable electronic exchange of data to expedite cargo clearance and lower the cost of doing business.[72] According to USAID officials, four ASEAN countries were ready to use the system as of January 2015, and it is planned to be operational by the end of the year.

- **ASEAN-U.S. Partnership for Good Governance, Equitable and Sustainable Development and Security.** This 5-year, $14 million program supported by USAID and State, also begun in 2013, seeks to support ASEAN integration by harmonizing approaches to the rule of law across countries; supporting people-to-people links through, for example, fellowships; collaboration on disaster response; and enhancing the ASEAN Secretariat's management capabilities, including information technology and public outreach capacities.[73]
- **U.S.-ASEAN Connectivity Cooperation Initiative.** Launched in 2011, this U.S. Trade and Development Agency (USTDA) initiative seeks to support ASEAN integration by leveraging private sector resources and expertise to support activities that increase connectivity and investment in the energy, transportation, and information and communications technology sectors. For example, USTDA has led reverse trade missions and workshops to increase U.S. trade and investment in electric smart grids, rail development, and other infrastructure areas in ASEAN countries. In September 2013, USTDA sponsored the ASEAN Connectivity through Rail Workshop in Indonesia that highlighted U.S. firms' capabilities in operation and maintenance of rail systems. In addition, USTDA is sponsoring the Global Procurement Initiative with the goal of fostering procurement systems that will make awards based on the best value offered, rather than on the lowest cost.[74]

Approximately $333 million of U.S. TCB assistance to ASEAN countries in fiscal years 2009 through 2013 was committed as part of a 5-year, $600 million Millennium Challenge Corporation (MCC) compact with Indonesia.[75] MCC commits funds at the time of compact signature, but disburses them over the 5 years of the compact. As of December 2014, MCC had expended $1.2 million of its $333 million commitment to Indonesia. For more information about U.S. TCB in ASEAN countries, see appendix V.

China Supports Trade Capacity Building and Infrastructure Development and Proposes Tens of Billions of Dollars for Future Infrastructure Projects

Like the United States, China has supported capacity-building efforts in ASEAN countries, but it also provides billions of dollars for infrastructure construction. According to the Chinese government's July 2014 white paper on foreign aid China's capacity-building efforts in ASEAN countries since 2010 have included setting up experimental crop stations, building three agricultural technology demonstration centers, dispatching 300 agricultural experts to provide technical guidance, and helping to establish systems for animal and plant disease prevention and control.[76] The paper states that China has also provided training to more than 5,000 officials and technicians from ASEAN countries in fields such as business promotion, culture and arts, Chinese language, finance, energy, and agriculture.

China has also contributed to regional development and integration through infrastructure construction, generally in the form of loans for specific projects, many of which are carried out by Chinese firms. The 2014 white paper states that China appropriated $14.4 billion for global foreign assistance from 2010 to 2012, 64 percent of which was interest-free or concessional loans. The white paper also indicates that China emphasized assistance in infrastructure construction, with 45 percent of China's total aid for economic infrastructure and 28 percent for social and public infrastructure. The white paper did not break out information on foreign aid in ASEAN countries.[77] According to expert testimony before the U.S.-China Economic and Security Review Commission in May 2015, as a result of overcapacity in the domestic Chinese construction market, projects overseas have become more attractive to Chinese state-owned enterprises.[78]

China has also provided loans to neighboring countries to finance transportation links that will facilitate trade and other exchanges. Some of these projects are part of the Greater Mekong Subregion (GMS) Economic Cooperation Program, supported by ADB.[79] Burma, Cambodia, Laos, Thailand, Vietnam, and China's Yunnan Province and Guangxi Zhuang Autonomous Region are members of the subregion. According to Chinese government publications and other sources, China funded construction of part of a highway in Laos on a route between Kunming and Bangkok, has upgraded its own highways that connect to other GMS countries, has built other roads financed by ADB, and has financed and built bridges in the subregion. The Chinese and Burmese governments recently completed construction of crude oil and natural gas pipelines from an Indian Ocean port in Burma to China. China also recently signed a memorandum of understanding with Thailand to build a railway in Thailand from the Thai-Laos border to Bangkok and the southeastern province of Rayong and is negotiating with Laos to build a railway connecting China with Laos' capital of Vientiane and the Thai border.

China has promised billions of dollars for new funds and multilateral institutions for the purpose of investing in infrastructure, including in ASEAN countries. For example:

- **Silk Road Fund.** China announced the creation of the $40 billion Silk Road Fund to finance infrastructure construction and other development in support of two initiatives announced by Chinese President Xi Jinping in 2013: the Silk Road Economic Belt and 21st Century Maritime Silk Road. According to a document released by the Chinese government in March 2015, these initiatives aim to improve land and maritime cooperation and connectivity along routes between China and the rest of Asia, the South China Sea, the Indian Ocean, Africa, and Europe.[80] In February 2015, the Chinese central bank announced that an initial $10 billion had been contributed to the fund by state-owned financial institutions and the Chinese foreign exchange reserves.[81] In April 2015, China announced the fund's first investment, in support of a hydropower project in Pakistan.
- **Asian Infrastructure Investment Bank (AIIB).** In 2013, Chinese President Xi Jinping proposed the creation of an international institution, AIIB, to finance infrastructure projects throughout the Asia-Pacific region.[82] Under the bank's initial agreement, the bank's authorized capital is $100 billion.[83] According to AIIB documents, 57 countries are prospective founding members of the bank, including each of the 10 ASEAN countries, and the bank anticipates beginning operations before the end of 2015.[84] The bank will be headquartered in Beijing. Chinese officials have said that all countries are welcome to join the bank; the United States and Japan have so far declined to do so. U.S. Treasury officials have stated that the United States welcomes the creation of new development institutions but have also expressed concerns about the governance and standards of the new bank.
- **Other funds.** In addition, in November 2014, Chinese Premier Li Keqiang pledged $20 billion in loans to boost infrastructure connectivity in Southeast Asia, including $10 billion in loans to ASEAN countries. He also announced that China would raise another $3 billion for the China-ASEAN Investment Cooperation Fund, a dollar-denominated equity fund that targets investment opportunities in infrastructure, energy, and natural resources in ASEAN countries.

As of June 2015, the fund reported that its current size was $1 billion, and it had set a target to ultimately raise $10 billion.

AGENCY COMMENTS

We are not making recommendations in this report. We sent a draft of this report for review and comment to the Departments of Agriculture, Commerce, State, and the Treasury and to MCC, OPIC, USAID, Ex-Im, USTDA, and USTR. We received technical comments from Agriculture, Commerce, State, the Treasury, and USTR, which we incorporated as appropriate.

David B. Gootnick,
Director International Affairs and Trade

APPENDIX I: OBJECTIVES, SCOPE, AND METHODOLOGY

We were asked to review the nature of the United States' and China's economic engagement in Southeast Asia.[1] Our objectives were to examine (1) what available data indicate about U.S. and Chinese trade and investment with the Association of Southeast Asia Nations (ASEAN) countries and (2) what actions the U.S. and Chinese governments have taken to further economic engagement with these countries.

As part of this review, we conducted fieldwork in Jakarta, Indonesia—where the ASEAN Secretariat is located—and Hanoi and Ho Chi Minh City, Vietnam. We based our selection of these two countries, among the 10 ASEAN countries, on the amounts of U.S. and Chinese exports and imports, foreign direct investment (FDI), and development assistance in each country. We also considered whether a country participated in U.S. and Chinese trade agreements or was a negotiating partner in the Trans-Pacific Partnership, whether a country was the location of any regional institutions, whether it was an emerging partner, and whether it was a South China Sea claimant. The information on foreign law in this report is not a product of GAO's original analysis but is derived from interviews and secondary sources.

To describe U.S. and Chinese engagement with ASEAN countries, we analyzed data on U.S. and Chinese trade in goods, trade in services, and FDI. We also analyzed trade and contract data to determine the extent to which U.S.

and Chinese firms compete. To assess the reliability of these data, where possible, we cross-checked the data with other sources, conducted checks on the data for internal consistency, and consulted with U.S. officials. Because of the limited availability of data and the context for different sets of data we report, the time period for each set of reported data varied. We determined that the data were sufficiently reliable for the purposes of our report and have noted caveats where appropriate to indicate limitations in the data.

- To obtain data on U.S. and Chinese trade in goods from 1994 through 2014, we accessed the United Nations' (UN) Commodity Trade Statistics Database by means of the Department of Commerce's (Commerce) Trade Policy Information System. This database provides data for comparable categories of exports and imports of goods for the United States and China. In reporting the value of exports, we used data on total exports, which include re-exports—goods that are imported but then exported in substantially the same condition. China does not report export data to the UN Commodity Trade database that separates re-exports from total exports. Therefore, we used data on total exports to ensure the comparability of U.S. and Chinese data on goods exports. For imports, we used data on general imports, which include goods that clear customs and goods that enter into bonded warehouses or foreign trade zones. We determined that data on trade in goods for the United States and China were generally reliable for comparing trends over time and the composition of trade.

  To categorize the U.S. and Chinese trade in goods into capital, intermediate, and consumer goods, we assigned each good from the UN Commodity Trade database to one of these three categories using the UN's Broad Economic Categories. For goods that the UN does not classify as capital, intermediate, and consumer goods, we created an unclassified category. For example, the UN does not classify passenger motor cars as capital or consumer goods.
- We analyzed data from the Organisation for Economic Co-operation and Development (OECD) and the World Trade Organization (WTO) on trade in value-added goods and services to illustrate the importance of accounting for components of a country's exports that originate in other countries.

  We analyzed data from the ASEANstats database for 2003, 2008, and 2013 to examine ASEAN countries' trade in goods with their trading partners over time. Because some of the ASEAN countries' trading partners do not report data to the UN Commodity Trade database, we used data from the ASEANstats database as a comprehensive set of data on trade in goods for all of ASEAN countries' trading partners. We compared trade data from the ASEANstats database and the UN Commodity Trade Database and found some differences in values of bilateral trade between ASEAN countries and their trading partners. Reasons for the differences include differences in the valuation of goods and differences in data quality.

- We calculated U.S. trade in services for 2011 and 2012, based on tabulations prepared for us by the Commerce's Bureau of Economic Analysis (BEA) and other sources, including the U.S. Census Bureau. BEA's data on trade in services for several categories—travel and passenger fares, transportation, education, and other private services—are based on data from various sources. According to BEA, its survey data are from mandatory surveys of primarily U.S. businesses with services trade that exceeds certain thresholds. BEA does not survey a random sample of U.S. businesses and therefore does not report the data with margins of error. Our estimates of U.S. trade in services represent broad estimates rather than precise values. We extrapolated values for certain services at the country level from broader data (e.g., travel service data are based on multiplying the number of travelers for a country by data on average expenditures for travelers and average passenger fees for the region) We calculated values for other services (e.g., business, professional, and technical services) from a range of estimates based on survey data. In instances where the volume of trade for a service was presented to us as a range, we used the midpoint value to estimate the volume of trade for that service. In instances where the volume of trade for a service was presented as a range and described by BEA as trending upward, we used the lowest value for the earlier years and the highest value for the later years and assumed that the growth was linear.

For China's trade in services in 2011, we used estimates from the UN Conference on Trade and Development, the World Trade Organization (WTO), and the International Trade Centre downloaded from the International Trade Centre's Trade Map database. The estimates for 2009 from the Trade Map database are the same as data on China's trade in services from a report by China's Ministry of Commerce.[2]

- For data on U.S. firms' investments from 2007 through 2012, we used data that we obtained directly from BEA. For Chinese firms' investments, we used data from the UN Conference on Trade and Development as reported by China's Ministry of Commerce. To identify patterns in, and to compare, U.S. and Chinese FDI, we report U.S. and Chinese data on FDI while noting their limitations. First, as we have previously reported, both U.S. and Chinese FDI may be underreported, and experts have expressed particular concern regarding China's data.[3] U.S. and Chinese firms set up subsidiaries in places such as the Netherlands and the British Virgin Islands, which can be used to make investments that are not captured by U.S. and Chinese data on FDI. Experts state that this could be a significant source of underreporting for China's data. For U.S. data, according to BEA, U.S. data on FDI are based on quarterly, annual, and benchmark surveys. BEA's benchmark survey is the most comprehensive survey of such investment and covers the universe of U.S. FDI. According to BEA, quarterly and annual surveys cover samples of businesses with FDI that exceed certain thresholds. BEA does not survey a random sample of businesses and therefore does not report the data with margins of error; therefore, we have not reported margins of error. Second, China does not report its definition of FDI when reporting its data. However, the types of data included by China in its FDI (e.g., equity investment data and reinvested earnings data) appear similar to data reported for U.S. FDI, which the United States defines on the basis of the OECD definition of FDI. Despite these limitations, various reports, including those published by international organizations such as the IMF, government agencies, academic experts, and other research institutions, use China's reported investment data to describe China's FDI activities. In addition, despite some potential underreporting of FDI data, we determined that the U.S. FDI data were reliable for reporting general patterns, when limitations are noted.

Given challenges in determining appropriate deflators for some data, we used nominal rather than inflation-adjusted values for U.S. and Chinese trade and for investments in ASEAN countries. However, we did test to see what the impact would be of deflating these data and found that deflating these values made a limited difference in describing the overall trends. For example, if the goods trade values that we report were adjusted using the U.S. gross domestic product (GDP) deflator, total Chinese trade in goods would surpass total U.S. trade in goods in 2007— similar to trends we found in nominal trade values. U.S. total trade in goods increased by a factor of 2.4 from 1994 through 2013 if not adjusted for inflation and by a factor of 1.7 if adjusted for inflation. Over the same period, Chinese total trade in goods increased by a factor of 30.9 if not adjusted for inflation and by a factor of 21.4 if adjusted for inflation.

To determine the extent to which U.S. and Chinese firms compete in ASEAN countries, we interviewed U.S. agency and private sector representatives and analyzed available data. To assess the extent to which exporters from the United States, China, and other countries compete, we calculated an export similarity index to compare U.S., Chinese, and other countries' exports to ASEAN countries from 2001 through 2014.[4] The export similarity index is a measure of the similarity of exports from two countries to a third country. For example, to calculate the index for U.S. and Chinese exports to ASEAN countries, for each type of good that the United States and China exports, we first calculate the share of that good in the United States' and China's total exports to ASEAN countries. We then identify the minimum of the United States' and China's shares. The index is the sum of the minimum shares for all types of goods that the United States and China export to ASEAN countries. We used data on goods exports from the UN Commodity Trade database at the four-digit level and calculated each country's export of a particular good as a share of that country's total exports to ASEAN countries.

We also analyzed data from Commerce's Advocacy Center on host-government contracts and data for contracts funded by the Asian Development Bank (ADB) and World Bank. Although these data represent a small share of activity in the region, they provide insights into the degree of competition between U.S. and Chinese firms for the projects represented.

- Commerce's Advocacy Center data were for a limited number of cases (184) where U.S. firms requested the agency's assistance in bidding for host-government contracts in ASEAN countries in 2009 through 2014. Because these data included the nationality of other firms bidding on a host-government contract, we used this information to determine the extent to which Chinese firms or firms of other nations were competing with U.S. firms for these contracts. We counted the numbers of contracts and summed the value of contracts in the Advocacy Center data for which each foreign country's firms competed against U.S. firms. We excluded 12 contracts for which the nationality of competitors was not identified, and in cases where the

U.S. firm(s) competed against a consortium of firms from different countries, we counted the whole value of the contract in each country's total. We also used the Advocacy Center's classification of contracts by sector to determine the sectors in which Chinese firms competed for the highest proportion of contracts. To determine the reliability of these data, we manually checked the data for missing values and reviewed information about how the data were collected. In addition, we interviewed Advocacy Center staff about the data. Advocacy Center staff told us that data from before 2010 may be less complete, because the center switched databases at that time, and some contracts that had been closed may not have been transferred. Overall, we found the data to be reliable for reporting on competition between U.S. and other firms, including Chinese firms, in ASEAN countries.

- The World Bank publishes data on the value, sector, and suppliers of its contracts in ASEAN countries. We used the World Bank's classification of contracts into procurement categories (goods, civil works, consultant services, and nonconsultant services) to compare the value and types of contracts that U.S. and Chinese firms were awarded from 2001 through 2014. However, we combined the consultant services and nonconsultant services categories into one category that we titled "consultant and other services". The data include contracts (generally large-value) that World Bank staff reviewed before the contracts were awarded. We analyzed all contracts in individual ASEAN countries as well as Mekong and ASEAN regional contracts. To determine the reliability of these data, we electronically checked the data for missing values and possible errors. We also contacted World Bank personnel to determine how the data were collected and any limitations of the data. We found that the data for contracts funded by the World Bank were generally reliable for the purpose of demonstrating U.S. and Chinese competition in ASEAN countries over time.
- To compare the value and types of contracts obtained by U.S. and Chinese firms, we used ADB's published data on the value, sector, and recipient of its contracts for consulting services, goods, and civil works provided as technical assistance or funded by loans and grants to ASEAN countries in 2013 and 2014. We also included regional contracts for Southeast Asia or the Greater Mekong Subregion in our analysis. ADB publishes data only for consulting contracts over $0.1

million in value and other contracts over $1.0 million, so our analysis of ADB contracts does not include some smaller ADB contracts. In addition, a portion of the ADB data did not have the contracts classified according to the nature of the contract (construction, consulting services, goods, turnkey, and others). Therefore, we classified contracts obtained by U.S. and Chinese firms that were missing these categories according to those used in the rest of the data. To determine the reliability of these data, we checked the data for missing values and other types of discrepancies. We found that the ADB data were generally reliable for our purpose of reporting on U.S. and Chinese competition in ASEAN countries in 2013 and 2014.

To examine the actions that the U.S. and Chinese governments have taken to further economic engagement, we reviewed regional and country studies and U.S., Chinese, and ASEAN agency documents and interviewed U.S. and third-country officials, officials from private sector business associations, and experts from think tanks. We tried to arrange visits with Chinese government officials in the ASEAN countries we visited and in Washington, D.C.; however, they were unable to accommodate our requests for a meeting. U.S. agencies included in the scope of our study are the U.S. Departments of Agriculture (USDA), Commerce, State (State), and the Treasury; the Office of the U.S. Trade Representative (USTR); the Millennium Challenge Corporation; the U.S. Agency for International Development (USAID); the Export-Import Bank of the United States (Ex-Im); the Overseas Private Investment Corporation (OPIC); and the U.S. Trade and Development Agency.

- To obtain information about U.S. and Chinese trade agreements with ASEAN countries, we reviewed the trade agreements; U.S., Chinese, and ASEAN documents; academic and government studies; prior GAO reports; and documents from multilateral organizations, such as the WTO. We also interviewed U.S. officials in Indonesia and Vietnam, officials from private sector business associations, and experts from think tanks. To calculate examples of tariff reductions from these trade agreements, we used data on trade in goods from the UN Commodity Trade database to identify top traded goods and data from the WTO and the U.S. International Trade Commission on U.S., Chinese, and ASEAN countries' tariffs.

- To calculate the percentage of world goods trade for the participants in the Trans-Pacific Partnership negotiations, the Regional Comprehensive Economic Partnership negotiations, and the North American Free Trade Agreement, we used data on trade in goods from the UN Commodity Trade Database. As of July 2015, some countries such as Malaysia and Italy had not reported data on trade in goods for 2013, so we used the average of those countries' available data from 2010 through 2012 as an estimate of its 2013 trade in goods.[5] In addition, Laos did not report data for 2010 through 2013, so we excluded it from the calculations. To calculate the total population and percentage of world GDP for these participants, we used data on population and GDP from the World Bank's World Development Indicators.
- To obtain information about U.S. financing, we compiled Ex-Im and OPIC data from these agencies' annual reports and congressional budget justifications and interviewed agency officials to provide additional context and to clarify elements of the data. Where relevant, we note that additional Ex-Im insurance may include ASEAN countries but do not include these in our totals. To determine the reliability of these data, we interviewed agency officials and checked their published annual reports against agency-provided summary data to determine any limitations of the data or discrepancies in the data. We determined that data from Ex-Im and OPIC were generally reliable to present trends and aggregate amounts by year.
- To document U.S. efforts to provide export promotion services in ASEAN countries, we reviewed State's Foreign Affairs Manual and information about Commerce and USDA's export promotion policies and trade missions. We also interviewed State, Commerce, and USDA officials in Washington, D.C., and in Vietnam and Indonesia. We obtained data from State, Commerce, and USDA on the agencies' staffing in ASEAN countries. To determine the reliability of the data, we obtained information about how the data were collected and tabulated. We determined that the data were sufficiently reliable to show staffing trends over time (see app. IV).
- To document Chinese financing and support for firms, we used publicly available information from the websites of the Export-Import Bank of China, the China Development Bank, and the China Export &

Credit Insurance Corporation. We converted financing numbers from Chinese yuan to U.S. dollars using exchange rates reported by the Federal Reserve. We supplemented this information with estimates from U.S. Ex-Im on Chinese export finance in 2013. We also used information reported by China's Ministry of Commerce about Chinese investment in special economic zones and from Xinhua, China's state press agency, about currency swap agreements between China and other countries' central banks.

- To obtain data on U.S. official development assistance, we used data from the OECD's Development Assistance Committee. To obtain data on China's grants and aid, we used data from China's 2014 white paper on foreign aid, which describes China's foreign assistance activities from 2010 through 2012.[6] To determine the reliability of U.S. development assistance data, we interviewed a knowledgeable USAID official about the definitions and collection of the data. We determined that U.S. development assistance data were generally reliable for showing the trends and composition of aid to ASEAN countries over time. China's white paper does not break out the data that it provides by country; thus, we were unable to provide data on China's provision of aid to ASEAN countries.
- To document U.S. support for economic development and integration in ASEAN countries, we used the USAID trade capacity building (TCB) database to capture U.S. development assistance efforts related to trade in ASEAN countries and at the ASEAN Secretariat. USAID collects data to identify and quantify the U.S. government's TCB activities in developing countries through an annual survey of agencies on behalf of USTR. We also reviewed agency project summaries and interviewed agency officials in Washington, D.C., Indonesia, and Vietnam. Where relevant, we noted that funds provided in a larger region (for example, funds provided to the East Asia and Pacific region) may include ASEAN countries, but we did not include these regional funds in our totals. To determine the reliability of these data, we interviewed agency officials regarding their methods for compiling and reviewing the data. We determined that data from the TCB database were sufficiently reliable for our purposes.
- To describe China's support for regional integration, we assessed publicly available information from China's July 2014 white paper on foreign aid; from Chinese ministries, such as the Ministry of Foreign

Affairs; and from Xinhua, China's state news agency. We determined that the white paper and web publications from the Ministry of Foreign Affairs represented official Chinese statements. We relied on Xinhua for translation of statements by Chinese officials about Chinese initiatives and strategies and for other factual information, such as the location of infrastructure built in ASEAN countries with Chinese support.

We conducted this performance audit from April 2014 to August 2015 in accordance with generally accepted government auditing standards. Those standards require that we plan and perform the audit to obtain sufficient, appropriate evidence to provide a reasonable basis for our findings and conclusions based on our audit objectives. We believe that the evidence obtained provides a reasonable basis for our findings and conclusions based on our audit objectives.

APPENDIX II: ROLES AND RESPONSIBILITIES OF U.S. AND CHINESE ENTITIES IN ASEAN COUNTRIES

Multiple U.S. and Chinese entities have roles in managing and conducting economic engagement with member countries of the Association of Southeast Asian Nations (ASEAN). Tables 6 and 7 provide more information about the roles and responsibilities of 10 U.S. entities and 6 Chinese entities that seek to promote trade and investment in, and provide aid to, ASEAN countries.

Six Chinese entities manage China's economic relationship with ASEAN countries. (See table 7.)

Table 6. Selected U.S. Government Entities' Roles and Areas of Involvement in Association of Southeast Asian Nations Countries

U.S. government entity	Role(s) and responsibilities	Area(s) of involvement
Department of Agriculture (USDA)	Expands and maintains access to foreign markets for U.S. agricultural products by removing trade barriers, enforcing U.S. rights under existing trade agreements, and providing market development programs; partners with the U.S. Agency for International Development to administer U.S. food aid programs.	Trade, investment, aid

Table 6. (Continued)

U.S. government entity	Role(s) and responsibilities	Area(s) of involvement
Department of State (State)	Oversees policy development and bilateral relations; provides diplomatic presence supporting U.S. aid, trade, and investment activities, including for other federal agencies as appropriate.	Trade, investment, aid
Department of the Treasury (Treasury)	Engages on macroeconomic, development, and financial policy-related issues, including through multilateral economic and financial institutions; provides bilateral technical assistance to support the development of strong financial sectors and public financial management; advocates for transparency, accountability, and effectiveness in helping to foster private sector investment through multilateral development banks, such as the World Bank.	Trade, investment, aid
Department of Commerce (Commerce)	Facilitates U.S. export and investment opportunities; helps U.S. firms resolve market access problems; assists U.S. firms competing for foreign-government contracts.	Trade, investment
Office of the U.S. Trade Representative (USTR)	Develops and coordinates implementation of U.S. trade and investment policy; leads discussions with trade and investment framework agreement partners; negotiates bilateral investment treaties and other trade agreements; seeks to reduce trade and investment barriers and distortions; enforces U.S. rights under trade agreements.	Trade, investment
U.S. Trade and Development Agency (USTDA)	Funds project-planning activities, such as feasibility studies, and U.S. visits for foreign decision makers to observe the design, manufacture, and operation of U.S. products and services to help them achieve their development goals.	Trade, investment
Export-Import Bank of the United States (Ex-Im)	Provides financing of U.S. goods and services—such as working capital guarantees (pre-export financing), export credit insurance, loan guarantees, and direct loans—to promote U.S. exports.	Trade
Overseas Private Investment Corporation (OPIC)	Provides development financing to assist U.S. private sector investors overseas through direct loans, loan guarantees, political risk insurance, and support for private equity investment funds.	Investment
Millennium Challenge Corporation (MCC)	Implements bilateral compacts for grant-funded development projects.	Aid
U.S. Agency for International Development (USAID)	Formulates and implements U.S. development policies to promote broad-scale human progress through the advancement of, among other things, economic prosperity, democracy, and good governance in developing countries.	Aid

Source: GAO analysis of information from State, Agriculture, Commerce, Treasury, USTR, USTDA, Ex-Im, OPIC, MCC, and USAID. | GAO-15-724.

Table 7. Selected Chinese Government Entities' Roles and Areas of Involvement in Association of Southeast Asian Nations Countries

Chinese government entity	Role(s) and responsibilities	Area(s) of involvement
China Development Bank	Provides medium- to long-term financing through loans for development projects.	Trade, investment, aid
Ministry of Commerce	Formulates and implements policies on foreign trade and investment activities; leads efforts to provide assistance to foreign countries.	Trade, investment, aid
Ministry of Foreign Affairs	Coordinates with other Chinese ministries on issues including foreign trade and economic cooperation and assistance.	Trade, investment, aid
Export-Import Bank of China	Provides export and import credits, international guarantees, and concessional loans for overseas construction and investment.	Trade, investment
SINOSURE – The China Export & Credit Insurance Corporation	Provides firms with short-, medium-, and long-term export credit insurance, investment insurance, loan guarantees, and credit rating services.	Trade, investment
Ministry of Finance	Supervises the implementation of the foreign aid budget.	Aid

Source: GAO analysis of information from the Brookings Institution, the Center for Global Development, the government of China, the World Bank, and China scholar Deborah Brautigam. | GAO-15-724.

APPENDIX III: U.S., CHINESE, EUROPEAN UNION, AND JAPANESE GOODS TRADE WITH ASEAN COUNTRIES

Machinery is the largest component of both the United States' and China's total goods exports and imports with the Association of Southeast Asian Nations (ASEAN) countries, but machinery's share of goods trade is falling. From 2007 through 2014, approximately 95 percent of U.S. and Chinese traded machinery was for industrial use, to produce other goods. For example, integrated circuits, a top machinery good, are used for producing computers and other electronic goods. The significant role of trade in machinery indicates that ASEAN countries are integrated into the U.S. and Chinese supply chains.

- **Imports.** From 2000 through 2014, U.S. imports of machinery from ASEAN countries declined from 61 percent to 40 percent of U.S.

imports from ASEAN countries. As of 2014, the next largest categories of U.S. imports from ASEAN countries consisted of "other" (23 percent); textiles (15 percent); chemicals, plastic, and rubber (11 percent); and animals, plants, and food (10 percent). Machinery as a percentage of Chinese imports from ASEAN countries ranged from a low of 41 percent in 2000 to a high of more than 60 percent in 2006 before falling to 43 percent in 2014. Other leading Chinese imports in 2014 were chemicals, plastic, and rubber (16 percent) and mineral products (15 percent).

- **Exports.** From 2000 through 2014, machinery declined from 64 percent to 34 percent of U.S. exports to ASEAN countries, as the export share of U.S. transportation products grew from a low of 5 percent in 2000 to a high of 15 percent in 2013. In 2014, the other large categories of U.S. exports to ASEAN countries were "other" (17 percent); animals, plants, and food (14 percent); chemicals, plastic, and rubber (12 percent); and mineral products (6 percent). Machinery as a percentage of Chinese exports to ASEAN countries fell from a high of 46 percent in 2004 to 33 percent in 2014. Other leading Chinese exports in 2014 were "other" (30 percent); metals (13 percent); chemicals, plastic, and rubber (10 percent); and transportation (5 percent).

Figure 15 shows the United States' and China's total goods imports from ASEAN countries, by type of goods, in 2000 through 2014.

Tables 8 through 11 show the top 10 exports by the United States, China, the European Union (EU), and Japan to ASEAN countries in 2014. In 2014, electronic integrated circuits and microassemblies was the top export to ASEAN countries for both the United States and China; otherwise, U.S. and Chinese top 10 exports to ASEAN countries did not overlap.[1] Electronic integrated circuits and microassemblies was also the only top 10 U.S. export to ASEAN that was among the top 10 EU exports to ASEAN. Three of the top 10 U.S. exports to ASEAN: (1) electronic integrated circuits and microassemblies; (2) diodes, transistors and similar semiconductor devices and photosensitive semiconductor devices, light emitting diodes; and (3) gold, nonmonetary (excluding gold ores and concentrates) were among the top 10 Japanese exports.

Figure 16 shows the United States' and China's total goods exports to ASEAN countries, by type of goods, from 2000 through 2014.

Table 8. Top 10 U.S. Exports to ASEAN Countries by Four-Digit Standard International Trade Classification Code and Share of Total Exports, 2014

	U.S. exports	Share of U.S. exportsto ASEAN countriesby value (percentage)
1	7764: electronic integrated circuits and microassemblies	13.9
2	2222: soybeans	3.0
3	7763: diodes, transistors and similar semiconductor devices; photosensitive semiconductor devices; light emitting diodes	2.7
4	0412: wheat (including spelt) and meslin, unmilled, not elsewhere specified	2.1
5	9710: gold, nonmonetary (excluding gold ores and concentrates)	1.7
6	2631: cotton (other than linters), not carded or combed	1.5
7	8722: instruments and appliances used in medical, surgical or veterinary sciences (excluding electrodiagnostic and radiological instruments and apparatus)	1.5
8	0222: milk and cream, concentrated or sweetened	1.4
9	8747: oscilloscopes, spectrum analyzers, etc. (except meters), for measuring, etc. electricity; instruments, etc. measuring or detecting ionizing radiations	1.4
10	7599: parts and accessories for use solely or principally with office machines (except photo- or thermo-copy) and automatic data process machines, etc.	1.3

Legend: ASEAN = Association of Southeast Asian Nations UN = United Nations.

Source: GAO analysis of data from the UN Commodity Trade database | GAO-15-724.

Notes: Our analysis does not include exports categorized as "9310: special transactions and commodities not classified according to kind" because these include many different types of goods. According to the UN, it developed the Standard International Trade Classification to classify traded goods not only on the basis of their material and physical properties, but also according to their stage of processing and economic functions.

Table 9. Top 10 Chinese Exports to ASEAN Countries by Four-Digit Standard International Trade Classification Code and Share of Total Exports, 2014

	Chinese exports	Share of Chineseexports to ASEANcountries by value(percentage)
1	7764: electronic integrated circuits and microassemblies	3.4
2	7649: parts and accessories suitable for use solely or principally with the apparatus of telecommunications and sound recording and reproducing equipment	2.8
3	7643: transmission apparatus for radiotelephony, telegraphy, broadcasting or television, whether or not including reception, sound recording, etc. apparatus	1.9
4	8719: liquid crystal devices, not elsewhere specified; lasers (other than laser diodes); other optical appliances and instruments, not elsewhere specified	1.8
5	8131: Lamps and lighting fittings (including searchlights and spotlights) not elsewhere specified	1.5
6	6842: aluminum and aluminum alloys, worked	1.4
7	6762: bars and rods of alloy steel, not elsewhere specified, not further worked than hot-rolled, drawn or extruded, but including those twisted after rolling	1.4
8	8442: suits, ensembles, jackets, blazers, dresses, skirts, divided skirts, trousers, bib and brace overalls, breeches and shorts, women's or girls' text fabric knit	1.4
9	7932: ships, boats and other vessels (other than pleasure craft, tugs, pusher craft, special purpose vessels and vessels for breaking up)	1.4
10	7522: digital automatic data processing machines containing in the same housing a central processing unit and an input and output unit	1.3

Legend: ASEAN=Association of Southeast Asian Nations UN = United Nations

Source: GAO analysis of data from the UN Commodity Trade database | GAO-15-724.

Notes: Our analysis does not include exports categorized as "9310: special transactions and commodities not classified according to kind" because these include many different types of goods. According to the UN, it developed the Standard International Trade Classification to classify traded goods not only on the basis of their material and physical properties, but also according to their stage of processing and economic functions.

Table 10. Top 10 EU Exports to ASEAN Countries by Four-Digit Standard International Trade Classification Code and Share of Exports, 2014

	EU exports	Share of EU exportsto ASEAN countriesby value(percentage)
1	7924: airplanes and other aircraft, mechanically propelled (other than helicopters), of an unladen weight exceeding 15,000 kg	7.2
2	7764: electronic integrated circuits and microassemblies	5.4
3	7149: parts of turbojet engines and gas turbines, not elsewhere specified	2.8
4	7812: motor vehicles for the transport of persons (other than public transport), not elsewhere specified	2.5
5	5429: medicaments, not elsewhere specified	2.0
6	7284: machinery and mechanical appliances specialized for a particular industry, not elsewhere specified	1.6
7	1124: spirits for beverages (except ethyl alcohol 80 percent or more alcohol by volume); liqueurs, etc., not elsewhere specified	1.5
8	7843: parts and accessories not elsewhere specified for tractors, motor cars and other motor vehicles, trucks, public-transport vehicles and road motor vehicles not elsewhere specified	1.4
9	5416: glycosides; glands or other organs and extracts; antisera, vaccines and similar products	1.4
10	7452: dish washing machines (not household type); machinery for cleaning, filling, sealing, labeling, etc. containers; machinery for aerating beverages	1.2

Legend: ASEAN=Association of Southeast Asian Nations; EU=European Union; UN = United Nations.

Source: GAO analysis of data from the UN Commodity Trade database | GAO-15-724.

Notes: Our analysis does not include exports categorized as "9310: special transactions and commodities not classified according to kind" because these include many different types of goods. According to the UN, it developed the Standard International Trade Classification to classify traded goods not only on the basis of their material and physical properties, but also according to their stage of processing and economic functions.

Table 11. Top 10 Japanese Exports to ASEAN Countries by Four-Digit Standard International Trade Classification Code and Share of Exports, 2014

	Japanese exports	Share of Japaneseexports to ASEANcountries by value(percentage)
1	7843: parts and accessories not elsewhere specified for tractors, motor cars and other motor vehicles, trucks, public-transport vehicles and road motor vehicles not elsewhere specified	5.8
2	7764: electronic integrated circuits and microassemblies	5.2
3	7812: motor vehicles for the transport of persons (other than public transport), not elsewhere specified	2.9
4	7284: machinery and mechanical appliances specialized for a particular industry, not elsewhere specified	2.6
5	9710: gold, nonmonetary (excluding gold ores and concentrates)	2.1
6	7821: motor vehicles for the transport of goods	2.1
7	7763: diodes, transistors and similar semiconductor devices; photosensitive semiconductor devices; light emitting diodes	1.9
8	7932: ships, boats and other vessels (other than pleasure craft, tugs, pusher craft, special purpose vessels and vessels for breaking up)	1.8
9	7139: parts, not elsewhere specified for internal combustion piston engines for road vehicles, etc., for marine propulsion engines and internal combustion engines, not elsewhere specified	1.8
10	7768: piezoelectric crystals, mounted, and parts, not elsewhere specified of thermionic, cold cathode or photocathode valves and tubes, diodes, transistors, etc.	1.7

Legend: ASEAN=Association of Southeast Asian Nations; UN = United Nations.

Source: GAO analysis of data from the UN Commodity Trade database | GAO-15-724.

Notes: Our analysis does not include exports categorized as “9310: special transactions and commodities not classified according to kind” because these include many different types of goods. According to the UN, it developed the Standard International Trade Classification to classify traded goods not only on the basis of their material and physical properties, but also according to their stage of processing and economic functions.

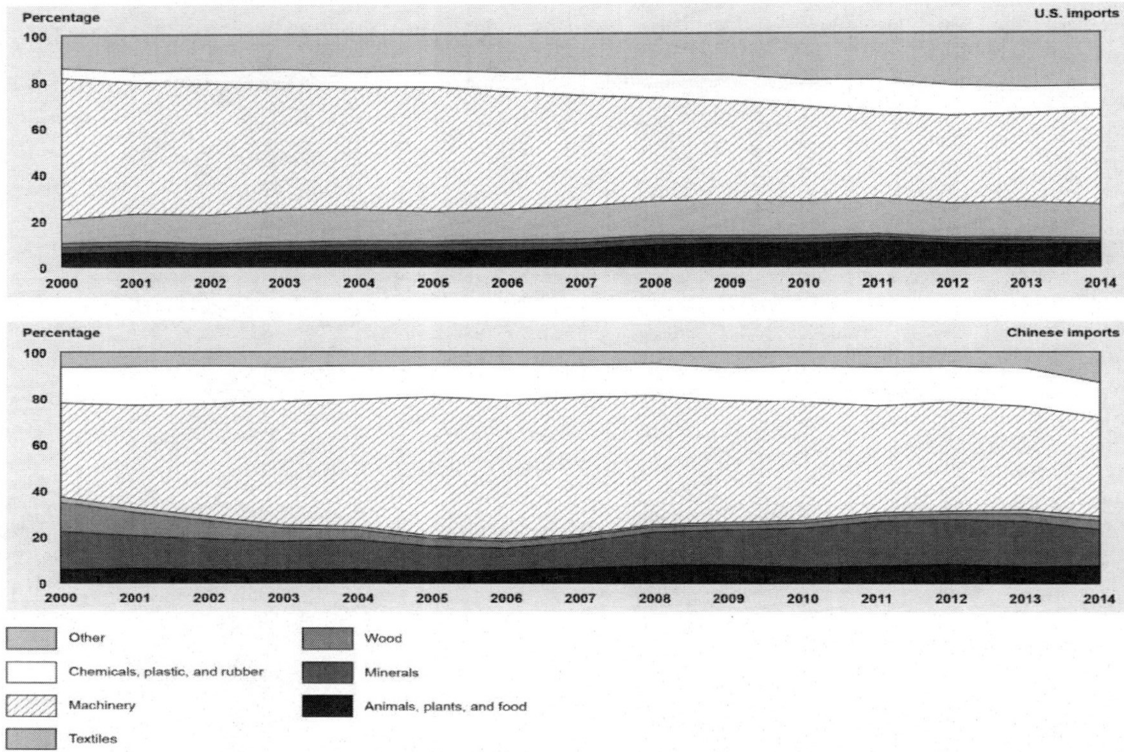

Source: GAO analysis of U.S. and Chinese data from the United Nations Commodity Trade database. | GAO-15-724.

Figure 15. U.S. and Chinese Imports of Goods from Association of Southeast Asian Nations Countries by Type, 2000-2014.

Commerce's FSO positions in ASEAN countries increased in fiscal years 2012 through 2014, while its locally employed staff (LES) positions remained about the same (see table 13).

Table 13. Department of Commerce FSO and LES Positions by ASEAN Country, Fiscal Years 2012-2014

Country	Type of position	2012	2013	2014
Brunei	FSO	0	0	0
	LES	0	0	0
Burma	FSO	0	0	1
	LES	0	0	0
Cambodia	FSO	0	0	0
	LES	0	0	0
Indonesia	FSO	3	3	3
Country	Type of position	2012	2013	2014
	LES	15	15	13
Laos	FSO	0	0	0
	LES	0	0	0
Malaysia	FSO	2	3	3
	LES	6	6	6
Philippines	FSO	2	2	2
	LES	12	12	12
Singapore	FSO	3	3	3
	LES	10	10	11
Thailand	FSO	2	2	2
	LES	13	14	12
Vietnam	FSO	4	4	4
	LES	18	17	18
Total	FSO	16	17	18
	LES	74	74	72

Legend: ASEAN=Association of Southeast Asian Nations. FSO = foreign service officer. LES = locally employed staff.

Source: GAO analysis of U.S. Department of Commerce data. | GAO-15-724.

Notes: The Department of Commerce's ASEAN FSO positions comprised about 7 percent of its worldwide FSO positions (excluding its Multilateral Development Bank staff) in fiscal year 2014. The department's ASEAN LES positions comprised about 10 percent of its worldwide LES positions in fiscal year 2014.

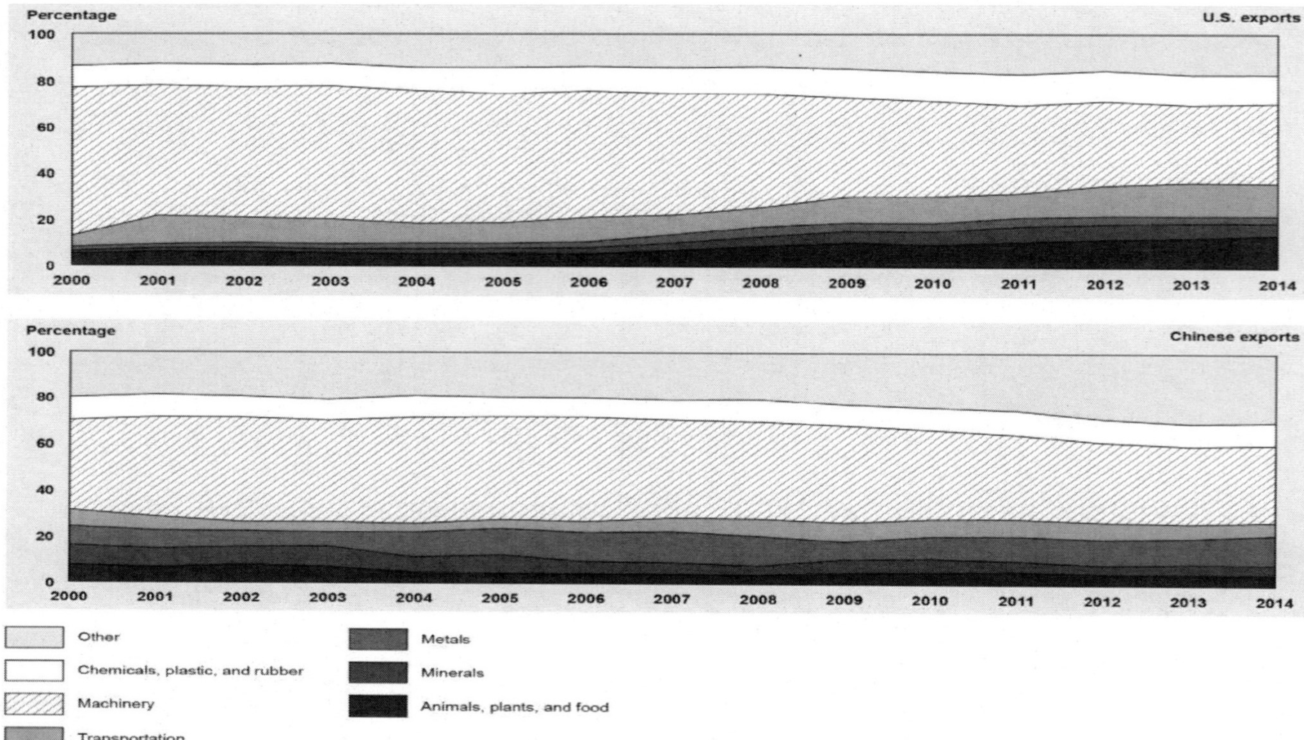

Source: GAO analysis of U.S. and Chinese data from the United Nations Commodity Trade database. | GAO-15-724.

Figure 16. U.S. and Chinese Exports of Goods to Association of Southeast Asian Nations Countries by Type, 2000-2014.

Appendix IV: Overseas Staffing in ASEAN Countries by Departments of State, Commerce and Agriculture

Overseas staffing in the member countries of the Association of Southeast Asian Nations (ASEAN) by the Departments of State (State) and Commerce (Commerce) generally increased in recent years, while the Department of Agriculture's (USDA) overseas staffing remained relatively constant.

State's economic foreign service officer (FSO) positions in ASEAN countries increased from 2008 through 2014, with the largest increase in positions from 2011 through 2012. However, State attributed the increase in positions in 2011 and 2012 to a worldwide reclassification of some positions from generalist interfunctional to economic. State economic FSO positions in ASEAN countries as a percentage of economic FSO positions worldwide remained from 6 to 7 percent from 2008 to 2014 (see table 12).

Table 12. Department of State Economic FSO Positions by ASEAN Country, Calendar Years 2008-2014

Country	2008	2009	2010	2011	2012	2013	2014
Brunei	0	0	0	0	1	1	2
Burma	2	3	3	3	4	5	6
Cambodia	1	2	2	2	3	3	3
Indonesia	13	14	15	16	18	17	17
Laos	0	1	1	1	3	4	4
Malaysia	6	6	6	6	6	6	6
Philippines	6	6	8	8	9	9	10
Singapore	4	4	4	4	4	4	4
Thailand	7	7	8	9	11	11	11
Vietnam	9	9	9	9	10	10	10
Total	48	52	56	58	69	70	73
Economic FSO positions in ASEAN countries as a percentage of such positions worldwide	6.4	6.8	6.6	6.8	6.4	6.5	6.8

Legend: ASEAN = Association of Southeast Asian Nations. FSO = foreign service officer.

Source: GAO analysis of U.S. Department of State data. | GAO-15-724.

Notes: Economic FSO positions are as of the end of each calendar year. These positions may include officers whose job responsibilities require that they work on both economic and political issues. According to the Department of State, the increase in economic FSO positions from 2011 to 2012 can be attributed to a reclassification of generalist interfunctional positions to economic positions.

Table 14. Department of Agriculture FSO and LES Positions by ASEAN Country, Fiscal Years 2009-2014

Country	Type of position	2009	2010	2011	2012	2013	2014
Brunei	FSO	0	0	0	0	0	0
	LES	0	0	0	0	0	0
Burma	FSO	0	0	0	0	0	0
	LES	1	1	1	1	1	1
Cambodia	FSO	0	0	0	0	0	0
	LES	1	1	1	0	0	0
Indonesia	FSO	2	2	2	2	2	2
	LES	10	10	10	7	7	8
Laos	FSO	0	0	0	0	0	0
	LES	1	1	1	0	0	0
Malaysia	FSO	1	1	1	1	1	1
	LES	5	5	5	5	4	4
Philippines	FSO	3	3	3	3	3	3
	LES	9	9	9	9	9	9
Singapore	FSO	0	0	0	0	0	0
	LES	2	2	2	2	2	2
Thailand	FSO	3	3	3	3	3	3
	LES	9	9	9	9	9	9
Vietnam	FSO	3	3	3	3	3	3
	LES	8	8	8	8	8	10
Total	FSO	12	12	12	12	12	12
	LES	46	46	46	41	40	43
Positions in ASEAN countries as a percentage of such positions worldwide	FSO	6.8	6.6	6.9	7.6	7.8	8.2
	LES	9.7	9.6	7.6	7.0	7.2	7.9

Legend: ASEAN=Association of Southeast Asian Nations. FSO = foreign service officer. LES = locally employed staff.

Source: GAO analysis of U.S. Department of Agriculture data. | GAO-15-724.

Notes: Department of Agriculture staff in Malaysia are responsible for supporting the department's activities, in accordance with its strategic goals, in Brunei, Papua New Guinea, and Singapore. Department of Agriculture staff in Vietnam provide support for the department's activities in Laos and Cambodia. The department plans to add one additional FSO position in Indonesia and one additional FSO and two LES positions in Burma.

The Department of Agriculture's (USDA) FSO and LES positions in ASEAN countries did not change significantly in fiscal years 2009 through 2014. USDA positions in ASEAN countries as a percentage of its global presence gradually increased for FSO positions during these years but decreased somewhat for LES positions from fiscal years 2009 through 2014 (see table 14).

APPENDIX V: U.S. TRADE CAPACITY BUILDING ASSISTANCE TO ASEAN COUNTRIES AND THE ASEAN SECRETARIAT

U.S. agencies have identified certain official development assistance to member countries of the Association of Southeast Asian Nations (ASEAN) and the ASEAN Secretariat as trade capacity building (TCB) assistance. TCB assistance addresses areas including the regulatory environment for business, trade, and investment; constraints such as low capacity for production and entrepreneurship; and inadequate physical infrastructure, for example, poor transport and storage facilities. Table 15 shows U.S. TCB assistance to ASEAN countries, including the ASEAN Secretariat, in fiscal years 2009 through 2013.

As table 15 shows, in fiscal years 2009 through 2011, U.S. TCB assistance to ASEAN countries and the ASEAN Secretariat remained relatively constant at approximately $45 million annually. In fiscal year 2012, the Millennium Challenge Corporation (MCC) signed a $600 million compact with Indonesia. MCC categorized its Indonesia compact's $332.5 million Green Prosperity Project as TCB assistance, resulting in an increase to $365.5 million in identified TCB assistance that year. In fiscal year 2013, U.S. TCB assistance fell to approximately $34 million.

Indonesia was the largest recipient of TCB assistance among ASEAN countries in recent years. Indonesia received almost 70 percent of the TCB funding in fiscal years 2009 to 2013, primarily because of funding from the MCC compact. The Philippines, Vietnam, and Cambodia were the next largest recipients of TCB assistance, with the Philippines receiving about 9 percent of total TCB assistance to ASEAN countries and the Secretariat in fiscal years 2009 through 2013, followed by Vietnam with 6 percent and Cambodia with about 5 percent. Singapore and Brunei did not receive TCB assistance during this period.

Table 15. U.S. TCB Assistance to the ASEAN Countries and Secretariat, Fiscal Years 2009-2013

Nominal dollars in millions	**2009**	**2010**	**2011**	**2012**	**2013**	**Total**	**TCB assistanceas percentageof total ASEANTCB assistance**
Brunei	-	-	-	-	-	-	0
Burma	-	-	0.2	-	6.4	6.6	1
Cambodia	4.2	4.5	3.9	11.7	3.0	27.4	5
Indonesia	13.4	3.8	7.4	339.3	9.1	373.1	70
Laos	2.4	2.2	2.0	1.6	0.7	8.9	2
Malaysia	1.2	1.8	0.8	0.8	1.1	5.7	1
Philippines	10.8	6.0	22.0	2.1	5.7	46.5	9
Singapore	-	-	-	-	-	-	0
Thailand	1.4	10.3	1.5	1.3	0.8	15.4	3
Vietnam	8.7	8.0	6.4	5.2	3.7	31.9	6
ASEAN Secretariat	3.5	9.1	1.0	3.4	3.8	20.8	4
ASEAN Total	**$45.5**	**$45.6**	**$45.2**	**$365.5**	**$34.3**	**$536.2**	**100**
TCB assistance to ASEAN countries as a percentage of TCB assistance worldwide	2	3	3	35	5	8	

Legend: ASEAN=Association of Southeast Asian Nations. TCB=trade capacity building.

Source: U.S. Agency for International Development TCB Database. | GAO-15-724.

Notes: The United States also provided TCB assistance categorized to the broader region during these years, such as to the Asia-Pacific Economic Cooperation Secretariat ($626,000), to Asia (countries not specified, $26.6 million), and to East Asia and Pacific (countries not specified, $2.6 million). Some of these funds may have been used in or benefitted ASEAN countries.

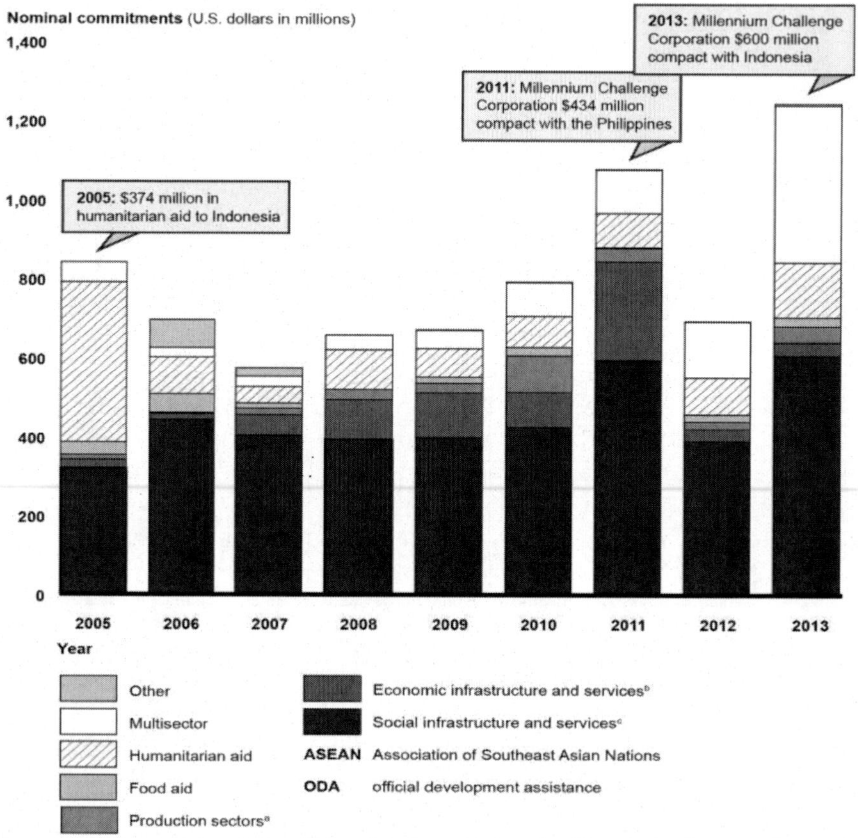

Source: GAO analysis of data from the Organisation for Economic Co-operation and Development. I GAO-15-724.

[a]Includes agriculture, forestry, fishing, industry, mining, construction, trade, and tourism.

[b]Includes transport, communications, energy, and financial services.

[c] Includes education, health, civil society, and water supply and sanitation.

Figure 17. U.S. ODA Commitments to ASEAN Countries, 2005-2013.

APPENDIX VI: U.S. AND CHINESE OFFICIAL DEVELOPMENT ASSISTANCE TO ASEAN COUNTRIES

U.S. official development assistance (ODA) to member countries of the Association of Southeast Asian Nations (ASEAN) has increased in recent years due to Millennium Challenge Corporation (MCC) commitments and has focused on social infrastructure and services. China does not report ODA by country and does not use the definitions used by the United States and other members of the Organisation for Economic Co-operation and Development's Development Assistance Committee (OECD-DAC).[1]

MCC Commitments Have Increased U.S. ODA to ASEAN Countries

In calendar years 2005 through 2013, the United States provided approximately $7.2 billion in ODA to ASEAN countries, approximately 2.8 percent of U.S. ODA worldwide for that period. In calendar year 2013, U.S. ODA to ASEAN countries was 4.5 percent of total U.S. ODA. More than half of U.S.-provided ODA to ASEAN countries was for "social infrastructure and services," which includes categories such as education, health, and assistance to government and civil society. In accordance with the 2005 Paris Declaration on Aid Effectiveness, the U.S. government generally does not condition its aid on, or tie it to, the recipient country's use of the aid to procure goods or services from the United States. From 2005 through 2013, the three highest U.S. ODA commitment levels to ASEAN countries resulted from large one-time commitments. In 2005, the United States committed $374 million in humanitarian aid to Indonesia. The 2011 and 2013 peaks reflect the entry-into-force of MCC compacts with the Philippines and Indonesia, respectively (see Figure 17).[2]

MCC's 5-year $434 million Philippines compact consists of rehabilitation of a 222-kilometer road on Samar to improve access to markets and social services ($214.4 million); funding for projects selected by communities, such as water systems, clinics, and schools ($120 million); efforts to improve tax administration ($54.3 million); and $45.1 million for program administration, monitoring, and evaluation.[3] MCC's 5-year, $600 million Indonesia compact consists of the Green Prosperity Project ($332.5 million) to provide technical and financial assistance for locally identified projects in renewable energy and natural resource management; the Community-Based Health and Nutrition to Reduce Stunting Project ($131.5 million) to improve child health and nutrition; and the Procurement Modernization Project ($50 million) to increase institutional capacity and employee knowledge of good procurement practices; and $86 million for program administration, monitoring, and evaluation.[4] Supported by the large commitments by MCC, Indonesia and the Philippines, the first and second-largest ASEAN countries by population, received the largest percentages of U.S. ODA to ASEAN countries in 2005 through 2013. Vietnam, the third largest, received the third-largest percentage (see table 16).

Table 16. U.S. ODA Commitments to ASEAN Countries, 2005 to 2013

Nominal dollars in millions		
Country	Total	Percentage of totalcommitments to ASEANcountries
Burma	$371.89	5.2
Brunei	-	0
Cambodia	706.24	9.8
Indonesia	2,950.19	40.9
Laos	69.75	1.0
Malaysia	130.93	1.8
Philippines	1670.35	23.1
Singapore	-	0
Thailand	550.19	7.6
Vietnam	770.88	10.7
Total	$7220.42	

Legend: ASEAN = Association of Southeast Asian Nations; ODA = official development assistance.

Source: GAO analysis of data from the Organisation for Economic Co-operation and Development's Development Assistance Committee database. | GAO-15-724.

Note: Numbers do not sum to totals because of rounding.

China Does Not Publish Aid Data Disaggregated by Country

China is not a member of the OECD-DAC and does not provide data according to OECD-DAC definitions and categories. In recent years, however, China has published some information about its foreign assistance. In 2011 and again in July 2014, China released a white paper on its foreign aid.[5] The white paper stated that China appropriated a total of $14.4 billion for global foreign assistance as grants (36 percent of the total), interest-free loans (8 percent), and concessional loans (56 percent) in 2010 through 2012. The white paper also stated that 31 percent ($4.4 billion) of China's aid was provided to Asia, but did not break out this aid by country. According to the white paper, 45 percent of China's total aid was for economic infrastructure, 28 percent was for social and public infrastructure, and from 2010 to 2012 China emphasized assistance in infrastructure construction. Unlike OECD-DAC countries, China has not agreed to eliminate tying aid to the use of its own goods and services.

End Notes

[1] The 10 members of ASEAN are Brunei Darussalam (Brunei), Burma (Myanmar), Cambodia, Indonesia, Laos, Malaysia, the Philippines, Singapore, Thailand, and Vietnam. In this report, "Southeast Asia" refers to the ASEAN members.

[2] An FTA is an agreement between two or more countries where the countries agree on certain obligations that affect trade in goods and services, and protections for investors and intellectual property rights, among other topics.

[3] Pub. L. No. 113-76, Div. K, § 7043.

[4] In 2013, we issued a report on U.S. and Chinese economic engagement in Sub-Saharan Africa. See GAO, *Sub-Saharan Africa: Trends in U.S. and Chinese Economic Engagement*, GAO-13-199 (Washington, D.C.: Feb. 7, 2013).

[5] We plan to issue a separate report with case studies of U.S. and Chinese economic engagement in Indonesia and Vietnam.

[6] Asian Development Bank Institute, *ASEAN 2030: Toward a Borderless Economic Community* (Tokyo: 2014).

[7] Economic Research Institute for ASEAN and East Asia, *ASEAN Rising: ASEAN and AEC Beyond 2015* (Jakarta: 2014).

[8] S. B. Das and C. R. James, *Addressing Infrastructure Financing in Asia*, (Singapore: Institute of Southeast Asian Studies, 2013). The study estimated the amount needed for ASEAN infrastructure investment in 2008 U.S. dollars.

[9] The U.S. Energy Information Administration is the U.S. Department of Energy's statistical and analytical agency.

[10] Transparency International, *Corruption Perceptions Index 2014* (Berlin: 2014). Transparency International is a global organization that publishes a corruption perceptions index based on expert opinion from around the world. The index measures the perceived levels of public sector corruption, where a ranking of 1 indicates the lowest levels of perceived corruption relative to other countries included in the index.

[11] World Bank, *Doing Business 2015: Going Beyond Efficiency* (Washington, D.C.: 2014).

[12] ASEAN, The ASEAN Charter, (Jakarta: 2008).

[13] Sanchita Basu et al., eds., *The ASEAN Economic Community: A Work in Progress* (Singapore: Asian Development Bank and Institute of Southeast Asian Studies, 2013). The Secretariat is headed by a secretary-general who serves a term of 5 years and has approximately 260 to 270 staff members, according to an ASEAN official. ASEAN is funded through a flat annual fee—$1.9 million per member in 2014, according to an ASEAN country representative.

[14] Asian Development Bank Institute and Institute of Southeast Asian Studies, *The ASEAN Economic Community: A Work in Progress*.

[15] Pub. L. No. 113-76, Div. K, § 7043.

[16] U.S.-China Economic and Security Review Commission, *2014 Report to Congress* (Washington, D.C.: 2014).

[17] The 2+7 cooperation framework proposes a two-part political consensus between China and ASEAN to (1) deepen strategic trust and friendship and (2) focus on economic development and expanding mutual benefit. The framework also lists seven action items for the China-ASEAN relationship, including upgrading the existing China-ASEAN FTA; accelerating construction of connectivity infrastructure, including a Trans-Asian Railway, and establishing the Asian Infrastructure Investment Bank; enhancing financial cooperation;

promoting maritime cooperation (including the Maritime Silk Road); and strengthening security cooperation.

[18] Information Office of the State Council, The People's Republic of China, China's Foreign Aid (2014), (Beijing, July 2014).

[19] We use the term goods for industrial use to refer to goods used in the production of other goods and include capital and intermediate goods. According to the Organisation for Economic Co-operation and Development, an intermediate good is an input to the production process that has itself been produced and, unlike capital, is used up or transformed in production. Examples of intermediate goods include electronic components used in the manufacture of computers and textiles. Capital goods include, for example, construction or mining equipment. In contrast to industrial goods, we use the term consumer goods to refer to goods used without further transformation for the satisfaction of needs or wants.

[20] Among consumer goods, cotton sweaters and pullovers were the top U.S. import from ASEAN countries, and cameras were China's.

[21] Among consumer goods, fresh grapes were a top U.S. export from ASEAN countries and women's and girls' cotton jackets and blazers were one of China's top exports.

[22] The data on trade in goods in this section are presented from the ASEAN countries' perspective. For example, ASEAN countries' exports to the United States are equivalent to U.S. imports from ASEAN countries. Because some of the ASEAN countries' trading partners do not report data to the UN Commodity Trade database, we used data from the ASEANstats database as a comprehensive set of data on trade in goods for all of ASEAN countries' trading partners. Reasons for the differences in trade values between the ASEANstats database and the UN Commodity Trade Database include differences in the valuation of goods, differences in data quality, and the omission of some ASEAN trading partners' data from the UN Commodity Trade Database. According to the Department of the Treasury, data on trade between ASEAN countries likely overstates the demand between ASEAN countries because the data likely capture the movement of intermediate goods across the value chain.

[23] See Organisation for Economic Co-operation and Development and World Trade Organization, *Trade in Value-Added: Concepts, Methodologies and Challenges*, Joint OECD-WTO Note (2012).

[24] OECD analyzed data for eight ASEAN countries: Brunei, Cambodia, Indonesia, Malaysia, the Philippines, Singapore, Thailand, and Vietnam. By this measure, only Vietnam imported more from China than the United States and all eight exported more to the United States than China.

[25] "Trade in services" refers to the buying and selling of intangible products and activities, such as tourism, financial services, and telecommunications. Contracted activities, such as construction and consulting services, are also examples of services. BEA has not released data on U.S. trade in services for several ASEAN countries because of confidentiality concerns and data limitations. BEA identified ways to estimate the value of U.S. trade in services for selected ASEAN countries that required us to make various assumptions. See app. I for details of our methodology.

[26] As we have previously reported, BEA faces several challenges to collecting comprehensive and accurate data. In 2005, we found that BEA had experienced challenges in identifying all U.S. service importers and obtaining high-quality survey data from importers. However, since 2005, BEA has implemented methods to better identify all U.S. service importers. In addition, BEA's data on trade in services may differ from other countries' data, including China's, because of differences in definitions, coverage, and methods used to measure

services. For example, we found that BEA's data on trade in services differed from data collected by India because of differences in the methodologies used to define and collect the data. See GAO, *International Trade: U.S. and India Data on Offshoring Show Significant Differences*, GAO-06-116 (Washington, D.C.: Oct. 27, 2005). According to BEA, its survey data are from mandatory surveys of U.S. businesses with services trade that exceed certain thresholds. BEA does not survey a random sample of U.S. businesses and therefore does not report the data with margins of error.

[27] BEA publishes data on U.S. imports of services from the five largest ASEAN economies—Indonesia, Malaysia, the Philippines, Singapore, and Thailand. According to BEA's data, the United States imported $14.1 billion in services from these five countries in 2012. The United States imported the most from Singapore at $5.6 billion, followed by $4.0 billion from the Philippines, $2.4 billion from Thailand, $1.4 billion from Malaysia, and $0.7 billion from Indonesia.

[28] BEA publishes data on U.S. exports of services to the five largest ASEAN economies by country: Indonesia, Malaysia, the Philippines, Singapore, and Thailand. According to BEA's data, U.S. exported $23.1 billion in services to these five countries in 2012. The United States exported the most to Singapore at $13.2 billion, followed by $2.6 billion to Malaysia, $2.6 billion to Thailand, $2.5 billion to the Philippines, and $2.2 billion to Indonesia.

[29] For example, U.S. and Chinese firms can set up subsidiaries in non-ASEAN countries, which can be used to make investments in ASEAN countries. Such investments would not be captured by U.S. and Chinese data on FDI in ASEAN countries. Conversely, U.S. and Chinese firms can set up subsidiaries in ASEAN countries, which can be used to make investments in ASEAN or non-ASEAN countries.

[30] According to OECD, FDI is the ownership by a foreign person or business of 10 percent or more of the voting equity of a firm located in the host country. FDI flows provide information about FDI activity within a given period of time, while FDI stock indicates the level of FDI at a given point in time. FDI flows are outflows (e.g., when the foreign investor establishes a firm in the host country) minus inflows (e.g., when the firm in the host country extends a loan to the foreign investor). We use data on FDI flows instead of data on FDI stock. According to BEA, data on FDI stock in ASEAN countries are available only by historical cost and do not reflect changes in the market value of FDI. When using a U.S. GDP deflator to deflate the nominal data, we calculated that cumulative U.S. and Chinese FDI flows for 2007 through 2012 were $94 billion and $22 billion, respectively, in 2009 dollars.

[31] A holding company typically does not produce goods or services itself but instead exists to own assets of other companies, which may be located in countries other than that of the holding company.

[32] We excluded U.S. FDI flows to the Philippines in this calculation because U.S. FDI flows to the Philippines from 2007 through 2012 were negative.

[33] The export similarity index is described in J. M. Finger and M. E. Kreinin, "A Measure of 'Export Similarity' and Its Possible Uses," *The Economic Journal*, 89.356 (1979), 905-912. The World Bank includes the export similarity index as an indicator to describe export trends. An IMF study stated that the index is a common indicator to gauge export competitiveness. See International Monetary Fund, *Changing Patterns of Global Trade* (June 15, 2011). Other academic studies have also used the index to compare the similarity of exports. For example, see Marcus Noland, "Has Asian Export Performance Been Unique?," *Journal of International Economics*, 43 (1997), 79-101, and Peter K. Schott,

"The Relative Similarity of China's Exports to the United States *vis a vis* Other U.S. Trading Partners" (July 2004). We provide a brief description of how we calculated the export similarity index in app. I.

[34] As of 2014, three of the top 10 U.S. exports to ASEAN are among the top 10 Japanese exports. One of the top 10 U.S. exports to ASEAN countries is among the top 10 Chinese exports to ASEAN and among the top 10 EU exports to ASEAN. Four of the top 10 U.S. exports to ASEAN countries are agricultural products. See app. III for lists of the top exports from each of these countries.

[35] According to the IMF study, among a selected group of countries, the United States' highest export similarity index in 2008 was 0.587 with Germany and its lowest was 0.312 with Hong Kong. The authors calculated the export similarity index using the more detailed six-digit product categories, whereas we calculated the index using four-digit product categories. Higher digit product categories tend to result in lower export similarity index values. See International Monetary Fund, *Changing Patterns of Global Trade*.

[36] Services provided by U.S. firms under World Bank-funded contracts represent a small fraction (less than 1 percent) of annual U.S. trade in service exports to ASEAN countries. However, World Bank contracts represent one of the few instances where data are available for examination of potential competition between U.S. and Chinese firms. According to the World Bank, the data include only major contract awards reviewed by World Bank staff prior to award, approximately one-fifth of all contracts. The nationality of a firm reflects the country where it is registered, although the firm's parent may be headquartered in another country. In addition, although subcontractors may perform a majority of the awarded contract, the data reflect the nationality of only the prime contractor.

[37] Domestic firms from the borrower countries obtained 71 percent of the total value of World Bank contracts in ASEAN countries.

[38] Commerce's Advocacy Center is responsible for coordinating the U.S. government's advocacy efforts on behalf of U.S. exporters bidding on public sector contracts overseas. From fiscal years 2009 through 2014, the Advocacy Center received applications from U.S. firms for commercial advocacy for 184 contracts in ASEAN countries. Our analysis excludes 12 contracts in which the nationality of competing firms was not identified. While the total number of contracts for which U.S. firms competed in ASEAN countries is unknown, contracts supported by the Advocacy Center represent only a portion of the total number of contracts.

[39] The United States has also signed trade and investment framework agreements (TIFAs) with ASEAN and with all ASEAN countries except Singapore and Laos. TIFAs, in contrast to FTAs, are short agreements that provide principles and structure for dialogue on trade and investment issues. Under the U.S.-ASEAN TIFA, the 2012 U.S.-ASEAN Expanded Economic Engagement (E3) Initiative seeks to increase efficiency and competitiveness of supply chains and other trade flows and to negotiate initiatives to lay the groundwork for ASEAN countries to prepare to join high-standard agreements. In addition, the U.S. Generalized System of Preferences extends trade preferences to Cambodia, Indonesia, Philippines, and Thailand that provides duty-free treatment for over 3,500 products for these countries and, according to USTR, an additional 1,473 products for Cambodia.

[40] The United States has also signed bilateral trade agreements with two ASEAN countries—Vietnam in 2000 and Laos in 2005. These agreements included elements modeled on WTO agreements and enabled the United States to extend normal trade relations.

[41] In 2010, the Congressional Research Service reported that Singapore made key concessions on financial services under the FTA and may have contributed to U.S. banks increasing their

presence in Singapore. See Congressional Research Service, *The U.S.- Singapore Free Trade Agreement: Effects After Five Years* (Washington, D.C.: Mar. 26, 2010).

[42] In 2003, the U.S. International Trade Commission stated that the U.S.-Singapore FTA's provisions on intellectual property rights protection generally go further than the WTO Agreement on Trade-Related Aspects of Intellectual Property Rights. For example, the FTA addresses Internet piracy by including provisions to ensure that only authors, composers, and other copyright holders have the right to make their works available online. See U.S. International Trade Commission, *U.S.-Singapore Free Trade Agreement: Potential Economy-wide and Selected Sectoral Effects*, USITC Publication 3603 (Washington, D.C.: June 2003).

[43] In 2009, we reported that Singapore generally had strong protections for workers before signing the FTA and had since improved them. We also reported that Singapore was continuing to strengthen its environmental laws and that the United States and Singapore had signed a memorandum of intent to cooperate on environmental matters. See GAO, *International Trade: Four Free Trade Agreements GAO Reviewed Have Resulted in Commercial Benefits, but Challenges on Labor and Environment Remain*, GAO-09-439 (Washington, D.C.: July 10, 2009).

[44] Office of the U.S. Trade Representative, *2015 National Trade Estimate Report on Foreign Trade Barriers* (March 2015). In 2009, we reported that the U.S.-Singapore FTA appeared to have helped increase bilateral trade in goods as well as improved market access for services and the climate for FDI. In addition, the enhanced intellectual property rights protections also appeared to have had a positive impact on commerce and investment. See GAO-09-439.

[45] Under the agreement, CLMV countries could designate up to 500 tariff lines as sensitive, while the ASEAN 6 and China could designate up to 400 lines as sensitive.

[46] See World Trade Organization, *Trade Policy Review Report by the Secretariat: China* (May 2014).

[47] The latest available World Trade Organization data on China's tariff schedule is for 2013.

[48] For example, according to WTO data, Singapore faces no tariff on a type of plastic, a key export from Singapore to China in 2014, for which other Chinese trading partners with normal trade relations face a tariff of 6.5 percent. See also Ministry of Trade and Industry Singapore, *Free Trade Agreement Between the People's Republic of China and The Republic of Singapore Media Info-Kit* (Oct. 23, 2008). The report cited Chinese beer exports and Singapore's exports of petrochemicals, processed foods, and electronics and electric products as key exports that the agreement would affect.

[49] In comparison, according to our analysis, the North American Free Trade Agreement between the United States, Canada, and Mexico, all of which are also engaged in TPP negotiations, had a combined population of about 470 million people; had a combined GDP of around $20 trillion, roughly 26 percent of global GDP; and covered about 15 percent of world goods trade in 2013.

[50] Although the potential impacts of TPP are uncertain, U.S. officials have cited a recent study that estimated gains from TPP for U.S. GDP of 0.4 percent in 2025 and 0.2 percent for world GDP over GDP without TPP. Since China is not a negotiating partner of TPP, the study estimated that TPP would decrease China's GDP by 0.2 percent in 2025. The study was based on a projection of TPP's impact on current trade flows. See Peter A. Petri and Ali Abdul Raheem, "Can RCEP and the TPP Be Pathways to FTAAP?" in *State of the Region, 2014-2015*, eds. Pacific Economic Cooperation Council (Singapore: Pacific Economic Cooperation Council, 2014), 31-43.

[51] The World Bank's world development indicators do not include data on GDP for Burma.

[52] The existing agreements between TPP negotiating partners and between RCEP negotiating partners may be bilateral or multilateral.

[53] APEC was established in 1989 to further enhance economic growth and prosperity for the region and to strengthen the Asia-Pacific community. Achieving region-wide free trade in the Pacific has been a long-standing goal of APEC. In 1994, APEC leaders established the goal of achieving free trade among all members by 2020. APEC consists of 21 member economies, including all ASEAN economies except for Burma, Cambodia, and Laos. APEC's 21 member economies are the United States; Australia; Brunei; Canada; Chile; China; Hong Kong, China; Indonesia; Japan; Malaysia; Mexico; New Zealand; Papua New Guinea; Peru; the Philippines; Russia; Singapore; South Korea; Chinese Taipei; Thailand; and Vietnam.

[54] Ex-Im is the United States' official export credit agency. Ex-Im makes fixed-rate loans directly to international buyers of goods and services and also guarantees loans made by private lenders to international buyers of goods or services, promising to pay the lenders if the buyers default. Export credit insurance products protect the exporter from the risk of nonpayment by foreign buyers for commercial and political reasons. For more information on Ex-Im products, see GAO, *Export-Import Bank: Recent Growth Underscores Need for Continued Improvements in Risk Management*, GAO-13-303 (Washington, D.C.: Mar. 28, 2013).

[55] OPIC supports U.S. investment projects in overseas countries by providing U.S. private sector investors with direct loans, loan guarantees, political risk insurance, and support for private equity investment funds.

[56] According to Ex-Im officials, Ex-Im does not maintain staff overseas. OPIC has one regional staff person in Bangkok, Thailand.

[57] This amount includes estimates of financing by the Export-Import Bank of China, the China Development Bank, and Sinosure in 2013. The estimates are based on extrapolated totals from data officially reported by China and press coverage of Chinese financing in 90 countries. For more information, see U.S. Export-Import Bank, *Report to the U.S. Congress on the Export-Import Bank of the United States and Global Export Credit Competition* (Washington, D.C.: June 2014).

[58] In our previous report on U.S. and Chinese economic engagement in sub-Saharan Africa, we analyzed specific Chinese government loans to Angola, Kenya, and Ghana and found that that these loans were generally less costly and more concessional than U.S. government loans to Angola, Kenya, and, to a lesser extent, Ghana. See app. II of GAO-13-199. According to Ex-Im officials, absence of information on the cost of China's loans may prevent Ex-Im from offering competitive loans for U.S. exports and thus disadvantage U.S. firms interested in exporting their goods and services. In rare cases, OECD rules allow Ex-Im to match a non-OECD participant's financing terms and conditions, if there is evidence or specific information about its offer. However, according to Ex-Im, such information is typically difficult to obtain from the borrower.

[59] These numbers are based on the December 31, 2014, exchange rate of 6.205 Chinese yuan per U.S. dollar. The largest category of credit provided to Chinese exporters—30 percent—was for the export of new and high-tech products, followed by 20 percent for exports of ships, 15 percent for overseas investment, 10 percent for exports of general mechanical and electronic products, and 8 percent for overseas construction projects. Import financing supported the import of products such as technical equipment and raw materials by Chinese enterprises.

[60] These numbers are based on the December 31, 2014, exchange rate of 6.205 Chinese yuan per U.S. dollar.

[61] Organization for Economic Co-Operation and Development, Trade and Agriculture Directorate, Trade Committee, Working Party on Export Credits and Credit Guarantees, *Chinese Export Credit Policies and Programmes*, TAD/ECG(2015)3 (March 16, 2015).

[62] Other U.S. entities, such as USTR, the Department of the Treasury, and the U.S. Trade and Development Agency, support U.S. business and investment in ASEAN countries by developing U.S. trade and investment policy, technical assistance to support the development of strong financial sectors, and feasibility studies to facilitate the export of U.S. goods and services, among other things. For more information about the roles and activities of U.S. agencies in ASEAN countries, see app. II.

[63] According to Commerce officials, the Singapore office offers U.S. firms a regional perspective on operating in ASEAN countries. Commerce's personnel in Thailand and Singapore are also responsible for providing support to U.S. businesses interested in exporting to Brunei, Cambodia, and Laos, where Commerce maintains no presence.

[64] Trade missions can include one-to-one meetings with foreign industry executives and government officials, networking events with local industry representatives, briefings and roundtables on local business practices and opportunities, and site visits to local facilities where U.S. firms' technologies or services may be applied. Commerce also provides support for trade missions organized by state and private sector organizations.

[65] While USDA does not maintain a presence in Brunei, Cambodia, or Laos, its personnel in Malaysia and Vietnam are responsible for supporting USDA activities in those countries in accordance with USDA's strategic goals.

[66] These programs provide, among other things, cost-share assistance to eligible U.S. organizations for activities such as consumer advertising, participation in trade fairs and exhibits, and market research and technical assistance. For more information about USDA's market development programs, see GAO, *Agricultural Trade: USDA Is Monitoring Market Development Programs as Required but Could Improve Analysis of Impact*, GAO-13-740 (Washington, D.C.: July 31, 2013).

[67] The exchange of currencies by the central banks of two countries is called a currency swap. Currency swap agreements allow countries to exchange local currency for foreign currency through another country's central bank or monetary authority's currency reserves. Currency swap agreements are generally designed for short-term support, with the exchange to be reversed at a future date.

[68] At the June 1, 2015, exchange rate of 6.199 Chinese yuan per U.S. dollar, China's currency swap agreements with ASEAN countries totaled $104.9 billion. China also has currency swap agreements in place with other countries, such as the United Kingdom and Russia.

[69] China is also part of a $240 billion multilateral currency swap agreement, the Chiang Mai Initiative Multilateralisation, with the 10 ASEAN countries, Japan and South Korea. The initiative provides for liquidity among participant economies experiencing short-term liquidity difficulties.

[70] Since at least 2001, the United States has committed to providing TCB assistance to developing countries to help them participate in, and benefit from, global trade. USAID maintains a database to track this assistance. For more information about TCB, see GAO, *Foreign Assistance: USAID Should Update Its Trade Capacity Building Strategy*, GAO-14-602 (Washington, D.C.: Aug. 11, 2014).

[71] Our analysis does not include any support provided by multilateral institutions to which the United States contributes funds, such as the World Bank.

[72] A national single window is a system that enables a synchronous processing of data for customs clearance through one channel. In addition to the single window, ASEAN Connectivity through Trade and Investment also includes efforts for trade and investment facilitation (such as harmonizing standards), small and medium-sized enterprise development, clean energy and energy efficiency, and information and communication technology development.

[73] ASEAN Connectivity through Trade and Investment and ASEAN-U.S. Partnership for Good Governance, Equitable and Sustainable Development and Security represent a continuation of a previous State and USAID project. From 2008 to 2013, State and USAID's ASEAN Development Vision to Advance National Cooperation and Economic Integration supported other technical support and capacity-building assistance for national single windows and support for the growth of supply chains in textiles and garments across ASEAN countries.

[74] For more than 10 years, USTDA has maintained an office in Bangkok, Thailand, supported with a personal service contractor, to advance and oversee its programs in ASEAN countries.

[75] MCC is a U.S. government corporation that seeks to reduce global poverty through economic growth. The Indonesia compact's Green Prosperity Project is designed to increase productivity in rural areas and reduce reliance on fossil fuels by expanding renewable energy, and to increase productivity and reduce greenhouse gas emissions by improving land use practices and management of natural resources.

[76] Information Office of the State Council, "China's Foreign Aid" (2014) (Beijing: July 2014).

[77] See app. VI for information on U.S. and Chinese official development assistance to ASEAN countries.

[78] U.S.-China Economic and Security Review Commission hearing, "China's Relations with Southeast Asia," May 13, 2015. The commission was created by Congress to report on the national security implications of the bilateral trade and economic relationship between the United States and the People's Republic of China.

[79] The GMS Program was established in 1992. The program supports regional development and economic cooperation through programs and projects that promote infrastructure linkages; facilitate cross border trade, investment, and tourism; enhance private sector competitiveness; develop human capital; and protect the environment.

[80] National Development and Reform Commission, Ministry of Foreign Affairs, and Ministry of Commerce of the People's Republic of China, *Vision and Actions on Jointly Building Silk Road Economic Belt and 21st-Century Maritime Silk Road* (Mar. 28, 2015).

[81] China's foreign exchange reserves provided the largest portion of the funds. Contributions also came from China Ex-Im, the China Investment Corporation, and the China Development Bank.

[82] The Chinese government stated that it was willing to subscribe up to 50 percent of AIIB's capital, but prospective members have since agreed to determine share allocation primarily by GDP; as a result, China will be the bank's largest shareholder but will contribute $29.8 billion of the $100 billion.

[83] In comparison, as of December 31, 2013, ADB's capitalization was $78.8 billion. The United States held 15.6 percent of total shares in ADB—slightly less than Japan's leading 15.7 percent—and China held 6.5 percent. The combined total resources of ADB and AIIB are still far below the $60 billion per year through 2020 that ADB estimates is needed to meet ASEAN countries' infrastructure needs.

[84] AIIB's 57 prospective founding members are Australia, Austria, Azerbaijan, Bangladesh, Brazil, Brunei, Burma, Cambodia, China, Denmark, Egypt, Finland, France, Georgia,

Germany, Iceland, India, Indonesia, Iran, Israel, Italy, Jordan, Kazakhstan, Kuwait, Kyrgyzstan, Laos, Luxembourg, Malaysia, the Maldives, Malta, Mongolia, Nepal, the Netherlands, New Zealand, Norway, Oman, Pakistan, the Philippines, Poland, Portugal, Qatar, Russia, Saudi Arabia, Singapore, South Africa, South Korea, Spain, Sri Lanka, Sweden, Switzerland, Tajikistan, Thailand, Turkey, the United Arab Emirates, the United Kingdom, Uzbekistan, and Vietnam.

End Notes for Appendix I

[1] In this report, Southeast Asia refers to the 10 countries of the Association of Southeast Asian Nations: Brunei, Burma, Cambodia, Indonesia, Laos, Malaysia, the Philippines, Singapore, Thailand, and Vietnam.

[2] China Ministry of Commerce, *China Trade in Services Report, 2010* (Apr. 6, 2012).

[3] GAO-13-199.

[4] The export similarity index is described in J. M. Finger and M. E. Kreinin, "A Measure of 'Export Similarity' and Its Possible Uses," *The Economic Journal*, 89.356 (1979): 905-912. The World Bank includes the export similarity index as an indicator to describe export trends. An IMF study stated that the index is a common indicator to gauge export competitiveness; see International Monetary Fund, *Changing Patterns of Global Trade* (June 15, 2011). Other academic studies have also used the index to compare the similarity of exports; for example, see Marcus Noland, "Has Asian Export Performance Been Unique?," *Journal of International Economics*, 43 (1997), 79-101, and Peter K. Schott, "The Relative Similarity of China's Exports to the United States *vis a vis* Other U.S. Trading Partners" (July 2004).

[5] To calculate the average, we did not include data on trade in goods for years when the country reported no exports or imports.

[6] Information Office of the State Council, The People's Republic of China, China's Foreign Aid (2014) (Beijing: July 2014).

End Note for Appendix I

[1] We ranked the value of U.S., Chinese, EU, and Japanese exports to ASEAN countries using the four-digit Standard International Trade Classification code. According to the United Nations (UN), it developed the Standard International Trade Classification to classify traded goods not only on the basis of their material and physical properties, but also according to their stage of processing and economic functions.

End Notes for Appendix VI

[1] OECD defines official development assistance as those flows to countries and territories on OECD's list of ODA recipients and to multilateral development institutions that are provided by official agencies, have the promotion of economic development and welfare of

developing countries as their main objective, and are concessional and convey a grant element of at least 25 percent.

[2] MCC's compacts with the Philippines and Indonesia entered into force several months after compact signature. MCC's Philippines compact was signed in September 2010 and entered into force in May 2011. MCC's Indonesia compact was signed in November 2011 and entered into force in April 2013. MCC funds are disbursed over the 5 years of the compact.

[3] None of the Philippines compact was categorized as trade capacity building assistance.

[4] The entirety of the Green Prosperity project was categorized as trade capacity building assistance.

[5] Information Office of the State Council, The People's Republic of China, China's Foreign Aid (2014) (Beijing: July 2014).

In: Southeast Asia
Editor: Pauline Nelson

ISBN: 978-1-63484-696-7

Chapter 2

SOUTHEAST ASIA: TRENDS IN U.S. AND CHINESE ECONOMIC ENGAGEMENT IN INDONESIA AND VIETNAM*

United States Government Accountability Office

WHY GAO DID THIS STUDY

The United States and China have each sought to increase their economic engagement in Southeast Asia. U.S. agencies have identified Indonesia and Vietnam as important emerging U.S. partners that contribute to regional stability and prosperity. Indonesia has the world's 10th largest economy in terms of purchasing power, and Vietnam is one of the most dynamic economies in East Asia. Both the United States and China have established comprehensive partnerships with each country that are designed to enhance their bilateral cooperation in key areas.

GAO was asked to examine the United States' and China's economic engagement in Southeast Asia. GAO issued a report on 10 Southeast Asian countries in August 2015. In this report, GAO presents case studies for two of these countries, Indonesia and Vietnam, providing greater detail about the United States' and China's trade and investment, competition, and actions to further economic engagement in the two countries. GAO analyzed publicly

---

* This is an edited, reformatted and augmented version of a United States Government Accountability Office publication, No. GAO-16-186, dated October 2015.

available economic data and documentation from 10 U.S. agencies and the Chinese government. The data that GAO reports have varying time periods because of the data sets' limited availability and differing contexts. GAO interviewed U.S., Indonesian, and Vietnamese officials and private sector representatives.

This is the public version of a sensitive but unclassified report that is being issued concurrently. GAO is not making any recommendations in this report.

WHAT GAO FOUND

Indonesia. In 2014, China's imports from, and exports to, Indonesia exceeded the United States' (see figure). The United States and China compete more often with other countries than with each other in goods exported to Indonesia and win contracts in different sectors. In contrast to the United States, which is not involved in a free trade agreement (FTA) with Indonesia, China is a party to a regional FTA that includes Indonesia and is negotiating the Regional Comprehensive Economic Partnership (RCEP) with Indonesia and 14 other countries. In fiscal years 2009 through 2014, U.S. agencies' financing for exports to, and investment in, Indonesia totaled about $2.5 billion, compared with at least $34 billion in Chinese financing, according to the Department of State. In 2007 through 2012, U.S. foreign direct investment (FDI) of $9.6 billion exceeded China's reported $2.7 billion, according to available data.

Vietnam. In 2014, U.S. imports from Vietnam exceeded China's, while Chinese exports to Vietnam exceeded U.S. exports (see figure). As in Indonesia, the United States and China compete more often with other countries than with each other in goods exported to Vietnam and win contracts in different sectors. The United States and Vietnam are both participants in the proposed regional Trans-Pacific Partnership, while China and Vietnam are both parties to a regional FTA and the RCEP negotiations. In fiscal years 2009 through 2014, U.S. agencies' financing for exports to, and investment in, Vietnam totaled about $205 million, compared with at least $4.5 billion in Chinese financing, according to the Department of State. In 2007 through 2012, China's reported FDI of $1.2 billion was more than twice the United States' reported FDI of $472 million, according to available data.

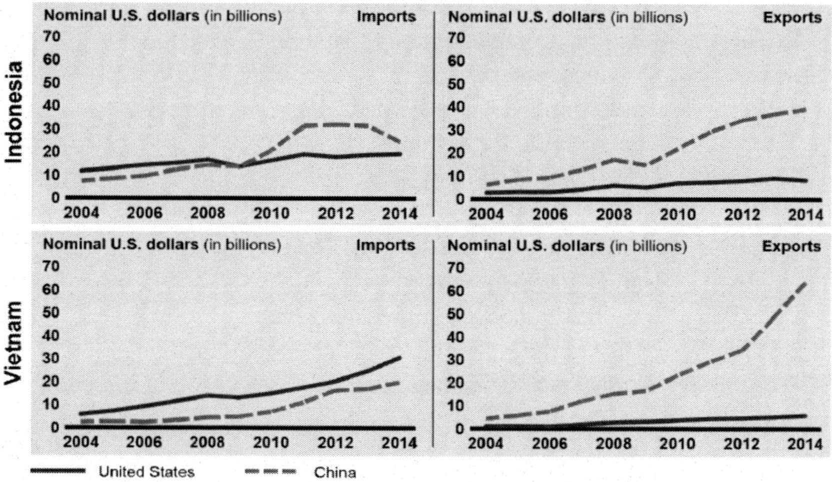

Source: GAO analysis of U.S. and Chinese data from the United Nations Commodity Trade database. | GAO-16-186.

U.S. and Chinese Goods Imports from, and Exports to, Indonesia and Vietnam, 2004-2014.

ABBREVIATIONS

ADB	Asian Development Bank
ASEAN	Association of Southeast Asian Nations
BEA	U.S. Bureau of Economic Analysis
BTA	Bilateral Trade Agreement
Commerce	U.S. Department of Commerce
EU	European Union
Ex-Im	Export-Import Bank of the United States
FDI	foreign direct investment
FTA	free trade agreement
GDP	gross domestic product
GMS	Greater Mekong Subregion
GSP	Generalized System of Preferences
IMF	International Monetary Fund
Labor	U.S. Department of Labor
MCC	Millennium Challenge Corporation
OECD	Organisation for Economic Co-operation and Development

OPIC	Overseas Private Investment Corporation
RCEP	Regional Comprehensive Economic Partnership
State	U.S. Department of State
TIFA	Trade and Investment Framework Agreement
TPP	Trans-Pacific Partnership
Treasury	U.S. Department of the Treasury
UN	United Nations
USAID	U.S. Agency for International Development
USDA	U.S. Department of Agriculture
USTDA	U.S. Trade and Development Agency
USTR	Office of the United States Trade Representative
WTO	World Trade Organization

* * *

October 29, 2015

The Honorable Steve Chabot
Chairman
Committee on Small Business
House of Representatives

The Honorable Matt Salmon
Chairman
The Honorable Brad Sherman
Ranking Member
Subcommittee on Asia and the Pacific
Committee on Foreign Affairs
House of Representatives

U.S. agencies have identified Indonesia and Vietnam as important emerging Southeast Asian economic powers that contribute to regional stability and prosperity. According to the World Bank, Indonesia is the 10th-largest economy in the world in terms of purchasing power, and Vietnam is one of the most dynamic economies in East Asia. The United States and China have sought to increase their economic engagement with both countries. For example, U.S. agencies have outlined specific goals to facilitate U.S. trade and investment in Indonesia and Vietnam, while China has fostered trade and investment opportunities for its firms operating in each country. The United

States and China have also established comprehensive bilateral partnerships with Indonesia and Vietnam, designed to enhance key aspects of their respective cooperation with the two countries.

You asked us to review the nature of the United States' and China's economic engagement in Southeast Asia. In August 2015, we issued a report examining U.S. and Chinese economic engagement with the 10 members of the Association of Southeast Asian Nations (ASEAN).[1] In this report, we present case studies of U.S. and Chinese trade and investment, competition, and actions to further economic engagement in two of these countries, Indonesia and Vietnam.

This report is a public version of a non-public sensitive but unclassified report that we are issuing concurrently. This report does not contain certain information, related to U.S. agency goals and characterization of other countries' economic activities, that the U.S. Department of State (State) and the U.S. Department of Agriculture (USDA) regarded as sensitive but unclassified.

To examine U.S. and Chinese trade and investment with Indonesia and Vietnam, we analyzed available data on U.S. and Chinese trade in goods, trade in services, and foreign direct investment (FDI). To determine the extent to which U.S. and Chinese firms compete in Indonesia and Vietnam, we analyzed data from the U.S. Department of Commerce (Commerce), the World Bank, and the Asian Development Bank (ADB). To identify actions that the U.S. and Chinese governments have taken to further economic engagement in Indonesia and Vietnam, we reviewed U.S., Chinese, and other countries' trade agreements, reports, and statements. We conducted fieldwork in both Indonesia and Vietnam and interviewed officials from U.S. and other countries' government agencies and private sector representatives. We requested meetings with Chinese government officials in Indonesia, Vietnam, and Washington, D.C.; however, they were unable to accommodate our requests. To assess the reliability of data, where possible, we cross-checked the data with other sources, evaluated the data for internal consistency, and consulted with U.S. officials and experts. Because of the limited availability of data and the differing contexts for the sets of data we report, these data sets have varying time periods. We consider the data we present to be reliable for our purposes and have noted caveats as appropriate regarding limitations of some of these data. See appendix I for additional information about our scope and methodology.

We conducted this performance audit from April 2014 to October 2015 in accordance with generally accepted government auditing standards. Those standards require that we plan and perform the audit to obtain sufficient, appropriate evidence to provide a reasonable basis for our findings and conclusions based on our audit objectives. We believe that the evidence obtained provides a reasonable basis for our findings and conclusions based on our audit objectives.

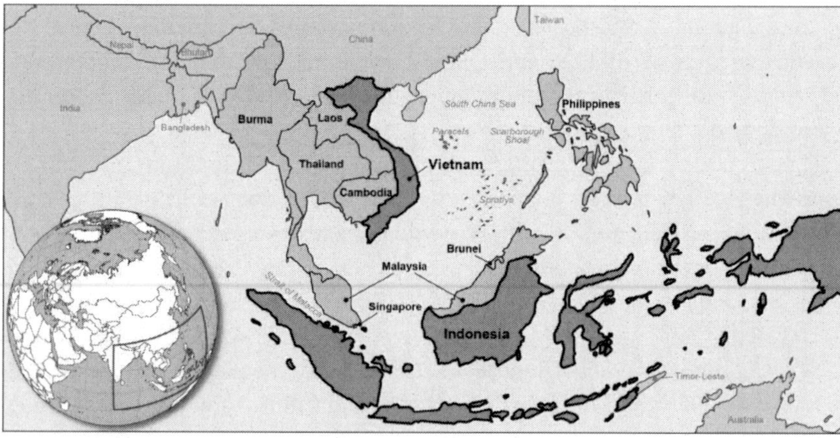

Source: Map Resources (maps). | GAO-16-186.

Figure 1. Members of the Association of Southeast Asian Nations (ASEAN).

BACKGROUND

As Southeast Asian countries, Indonesia and Vietnam are in a region of growing economic power. ASEAN, to which both countries belong, is seeking to form an economic community by the end of 2015 that would deepen economic integration among the 10 ASEAN member states (see fig. 1). World Bank data show that from 2000 through 2014, the collective real gross domestic product (GDP) of ASEAN countries increased by approximately 98 percent.[2] According to International Monetary Fund (IMF) data, if the ASEAN countries were a single nation, their collective GDP in 2014 would represent the seventh-largest economy in the world. ASEAN countries are also important strategically, in part because they are located astride key sea lanes between the Persian Gulf and the economic centers of East Asia. On the basis of a 2011 United Nations (UN) Conference on Trade and Development Review Maritime Transport, the U.S. Department of Energy estimated that more than half of the world's annual merchant fleet tonnage passed through the South China Sea, which is bordered by Indonesia and Vietnam.

Indonesia's Economy and Relations with the United States and China

According to data from the World Bank, Indonesia's real GDP increased by around 108 percent from 2000 to 2014. However, the World Bank estimated that in 2011, 16 percent of Indonesians lived below the poverty line of $1.25 per day.[3] Indonesia is the world's fourth-largest country by population.

The United States established diplomatic relations with Indonesia in 1949, after Indonesia gained independence from the Netherlands. According to State, Indonesia's democratization and reform process since 1998 has increased its stability and security and resulted in strengthened U.S.- Indonesia relations. In 2010, the United States and Indonesia officially launched the United States–Indonesia Comprehensive Partnership to broaden, deepen, and elevate bilateral relations between the two countries on a variety of issues, including economic and development cooperation. However, according to U.S. agencies, the U.S.-Indonesia bilateral relationship continues to face significant challenges because of Indonesia's implementation of protectionist laws, limited infrastructure, and unevenly applied legal structure. U.S. agencies' stated goals for Indonesia include supporting the facilitation of U.S. trade and investment between the two countries.[4] The U.S. Embassy in Indonesia is located in Jakarta, with U.S. consulates in Surabaya and Medan and a U.S. consular agency in Bali.

China and Indonesia have a long-standing history of trade and interchange. The two countries established diplomatic relations in 1950, 5 years after Indonesia gained independence from the Netherlands. Relations between China and Indonesia were suspended in 1967, after the Indonesian government suspected China of complicity in planning a 1965 coup, but were restored in 1990. Since then, trade and economic relations between the two countries have grown rapidly and in 2013, both countries agreed to elevate bilateral relations to a comprehensive strategic partnership. The partnership seeks to strengthen cooperation in several key areas, including trade, investment, and economic development. In 2015, the countries reaffirmed their support of the partnership and agreed, among other things, to expand market access and two-way investment for firms and to deepen their infrastructure and industrial cooperation. In April 2015, the Presidents of China and Indonesia released a statement setting a bilateral trade target of $150 billion by 2020—an increase of $70 billion from the 2015 target of $80 billion. The two Presidents stated that they will work toward the reduction of tariff and nontariff trade barriers and increase the frequency of trade missions between the two countries. China maintains an embassy in Jakarta and consulates in Medan, Surabaya, and Denpasar.

Vietnam's Economy and Relations with the United States and China

Vietnam has experienced rapid economic growth in the past 15 years, primarily because of economic reforms it began implementing in the late 1980s that transformed it from a centrally planned economy to a type of socialist market economy. Data from the World Bank show that Vietnam's real GDP increased by around 137 percent from 2000 to 2014. Vietnam has also made great progress in reducing poverty since the 1990s, according to the World Bank. In 2012, the World Bank reported that about 2 percent of Vietnamese lived below the poverty line of $1.25 per day.

The United States established diplomatic relations with Vietnam in 1950, after Vietnam achieved limited independence from France. The United States and Vietnam suspended diplomatic relations at the end of the Vietnam War in 1975 but restored them in 1995. Since then, common strategic and economic interests have led Vietnam and the United States to improve relations across a wide range of issues. In 2006, Congress passed a comprehensive trade and tax bill that granted Vietnam permanent normal trade relations. In July 2013, the United States and Vietnam established the United States–Vietnam Comprehensive Partnership, an overarching framework for advancing the bilateral relationship in areas such as economic engagement. In October 2014, the United States relaxed an arms embargo, which it had imposed on Vietnam in 1984, to permit Vietnamese acquisition of maritime military materiel. However, the United States continues to express concerns about Vietnam's human rights record and designates Vietnam as a nonmarket economy in antidumping procedures.[5] Vietnam has expressed opposition to aspects of U.S. trade policy, including U.S. restrictions on its export of catfish into the U.S. market. U.S. agencies' stated goals for Vietnam include supporting Vietnam's economic governance. The U.S. Embassy in Vietnam is located in Hanoi, and the U.S. Consulate General is in Ho Chi Minh City.

For centuries, China and Vietnam have had a turbulent relationship that continues to be affected by long-standing territorial disputes in the South China Sea. China has claimed sovereignty over the South China Sea, illustrating its claims by marking its maps with a "nine dash line" that overlaps with Vietnamese claims and encircles most of the South China Sea, including the Paracels and Spratlys. During the Vietnam War, China served as a close ally of the North Vietnamese. In 1974, shortly before the war ended, China seized control of the Paracel Islands from the South Vietnamese. After the war, underlying tensions between the two countries surfaced and China-Vietnam relations deteriorated. China opposed Vietnam's invasion of Cambodia in 1978, and following a series of disputes, the Chinese army crossed the Vietnamese border in February 1979 and fought a 2-week battle before the Chinese withdrew.

In 1991, China and Vietnam renormalized relations. Since then, China and Vietnam have established close economic relations. In 2008, the two countries agreed to establish a comprehensive strategic partnership that enhanced cooperation in multiple areas, such as trade and investment. However, in May 2014, tensions were reawakened when China placed an oil rig near the disputed Paracel Islands, sparking widespread protests in Vietnam; some of these protests turned violent and included attacks on Chinese and Taiwanese individuals and firms. Despite continuing tensions, in April 2015, the leaders of both countries pledged to strengthen their partnership, for example, by increasing cooperation on infrastructure development. China maintains an embassy in Hanoi and a consulate in Ho Chi Minh City.

U.S. AND CHINESE TRADE AND INVESTMENT, COMPETITION, AND ACTIONS TO FURTHER ECONOMIC ENGAGEMENT IN INDONESIA

China Has Surpassed the United States in Trade in Goods with Indonesia, but U.S. Investment Has Exceeded Chinese Investment

The value of China's total trade in goods with Indonesia surpassed the United States' in 2005 and was more than double the United States' in 2014, when Chinese imports and exports both exceeded U.S. imports and exports.[6] The United States and China are Indonesia's fifth and second-largest trading partners, respectively, while other ASEAN countries collectively represent Indonesia's largest trading partner. Available data on U.S. and Chinese FDI, although limited, indicate that U.S. FDI greatly exceeded Chinese FDI in Indonesia from 2007 through 2012.[7] However, Chinese FDI has significantly increased since 2010 and nearly reached U.S. levels of FDI in 2012.

China's Total Trade in Goods with Indonesia Has Surpassed U.S. Trade in Goods, Both Imports and Exports

The value of China's total trade in goods with Indonesia surpassed the United States' in 2005 and was more than double the United States' total trade in goods—$64 billion versus $28 billion, respectively—in 2014 (see fig. 2). China's total goods trade in Indonesia increased in nominal terms every year after 2001 except 2008 and 2009, when the global economic crisis occurred, and 2013 and 2014, when Chinese imports of minerals from Indonesia declined.[8] From 1994 through 2014, China's total trade in goods in Indonesia grew much more rapidly than U.S. total trade in goods, with a slight decline in 2014.

As figure 2 illustrates, from 1994 through 2014, China's imports from, and exports to, Indonesia grew to exceed the United States'. Moreover, while the United States had a nearly continuous annual trade deficit with Indonesia during this period, China had an increasing trade surplus almost every year after 2007.

- Chinese imports from Indonesia surpassed U.S. imports from Indonesia in 2009 and increased significantly in 2010 and 2011. However, in 2013 and 2014, Chinese imports declined sharply, primarily because of a significant decrease in Chinese imports of minerals and slowing economic growth in China, according to an IMF report.[9] The IMF report stated that in 2014, Indonesia implemented a ban of Indonesia's raw mineral ore exports, requiring all raw mineral ores to be processed in Indonesia to increase domestic value added.[10]
- Chinese exports to Indonesia surpassed U.S. exports in 2000 and continued to grow through 2014.
- The United States had a trade deficit with Indonesia every year from 1994 through 2014, with the deficit growing from $4.2 billion in 1994 to $11.1 billion in 2014. China had a trade deficit with Indonesia every year from 1994 through 2006 but, with the exception of 2011, had a trade surplus every year from 2007 through 2014. China's trade

surplus increased dramatically from 2012 through 2014, from $2.3 billion to $14.6 billion.

From 2000 through 2014, the composition of U.S. and Chinese trade in goods with Indonesia remained relatively stable, except for a significant overall increase in China's mineral imports that peaked in 2013. In 2014, textiles represented the largest share of U.S. imports (26 percent) while minerals represented the largest share of Chinese imports (42 percent). Animals, plants, and food represented the largest share of U.S. exports in 2014 (32 percent), and machinery represented the largest share of Chinese exports (33 percent). Most of China's, and almost half of the United States', trade in goods with Indonesia in 2014 consisted of goods for industrial use (i.e., goods, such as rubber and coal, used in the production of other goods). See appendix II for more information about the composition and use of U.S. and Chinese trade in goods with Indonesia.

China and the United States Are Significant Trading Partners of Indonesia, but Other ASEAN Countries Are Its Largest Partner

In 2013, other ASEAN countries collectively represented Indonesia's largest trading partner in total trade in goods, followed by China, Japan, the European Union (EU), and the United States.[11]

- **Exports.** Indonesia exported $16 billion in goods to the United States, its fifth-largest export market, and $23 billion in goods to China, its third-largest export market, in 2013. Other ASEAN countries, Japan, and the EU represented Indonesia's first, second, and fourth-largest goods export markets, respectively. The United States' share of total Indonesian goods exports decreased from 12.1 percent in 2003 to 8.6 percent in 2013, while China's share of total Indonesian goods exports increased from 6.2 percent to 12.4 percent during the same period.
- **Imports.** Indonesia imported $9 billion in goods from the United States, its sixth-largest import market, and $30 billion in goods from China, its second-largest import market, in 2013. Other ASEAN countries, Japan, the EU, and South Korea represented Indonesia's first-, third-, fourth-, and fifth-largest goods import markets, respectively. The United States' share of total Indonesian goods imports decreased from 8.3 percent in 2003 to 4.9 percent in 2013. China's share of total Indonesian goods exports increased from 9.1 percent in 2003 to 16 percent in 2013.

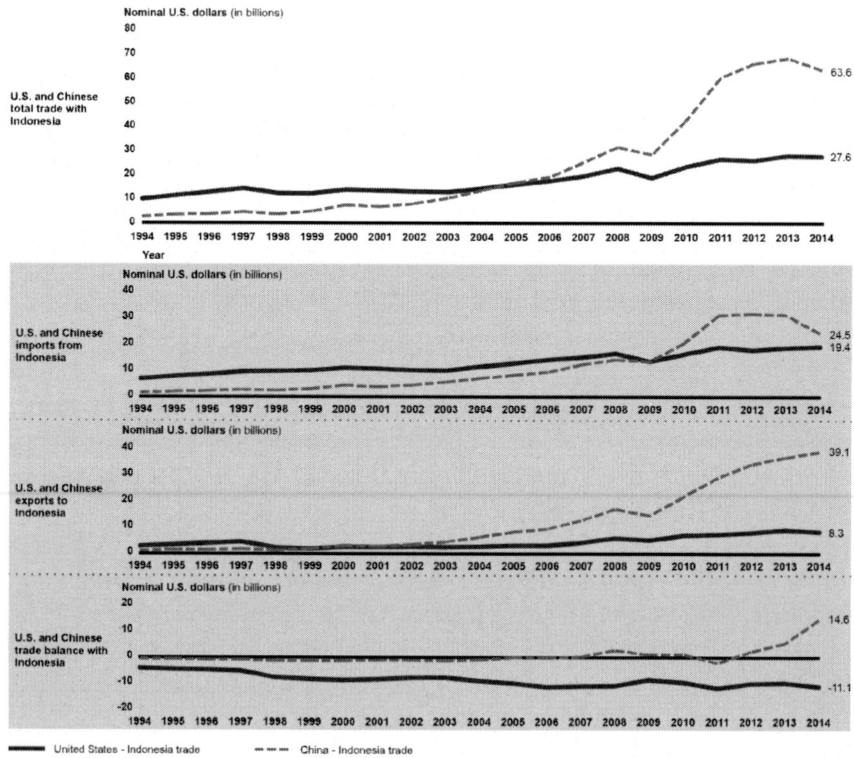

Source: GAO analysis of U.S. and Chinese data from the United Nations Commodity Trade database. | GAO-16-186. Note: The trade values shown are nominal—that is, not adjusted for inflation. Changes in values over time are due in part to changes in the prices of traded goods.

Figure 2. U.S. and Chinese Trade in Goods with Indonesia, 1994-2014.

Figure 3 shows Indonesia's exports and imports in 2003, 2008, and 2013, by trading partner.

Indonesia ranks higher as an export and import partner of China than of the United States.

- Indonesia is China's 15th-largest export market and the United States' 34th-largest by value. In 2014, China exported $39.1 billion in goods to Indonesia, or 1.7 percent of global Chinese goods exports. In the same year, the United States exported $8.3 billion in goods to Indonesia—0.5 percent of global U.S. goods exports.

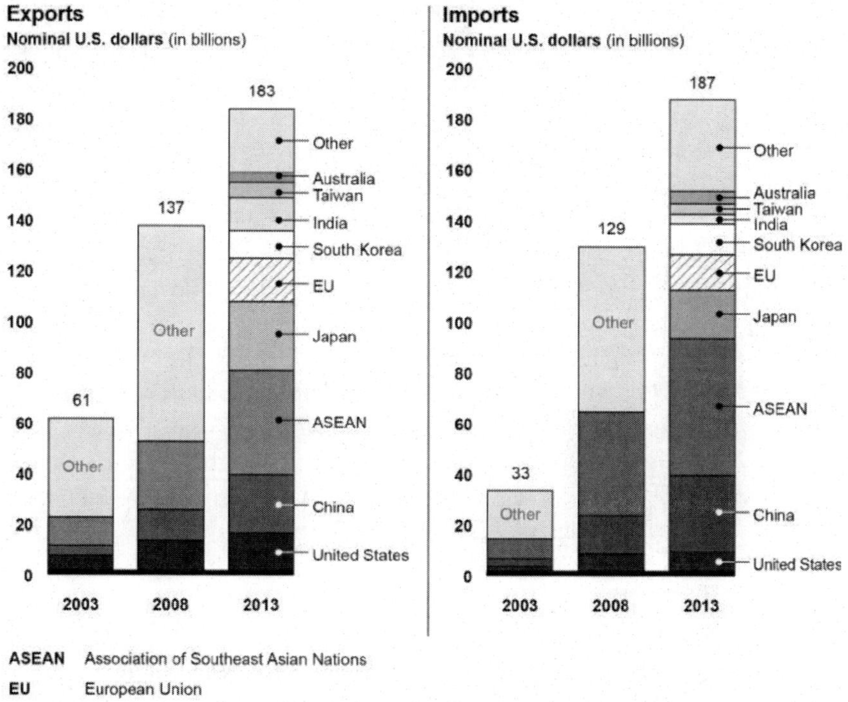

Source: GAO analysis of data from ASEANstats database. | GAO-16-186.

Notes: The trade values shown are nominal—that is, not adjusted for inflation. Changes in values over time are due in part to changes in the prices of traded goods.

Although the United States does not have diplomatic relations with Taiwan, we have listed Taiwan as a separate country, because whenever the laws of the United States refer or relate to foreign countries, nations, states, governments, or similar entities, such terms shall include and shall apply to Taiwan.

Figure 3. Value of Indonesian Exports and Imports of Goods in 2003, 2008, and 2013, by Trading Partner.

- Indonesia is China's 20th-largest source of imported goods and the United States' 24th-largest by value. In 2014, China imported $24.5 billion in goods from Indonesia, or 1 percent of global Chinese goods imports. In the same year, the United States imported $19.4 billion in goods from Indonesia—0.8 percent of global U.S. goods imports.

The United States' role relative to China's in Indonesia's trade of goods as well as services may be greater when the amount of intermediate U.S. inputs to the traded goods and services is taken into account. Because of the nature of global supply chains, for example, a consumer phone from a U.S. company might be assembled in China but includes components manufactured by Germany, Japan, South Korea, and other countries.[12] Data from the UN Commodity Trade database, which counts the full value of the export only for the exporting country, showed that in 2011, China exported $29.2 billion in goods to Indonesia, almost four times the $7.4 billion in goods that the United States exported to Indonesia.[13] However, data from the Organisation of Economic Co-operation and Development (OECD) and the World Trade Organization (WTO), which attempt to account for value added to a finished export by each contributing country, show that China's exports of value-added goods and services to Indonesia were around 1.8 times those of the United States. The OECDWTO data suggest that Chinese exports to Indonesia contained a higher portion of components produced elsewhere than U.S. exports contained.

Total U.S. Trade in Services with Indonesia Was Almost $3 Billion in 2013, While Data on China's Trade in Services Are Unavailable

Available data from the U.S. Bureau of Economic Analysis (BEA)[14] indicate that U.S. trade in services with Indonesia totaled approximately $2.9 billion in 2013.[15] The United States

- exported $2.2 billion in services to Indonesia in 2013, with travel and business services, respectively, as the largest and second-largest categories by value,[16] and
- imported $692 million in services from Indonesia in 2013, with travel and business services, respectively, as the largest and second-largest categories by value.

In 2013, total U.S.-Indonesian services trade represented 10 percent of the value of U.S.-Indonesian goods trade.

China does not publish data on its trade in services with Indonesia.

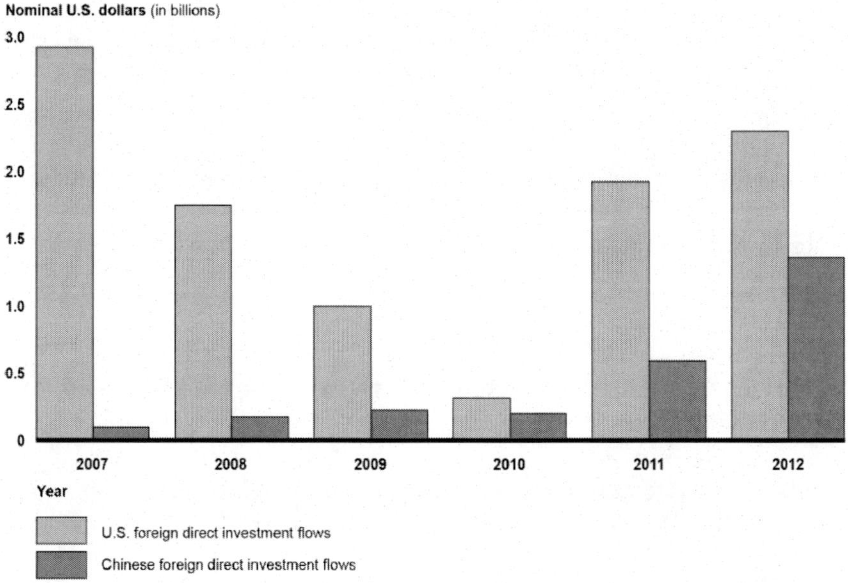

Source: GAO analysis of data from the U.S. Bureau of Economic Analysis and Chinese data from the United Nations Conference on Trade and Development. | GAO-16-186.

Notes: Foreign direct investment (FDI) flows represent FDI activities in a given period of time.

Although China has reported investment data since 2003, China began including financial investment in its total investment data in 2007. Chinese FDI data do not include Hong Kong's investments in Indonesia.

The investment data shown are nominal values—that is, not adjusted for inflation. When using a U.S. gross domestic product deflator, we calculated cumulative U.S. and Chinese FDI flows in 2007 through 2012 at $10.1 billion and $2.6 billion, respectively, in 2009 dollars.

Figure 4. U.S. and Chinese Foreign Direct Investment Flows to Indonesia, 2007-2012.

U.S. Investment Flows to Indonesia Exceeded Chinese Investment Flows in 2007- 2012, but Available Data Have Limitations

Data on FDI in Indonesia from the United States and China have limitations, in that these data may not accurately reflect the countries to which U.S. and Chinese FDI ultimately flows. For example, U.S. and Chinese data on FDI in Indonesia do not reflect investments by subsidiaries that U.S. and Chinese firms may set up in other countries and use to make investments in Indonesia. Conversely, U.S. and Chinese firms may set up subsidiaries in

Indonesia that can be used to make investments in other countries. Given these limitations, available data show that U.S. FDI flows to Indonesia in 2007 through 2012 totaled about $10.2 billion, exceeding China's reported FDI flows of about $2.7 billion. However, annual Chinese FDI flows increased significantly during this time, from $100 million in 2007 to $1.4 billion in 2012 in nominal terms (see fig. 4). According to BEA, over 90 percent of total U.S. FDI flows to Indonesia in 2007 through 2012 were concentrated in holding companies and mining.[17]

United States and China Compete Most Often with Other Countries in Goods Exports and Win Government Contracts in Different Sectors

Data on U.S. and Chinese goods exports to Indonesia indicate that from 2006 through 2014, U.S. exports of goods to Indonesia were more similar to Japanese and EU exports than to Chinese exports, suggesting that the United States is more likely to compete directly with Japan and EU countries than with China.[18] Figure 5 presents a commonly used index for assessing the similarity of the United States' goods exports to Indonesia to those of China and other countries.[19]

Data from Commerce's Advocacy Center, the World Bank, and ADB provide some information about Indonesian government contracts that U.S. and Chinese firms competed for or won. Although these data represent a small share of U.S. and Chinese economic activity in Indonesia, they offer insights into the degree of competition between U.S. and Chinese firms for the projects represented. These data indicate that U.S. firms in Indonesia have competed more often with firms from other countries than with Chinese firms and have tended to win contracts in different sectors.

- **Commerce Advocacy Center.** Data from Commerce's Advocacy Center show that U.S. firms that the center supported in fiscal years 2009 through 2014 competed for Indonesian government contracts most often, and for highest total contract value, with French firms, followed by Chinese firms and firms from other countries (see table 1).[20] According to the center's data, Chinese firms competed with the U.S. firms for 8 of 32 contracts covering a range of sectors, including energy and power; defense; transportation; telecommunications; and computers, information technology, and security. The 8 contracts for which Chinese firms competed had a total value of $3.6 billion—34 percent of the $10.4 billion in total contract value for which the U.S. firms competed. In contrast, French firms competed against U.S. firms for 11 contracts with a total value of about $8.3 million.

Table 1. Nationalities of Firms That Competed with U.S. Firms Supported by the Department of Commerce's Advocacy Center for Indonesian Government Contracts, Fiscal Years 2009-2014

	Contracts competed	
Nationalities of firms competing with U.S. firms[a]	**Total value (millions)**	**Number**
France	$8,301	11
China	3,565	8
South Korea	3,290	5
Germany	2,392	6
Italy	2,071	7
Japan	2,000	1
Spain	1,080	5
All contracts for which U.S. firms competed	**10,395**	**32**

Source: U.S. Department of Commerce Advocacy Center. I GAO-16-186.

Note: The value and number of contracts do not sum to the totals shown for "all contracts for which U.S. firms competed" because firms from multiple countries competed for some contracts. The number and value of these contracts are included in each bidding country's total.

[a]Firms from at least 17 additional countries competed against U.S. firms for contracts, but none of those countries' firms competed for more than $1 billion in total contract value.

- **World Bank.** From 2000 through 2014, U.S. and Chinese firms won a relatively small share of World Bank-financed contracts in Indonesia and tended to win contracts in different sectors.[21] U.S. and Chinese firms won a combined $33 million (1.1 percent) of the $2.94 billion in total contract dollars that the World Bank awarded in Indonesia.[22] Of the $26 million that U.S. firms won, $24 million (94 percent) was for consultant services and the remainder was for goods. In contrast, of the $7 million contract dollars that Chinese firms won, $6.9 million (96 percent) was for goods. Indonesian firms won $2.54 billion (86 percent) of the World Bank's total contract dollars, while Japanese, French, Korean, and Australian firms won a combined $267 million (9 percent).

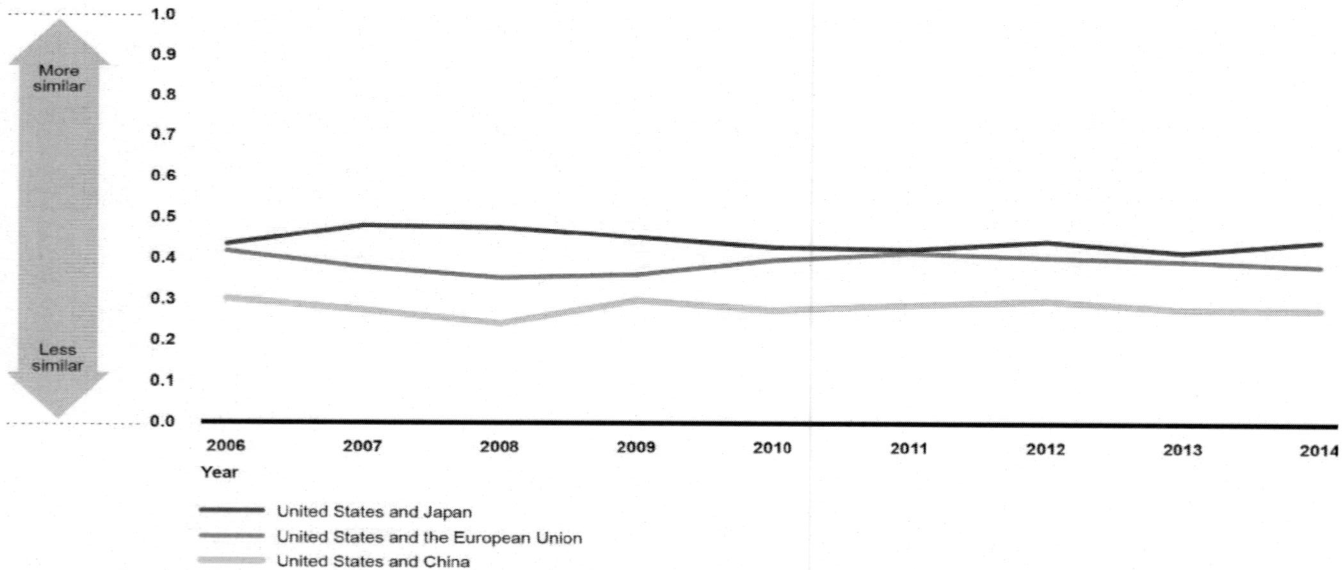

Source: GAO analysis of U.S., Chinese, European Union countries', and Japanese data from the United Nations Commodity Trade database. | GAO-16-186.

Notes: An index value of 1 would indicate that each good exported to Indonesia represented the same percentage of total exports to Indonesia for both of the paired countries. A zero value would indicate no overlap—that is, the two countries exported entirely different goods. We excluded exports of special transactions and commodities not classified by kind, because those exports include many different types of goods.

Figure 5. Export Similarity Index of U.S. Goods Exports to Indonesia Relative to Chinese, European Union, and Japanese Exports to Indonesia, 2006-2014.

- **ADB.** U.S. firms won a small share of ADB contracts in Indonesia in 2013 and 2014, while Chinese firms won no ADB contracts. During this period, U.S. firms won three ADB contracts for a combined $10 million of the $410 million in total contract dollars that ADB awarded in Indonesia. One of the three contracts was for a geothermal power project, and the other two were consulting contracts worth less than $0.5 million each.

U.S. Firms Face a Challenging Business Environment in Indonesia

U.S. agencies and private sector representatives have cited multiple challenges to trading and investing in Indonesia.

- **Restrictive regulatory environment.** According to officials from the Office of the U.S. Trade Representative (USTR), Indonesia's regulatory environment constitutes the biggest market access barrier for U.S. firms. In 2014 and 2015, USTR reported that Indonesia's trade and investment climate was characterized by, among other things, growing protectionism toward local business interests.[23] According to the USTR reports, in recent years, Indonesia has enacted numerous regulations on imports, such as those relating to local content and domestic manufacturing requirements, which have increased the burden for U.S. exporters. In 2013, the United States initiated a WTO dispute settlement process with Indonesia because of Indonesia's import licensing restrictions on horticulture and meat products.[24] A representative of one U.S. firm whom we spoke with in Indonesia said that the firm had stopped importing soybeans into Indonesia for about a year because of Indonesian quotas, rising import taxes, and local origination requirements. Moreover, according to an official representing an American regional trade association, regulations may appear without advance notice or consultations with affected industries and may not be uniformly enforced. In addition, USDA's 2014 Country Strategy Statement for Indonesia states that market access challenges for U.S. exports to Indonesia, such as Indonesia's import licensing requirements, have dominated the U.S.-Indonesia bilateral relationship. The World Bank's 2015 ease of doing business ranking of 189 economies, where a ranking of 1 indicates the most business-friendly regulations relative to other countries in the rankings, ranked Indonesia at 114.[25] Indonesia ranked least favorably in *enforcing contracts* (172) and most favorably in *ensuring protections for minority investors* (43). In assigning the ranking, the World Bank said that Indonesia implemented reforms that reduced the tax burden on companies and made it easier for them to start a business and obtain access to electricity.

- **Corruption.** Although the Indonesian government investigates and prosecutes high-profile corruption cases, many investors consider corruption a significant barrier to doing business in Indonesia, according to USTR's 2015 report on foreign trade barriers.[26] A representative of one U.S. firm told us that after paying taxes to the Indonesian government, the firm may be asked to pay additional fines. U.S. firms and representatives of American regional trade associations also noted that while U.S. firms are bound by U.S. law not to engage in corrupt practices, some of the firms' competitors do not face similar restrictions.[27] Transparency International's 2014 Corruption Perceptions Index ranked Indonesia at 107 of 175 countries and territories, where a ranking of 1 indicates the lowest perceived level of public sector corruption relative to other countries in the index.[28]
- **Weak infrastructure.** Indonesia has weak and underdeveloped public infrastructure, such as ports, rail, and land transport, which increases transaction costs and inefficiencies and hampers exporters and investors, according to a report by Commerce and State.[29] A representative of a private sector consulting firm operating in Indonesia said that Indonesia has poor infrastructure for transporting goods from factories to port. According to a State official, Indonesia's economic growth is not likely to increase without significant investment in infrastructure.
- **Violations of intellectual property rights.** In 2015, USTR reported that Indonesia was one of 13 countries designated as a Priority Watch List country because of particular problems with respect to intellectual property rights protection, enforcement, or market access for persons relying on such rights.[30] According to the report, the United States is concerned that, among other things, Indonesia's efforts to enforce intellectual property rights have not been effective in addressing rampant piracy and counterfeiting.
- **Limited access to land.** An absence of clear Indonesian laws regarding the acquisition and use of land by investors has slowed

infrastructure development projects, according to a State document. For example, the document stated that construction on a hydroelectric dam in West Java, although nearly complete as of January 2015, had been delayed because of land use disputes. A new regulation on land use is scheduled to go into effect in 2015, but a State document noted that this law is untested and that implementation may be erratic, especially in its initial years.

United States and China Are Both Engaging Economically with Indonesia, but China Has Free Trade Agreements with Indonesia and Has Provided More Financing

Although the United States is engaging economically with Indonesia, the two countries have no free trade agreement (FTA), while China has both trade and investment agreements with Indonesia through its agreements with ASEAN countries. Also, the United States is not negotiating any existing or proposed regional trade agreements with Indonesia, whereas China is engaging Indonesia through a proposed regional trade agreement. Both the United States and China support their domestic firms in Indonesia through financing and other means, although U.S. agencies estimate that Chinese financing has greatly exceeded U.S. financing. The United States and China also have provided support for economic development, with U.S. efforts focused on capacity building and Chinese efforts focused on physical infrastructure development.

United States Has No FTA with Indonesia, while China Has Free Trade and Investment Agreements with Indonesia

The United States has not established an FTA with Indonesia, although the two countries have a limited trade framework agreement to facilitate trade relations. The United States–Indonesia Trade and Investment Framework Agreement (TIFA) is intended to facilitate discussions of trade and investment issues. In contrast to FTAs, TIFAs are short agreements that provide strategic frameworks and structure for dialogue on trade and investment issues and prepare countries for eventual accession to high-standard trade agreements. The United States–Indonesia TIFA was signed in 1996 by USTR and Indonesia's Ministry of Trade. According to USTR, U.S. officials meet regularly with Indonesian officials in both formal TIFA meetings and informal meetings to address bilateral trade and investment issues. The last two formal meetings that U.S. and Indonesian officials held under the TIFA occurred in September 2015 and June 2013, according to USTR. In the September 2015 meeting, officials discussed a range of issues, such as policies related to the information and communications technology sector and Indonesia's Economic Policy Package.[31]

In addition, in June 2015, Congress reauthorized the Generalized System of Preferences (GSP), which provides duty-free treatment for 3,500 tariff lines from many developing countries, including Indonesia, through the end of 2017. According to a report by the Congressional Research Service, in 2012—the last full year of GSP implementation—Indonesia ranked fourth of 127 beneficiary countries in the value of U.S. imports that entered duty free through GSP.[32] According to data in the report, of the $18 billion in U.S. imports from Indonesia in 2012, about 12 percent, or $2.2 billion, entered the United States duty free through GSP.

In contrast, China has trade and investment agreements with Indonesia through the China-ASEAN Framework Agreement on Comprehensive Economic Cooperation. The China-ASEAN Framework Agreement on Comprehensive Economic Cooperation comprises a series of agreements on trade and investment to expand access to each other's markets.[33]

- The China-ASEAN Trade in Goods Agreement, which entered into force in 2005, is intended to give China and Indonesia, as well as other ASEAN countries, tariff-free access to each other's market for many goods and reduced most duties for Indonesia's trade in goods with China to zero by 2012. According to a study by the ADB, in 2010, the average tariff on exports from six ASEAN countries, including Indonesia, to China was 0.1 percent, while the average tariff on Chinese exports to Indonesia was 0.6 percent.[34]
- The China-ASEAN Trade in Services Agreement, which entered into force in 2007, is intended to provide market access in agreed-on sectors of China and Indonesia, as well as other ASEAN countries, to foreign companies and firms that is equivalent to domestic service providers' market access in their own countries.
- The China-ASEAN Investment Agreement, which entered into force in 2010, committed China and Indonesia, as well as other ASEAN countries, to treat each other's investors as equal to their domestic investors.

Selected studies have projected that the China-ASEAN Trade in Goods Agreement generally increases trade for China and Indonesia and improves Indonesia's economy.[35] All but one of these studies also estimated that the agreement improves China's economy.[36] In addition, one study estimated that the agreement increases investment in China and Indonesia.[37] In August 2014, China and Indonesia, as well as the other ASEAN countries, announced discussions to upgrade these agreements. In August 2015, China's Commerce Minister announced that China and ASEAN had agreed to the goal of finalizing negotiations to upgrade these agreements by the end of 2015.

Unlike the United States, China Is Engaging Indonesia through a Proposed Regional Free Trade Agreement

Although the United States has concluded negotiations for a regional trade agreement known as the Trans-Pacific Partnership (TPP), Indonesia was not a party to these negotiations.[38] In contrast, China and Indonesia are both parties to ongoing negotiations for the Regional Comprehensive Economic Partnership Agreement (RCEP), which negotiating parties have said they hope to complete in 2015.[39] Indonesia's trade with China and with the 14 other countries negotiating RCEP represented 66 percent of its total trade in goods in 2013.[40] RCEP negotiating parties seek to expand access to trade and investment among the parties by combining their existing FTAs into a single comprehensive agreement. The United States is not a party to the RCEP negotiations.

U.S. Agencies Have Provided Less Financing for Investment Projects in Indonesia Than Chinese Agencies

Our analysis of U.S. agency data showed that in fiscal years 2009 through 2014, the Export-Import Bank of the United States (Ex-Im) and the Overseas Private Investment Corporation (OPIC) provided about $2.5 billion in financing to support U.S. exports to, and investment in, Indonesia (see table 2). Although China does not publish data on its financing in Indonesia, our analysis of State data found that China has financed at least $36.4 billion in investment projects in Indonesia since 2009.

Our analysis of Ex-Im and OPIC information for fiscal years 2009 through 2014 found the following.

- Ex-Im authorized about $2.4 billion in loans, loan guarantees, and insurance to support U.S. exports to Indonesia during this period.[41] Ex-Im's authorizations in Indonesia consisted mostly of loan guarantees. Ex-Im authorized its two largest loan guarantees in fiscal years 2011 and 2013, when it authorized more than $1.6 billion in guarantees for the purchase of commercial aircraft.

- OPIC committed about $86 million in financing to U.S. investment projects in Indonesia during this period.[42] OPIC's largest commitment in Indonesia consisted of a $50 million investment guarantee in fiscal year 2013 for a facility to help expand lending to small and medium-sized enterprises investing in Indonesia.

China does not publish data on its financing for exports, imports, and investment in Indonesia by private and state-owned enterprises, but State reported that China has made available at least $36.4 billion in financing for investment projects in Indonesia since 2009.[43] According to State, Chinese financing is generally offered in the form of soft loans by China's Development Bank and Export-Import Bank.[44] For example, State reported that in 2013, China's Export-Import Bank financed a $6 billion coal mining infrastructure and transportation project in Papua and Central Kalimantan. In April 2015, China's President reiterated China's commitment to provide financing in support of Indonesia's infrastructure and connectivity development.

Table 2. Ex-Im Authorizations and OPIC Commitments in Indonesia, Fiscal Years 2009-2014

Nominal U.S. dollars in millions			
Fiscal year	**Ex-Im authorizations[a]**	**OPIC commitments**	**Total**
2009	$279.5	$0	**$279.5**
2010	328.3	0.4	**$328.7**
2011	550.7	14	**$564.7**
2012	19.9	21.5	**$41.4**
2013	1,220.2	50.0	**$1,270.2**
2014	0.5	0	**$0.5**
Total[b]	**$2,399**	**$86.0**	**$2,485.1**

Legend: Ex-Im = Export-Import Bank of the United States; OPIC = Overseas Private Investment Corporation

Source: GAO analysis of Ex-Im annual reports and data and OPIC data. | GAO-16-186.

[a]Ex-Im generally provides financing to businesses when private financing is unavailable; therefore, fluctuations in its financing activity may reflect changes in the business and banking environment rather than Ex-Im's initiative.

[b]These data do not include Ex-Im multibuyer insurance, which may include multiple countries, or OPIC funds recorded as provided to the Asia and the Pacific Region, some of which may be used in Indonesia.

United States and China Provide a Variety Services to U.S. and Chinese Firms in Indonesia

State, Commerce, and USDA maintain staff in Indonesia to provide export promotion services and to advocate for policies favorable to U.S. firms operating in Indonesia.[45]

- **State.** State maintains an Economic and Environment Section at the U.S. Embassy in Jakarta that is organized into three focus areas: environment, science, technology, and health; trade and investment; and macroeconomics and finance. According to State officials, improving economic relations with Indonesia to facilitate greater U.S. trade and investment is a key priority of the section.
- **Commerce.** According to a senior Commerce official in Indonesia, Commerce personnel based in Indonesia work to help U.S. firms find local partners, obtain the appropriate licenses and registrations for conducting business in Indonesia, and interpret existing or new laws and regulations, among other duties.[46] The officials said that they also advocate for U.S. firms and lead or support trade missions.[47] For example, Commerce officials led a trade mission focused on clean energy business practices in 2010 and led a trade mission focused on education in 2011.
- **USDA.** USDA personnel in Indonesia offer U.S. firms assistance with market access and market development issues, according to a USDA official. For example, according to the official, when Indonesia restricted imports on all U.S. live and processed poultry in response to an avian flu outbreak in Washington and Oregon in late 2014, USDA personnel worked with Indonesia to lift the restriction for U.S. poultry not affected by the outbreak. USDA also cooperates with industry commodity groups and provides market intelligence reports to U.S. firms, according to the official.

The Chinese government has pursued agreements with Indonesia to support Chinese firms that do business there. For example:

- **Special economic zones.** China's Ministry of Commerce has worked with Indonesia to establish at least one special economic zone to facilitate cross-border trade and investment, according to Chinese embassy websites.[48] According to the Chinese Ministry of Commerce, the government of China supports Chinese firms that establish and invest in a zone by offering financing and facilitating movement of materials, equipment, labor, and foreign exchange between China and the zone. In establishing these zones, China negotiates with Indonesia and other host governments in the areas of tax, land, and labor policies to support firms that choose to invest in the zones.

- **Currency swaps.** China has facilitated cross-border trade in local currencies in Indonesia through the establishment and renewal of a bilateral currency swap arrangement totaling 100 billion Chinese yuan, according to the Central Bank of Indonesia's website.[49] The bank's website states that the arrangement promotes bilateral trade and direct investment for economic development between the two countries and helps guarantee stabilized financial markets by ensuring the availability of short-term liquidity.[50] The People's Bank of China and the Central Bank of Indonesia established the arrangement in March 2009 and renewed it in October 2013 for 3 more years.[51]

United States and China Generally Foster Economic Development in Different Areas

The United States has fostered economic development in Indonesia through assistance to strengthen governance and energy development. In fiscal years 2009 through 2013, U.S. agencies provided about $373 million in trade capacity building assistance—that is, development assistance intended to improve a country's ability to benefit from international trade—to Indonesia.[52] U.S. trade capacity building assistance to Indonesia has supported initiatives aimed at, among other things, providing economic policy advisory services to the Indonesian government; strengthening key trade and investment institutions; improving Indonesia's competiveness in global supply chains; and strengthening the capacity of the government Indonesia to analyze, negotiate, and implement bilateral and multilateral trade agreements. The majority of U.S. trade capacity assistance provided to Indonesia during this period—about 90 percent—was committed as part of a 5-year, $600 million Millennium Challenge Corporation (MCC) compact with Indonesia for a project that is designed to help the government of Indonesia to, among other things, increase productivity and reduce reliance on fossil fuels.[53] (For more information about U.S. trade capacity building assistance to Indonesia, see app. IV.) The United States has also sought to ensure affordable, secure, and cleaner energy supplies in Indonesia and across the Asia-Pacific region through the U.S.-Asia Pacific Comprehensive Energy Partnership with Indonesia, which, according to State, was launched in 2012.[54]

China has assisted economic development in Indonesia by supporting Indonesia's connectivity and infrastructure development as well as its role in regional initiatives. According to a joint statement issued by Chinese President Xi Jinping and Indonesia's President Widodo in April 2015, China plans to support Indonesia's infrastructure and connectivity development by providing financing for railways, highways, ports, docks, dams, airports, and bridges, among other things. According to a speech by a senior Chinese official posted on a Chinese embassy website, the power plants built by Chinese firms make up one-quarter of Indonesia's power supply, and Chinese firms have built Indonesia's longest cross-sea bridge to facilitate the transport and flow of commerce between the Java and Madura Islands. State reported that between 2006 and 2015, China undertook six power plants, including two coal-fired power plants and a $17 billion, 7,000-megawatt hydropower plant; three rail projects; and a coal mining infrastructure and transportation project.

China's Foreign Minister has publicly stated that Indonesia is the most important partner in its 21st Century Maritime Silk Road Initiative, which, according to a document released by the Chinese government in March 2015, aims to improve maritime cooperation and regional connectivity. In November 2014, China announced the creation of a $40 billion Silk Road Fund to help implement this initiative. In addition, Indonesia is one of 57 prospective founding members of China's proposed Asian Infrastructure Investment Bank, an international institution to finance infrastructure projects throughout the Asia-Pacific region.[55] Under the bank's initial agreement, the bank's authorized capital is $100 billion, of which China has pledged $29.8 billion and Indonesia has pledged $3.4 billion.[56] Bank documents indicate that the bank anticipates beginning operations before the end of 2015.

U.S. and Chinese Trade and Investment, Competition, and Actions to Further Economic Engagement in Vietnam

China's Total Trade in Goods with, and Investments in, Vietnam Have Exceeded the United States'

The value of China's total trade in goods with Vietnam surpassed that of the United States in 2007 and was more than double the value of the United States' total trade in goods with Vietnam in 2014.[57] However, U.S. imports from Vietnam exceed Chinese imports, while China's exports to Vietnam exceed the United States'. The United States is Vietnam's fourth largest trading partner, and China is Vietnam's largest trading partner. Available data on U.S. and Chinese FDI, although limited, indicate that Chinese FDI in Vietnam from 2007 through 2012 was more than double U.S. FDI in Vietnam during this time.

China's Total Goods Trade with Vietnam Has Surpassed the United States', but U.S. Imports Exceed Chinese Imports

The value of China's total trade in goods with Vietnam surpassed the United States' in 2007, and the gap has continued to grow. In 2014, China's total goods trade with Vietnam was $83.6 billion, while the United States' was $36.3 billion (see fig. 6). According to Vietnamese and U.S. government officials, an unknown amount of Chinese-Vietnamese trade occurs across the countries' porous border and outside official channels.

Figure 6 illustrates the following:

- From 1994 through 2014, the United States' imports from Vietnam exceeded China's every year except 1994, 1995, and 2000.
- Chinese exports grew faster than U.S. exports from 1994 through 2014.
- The United States had an annual trade deficit with Vietnam from 1997 through 2014, while China had an annual trade surplus with Vietnam from 1994 through 2014. Both the U.S. deficit and Chinese surplus have accelerated in recent years.

From 2000 through 2014, the composition of U.S. and Chinese total trade in goods with Vietnam shifted from predominantly raw commodities to manufactured goods. In 2014, textiles represented the largest share of U.S. imports from Vietnam (31 percent) and machinery represented the largest share of Chinese imports from Vietnam (47 percent). Animals, plants, and food represented the largest share of U.S. exports to Vietnam (36 percent) in 2014,[58] while machinery represented the largest share of Chinese exports to Vietnam (31 percent). In 2014, the majority of U.S. imports from Vietnam consisted of goods for consumer use, such as wooden bedroom furniture. The majority of U.S. exports to Vietnam and of Chinese imports from, and exports to, Vietnam in 2014 consisted of goods for industrial use, which are used in the production of other goods, such as microchips. See appendix III for more information about the composition and use of the United States' and China's trade in goods with Vietnam.

China Is Vietnam's Largest Trading Partner, While the United States Ranks Fourth

China and the United States are Vietnam's largest and fourth-largest trading partners, respectively, in terms of their combined exports and imports of goods.[59] Other ASEAN countries and the EU are Vietnam's second and third-largest trading partners.

- **Exports.** In 2013, Vietnam exported $24 billion in goods to the United States and $13 billion in goods to China. After the EU, the United States was the second-largest market for Vietnamese goods exports, while China was the fifth-largest market for Vietnamese goods exports in 2013. In both 2004 and 2013, the United States' share of Vietnam's exports was around 18 to 19 percent. China's share of Vietnam's exports was around 10 percent in both 2004 and 2013.
- **Imports.** Vietnam imported $5 billion in goods from the United States, its seventh-largest import market, and $37 billion in goods from China, its largest import market, in 2013. Other ASEAN countries, South Korea, Japan, Taiwan, and the EU represented Vietnam's second-, third-, fourth-, fifth-, and sixth-largest goods import markets, respectively, in 2013.[60] In both 2004 and 2013, the United States' share of Vietnam's imports was around 3 to 4 percent. China's share of Vietnam's imports increased significantly during the same period, from 14 percent in 2004 to 28 percent in 2013.

Figure 7 shows Vietnam's exports and imports by trading partner in 2004, 2008, and 2013.

Vietnam is a larger export market for China than the United States, but is a larger source of imported goods for the United States than it is for China.

- Vietnam was China's seventh-largest export market by value in 2014 but the United States' 44th-largest. In 2014, China exported $63.7 billion in goods to Vietnam, which accounted for 2.7 percent of China's global goods exports. In the same year, the United States exported $5.7 billion in goods to Vietnam, which accounted for 0.4 percent of total U.S. global goods exports.

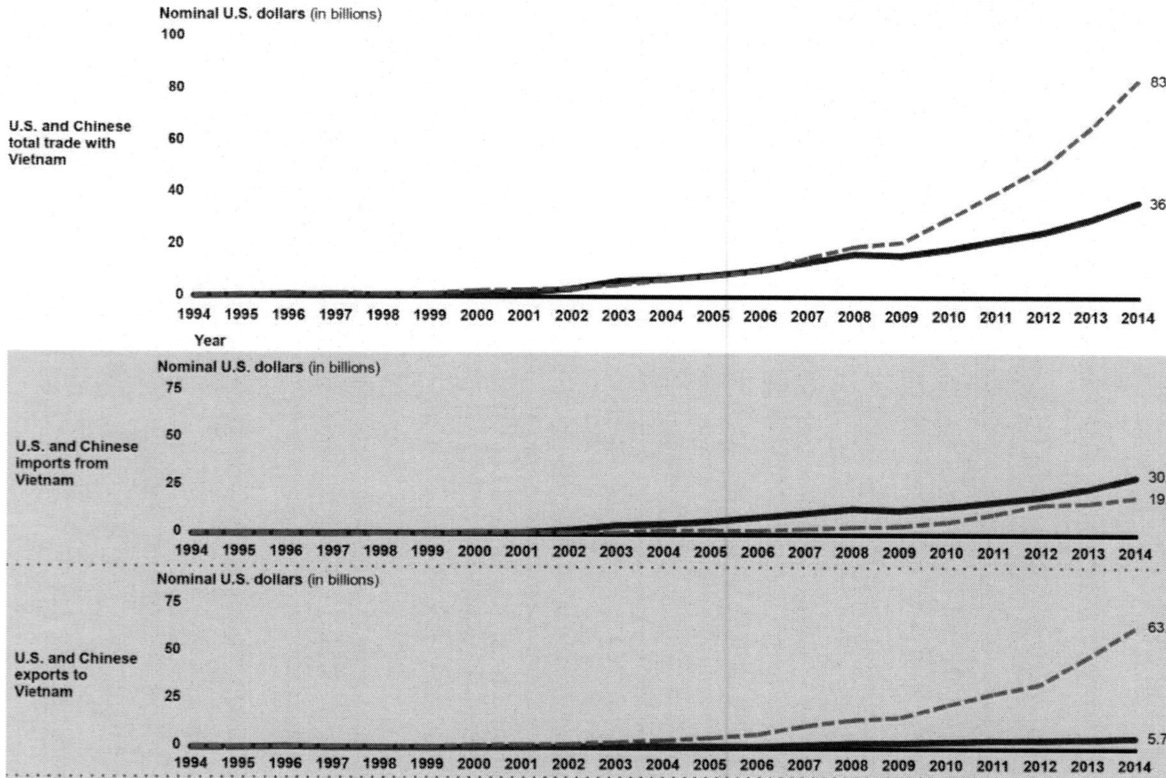

Nominal U.S. dollars (in billions)
100
80
60
40
20
0
U.S. and Chinese total trade with Vietnam
83.6
36.3
1994 1995 1996 1997 1998 1999 2000 2001 2002 2003 2004 2005 2006 2007 2008 2009 2010 2011 2012 2013 2014
Year
Nominal U.S. dollars (in billions)
75
50
25
0
U.S. and Chinese imports from Vietnam
30.6
19.9
1994 1995 1996 1997 1998 1999 2000 2001 2002 2003 2004 2005 2006 2007 2008 2009 2010 2011 2012 2013 2014
Nominal U.S. dollars (in billions)
75
50
25
0
U.S. and Chinese exports to Vietnam
63.7
5.7
1994 1995 1996 1997 1998 1999 2000 2001 2002 2003 2004 2005 2006 2007 2008 2009 2010 2011 2012 2013 2014

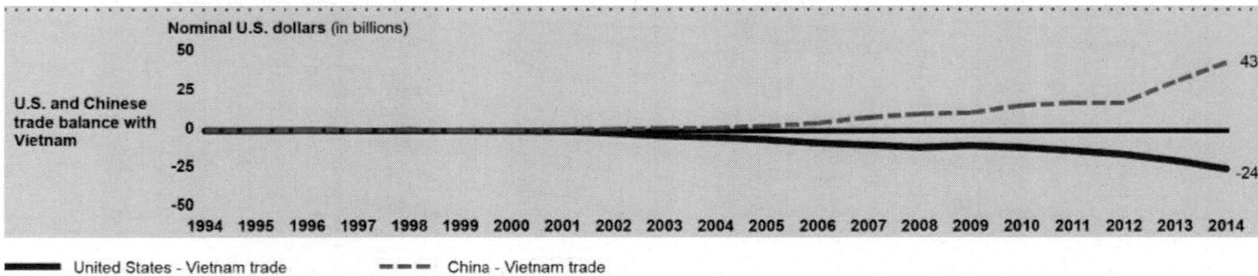

Source: GAO analysis of U.S. and Chinese data from the United Nations Commodity Trade database. | GAO-16-186.

Note: The trade values shown are nominal—that is, not adjusted for inflation. Changes in values over time are due in part to changes in the prices of traded goods.

Figure 6. U.S. and Chinese Total Trade in Goods with Vietnam, 1994-2014.

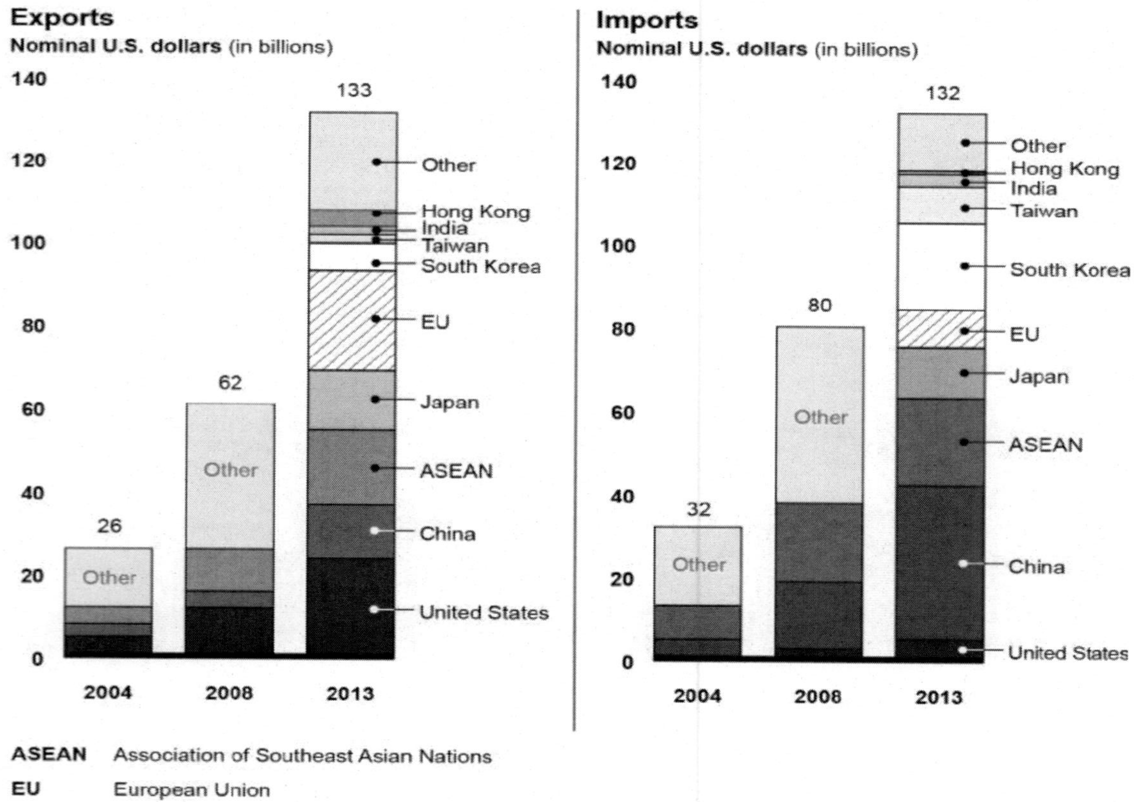

Source: GAO analysis of data from ASEANstats database. | GAO-16-186.

Notes: The trade values shown are nominal—that is, not adjusted for inflation. Changes in values over time are due in part to changes in the prices of traded goods.

Hong Kong is a special administrative region of China, but we have included it in this report as a separate country because it is an economic entity separate from the rest of China and is able to enter into international agreements on its own behalf in commercial and economic matters.

Although the United States does not have diplomatic relations with Taiwan, we have listed Taiwan as a separate country, because whenever the laws of the United States refer or relate to foreign countries, nations, states, governments, or similar entities, such terms shall include and shall apply to Taiwan.

Figure 7. Value of Vietnamese Exports and Imports in 2004, 2008, and 2013, by Trading Partner.

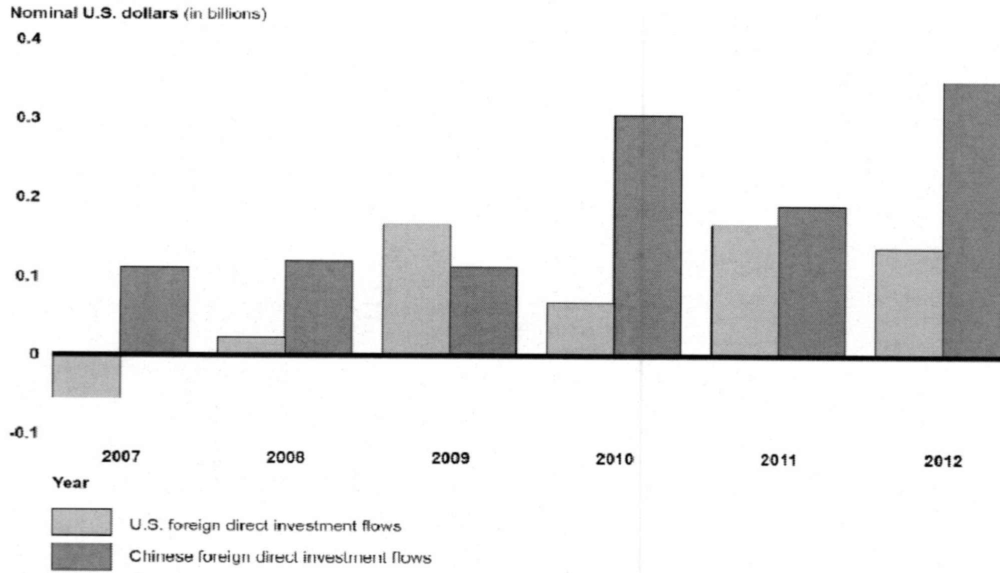

Source: GAO analysis of data from the U.S. Bureau of Economic Analysis and Chinese data from the United Nations Conference on Trade and Development. | GAO-16-186.

Notes: Foreign direct investment (FDI) flows represent FDI activities within a given period of time.

In 2007, U.S. FDI flows to Vietnam were negative—that is, flows from U.S. affiliates in Vietnam to the U.S. parent companies were larger than flows from the U.S. parent companies to U.S. affiliates in Vietnam.

Although China has reported investment data since 2003, China began including financial investment in its total investment data in 2007. Chinese FDI data do not include Hong Kong.

The investment data shown are nominal values—that is, not adjusted for inflation. When using a U.S. GDP deflator, we calculated cumulative U.S. and Chinese FDI flows for 2007 through 2012 at $490 million and $1.2 billion, respectively, in 2009 dollars.

Figure 8. U.S. and Chinese Foreign Direct Investment Flows to Vietnam, 2007-2012.

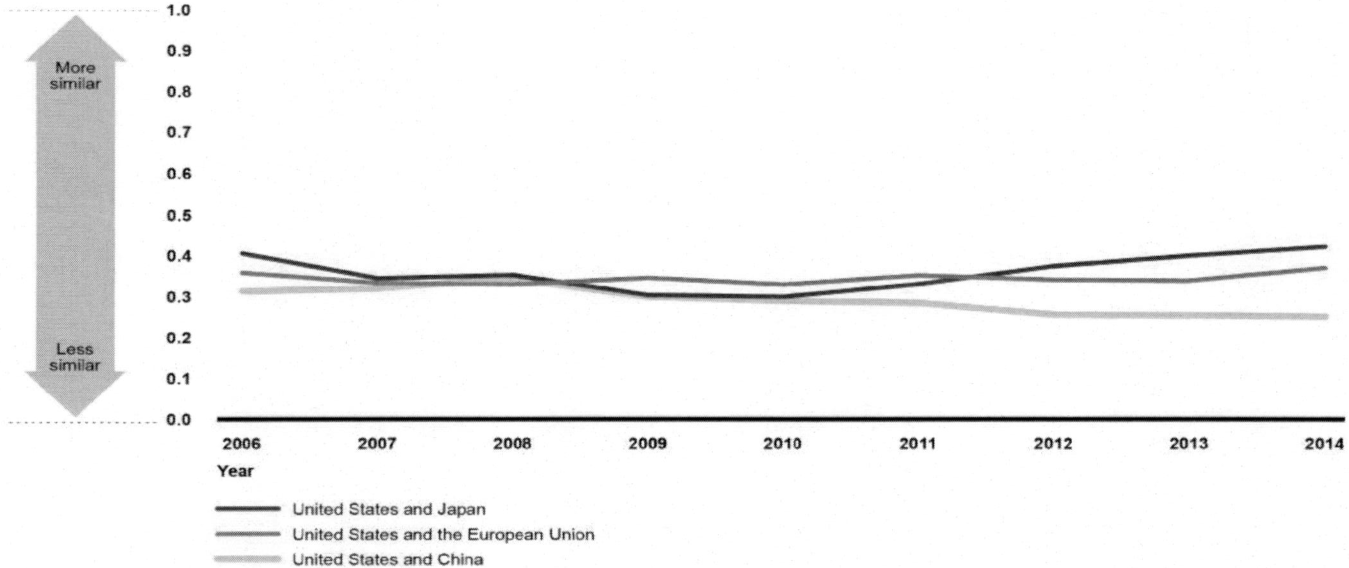

Source: GAO analysis of U.S., Chinese, European Union countries', and Japanese data from the United Nations Commodity Trade database. | GAO-16-186.

Notes: An index value of 1 would indicate that each good exported to Vietnam represented the same percentage of total exports to Vietnam for both of the paired countries. A value of 0 would indicate no overlap—that is, each country exported entirely different goods. We excluded exports of special transactions and commodities not classified by kind, because those exports include many different types of goods.

Figure 9. Export Similarity Index of U.S. Goods Exports to Vietnam Relative to Chinese, European Union, and Japanese Exports to Vietnam, 2006-2014.

- Vietnam was China's 26th-largest source of imported goods by value in 2014 and was the United States' 15th-largest. In 2014, China imported $19.9 billion in goods from Vietnam, which accounted for 1.0 percent of China's global goods imports. In the same year, the United States imported $30.6 billion in goods from Vietnam, which accounted for 1.3 percent of total U.S. goods imports from the world.

The United States' role relative to China's in Vietnam's trade of goods as well as services may be greater when the amount of intermediate U.S. inputs to the traded goods and services is taken into account. Because of the nature of global supply chains, for example, a consumer phone from a U.S. company might be assembled in China but include components manufactured by Germany, Japan, South Korea, and other countries.[61] Data from the UN Commodity Trade database, which counts the full value of an export for only the exporting country, showed that China exported $29.1 billion in goods to Vietnam in 2011, almost seven times the $4.3 billion in goods that the United States exported to Vietnam that year.[62] However, data from the OECD and the WTO, which attempt to account for the value added to a finished export by each contributing country, show that China exported only about 2.5 times more in value-added goods and services to Vietnam than the United States did. The OECDWTO data suggest that Chinese exports to Vietnam contained a higher portion of components produced elsewhere than did U.S. exports.

Total U.S. Trade in Services with Vietnam Was Approximately $3 Billion in 2012, but Data on China's Trade in Services Are Unavailable

Our analysis of data from BEA[63] and other sources on U.S. trade in services in Vietnam[64] provides broad estimates rather than precise values. However, our calculations indicate that U.S. total trade in services with Vietnam totaled approximately $3.1 billion in 2012.[65] Our analysis shows that the United States

- exported approximately $1.7 billion in services to Vietnam in 2012, with (1) business, professional, and technical services and (2) education as the largest and second-largest service categories by value, and
- imported approximately $1.4 billion in services from Vietnam in 2012, with (1) travel and passenger fares and (2) transportation services as the largest and second-largest service categories by value.

In 2012, the value of U.S.-Vietnamese services trade was about 12 percent of the value of U.S.-Vietnamese goods trade.

China does not publish data on its trade in services with Vietnam.

Chinese Investment Flows to Vietnam Were More Than Double U.S. Investment Flows in 2007-2012, but Available Data Have Limitations

Data on FDI in Vietnam from the United States and China have limitations, in that these data may not accurately reflect the countries to which U.S. and Chinese FDI ultimately flows. [66] For example, U.S. and Chinese firms may set up subsidiaries in other countries, which are then used to make investments in Vietnam. Such investments would not be captured by U.S. and Chinese data on FDI in Vietnam. Conversely, U.S. and Chinese firms can set up subsidiaries in Vietnam, which can be used to make investments in other countries. Given these limitations, available data show that from 2007 through 2012, China's reported FDI flows to Vietnam totaled approximately $1.2 billion, more than twice the U.S. FDI flows of approximately $500 million. During this period, China's reported annual FDI flows to Vietnam fluctuated but continued to exceed U.S. FDI flows every year except 2009 (see fig. 8). Although BEA does not publicly report data on U.S. FDI flows to Vietnam by type of investment, information that BEA provided to us indicates that from 2003 through 2013, on average, one-third of total U.S. FDI stock in Vietnam was in mining and manufacturing. Mining increased from 22 percent of U.S. FDI stock in Vietnam in 2003 to more than 50 percent in 2013, while manufacturing's share of total U.S. FDI stock in Vietnam fell from a high of 60 percent in 2006 to 28 percent in 2013. According to officials from Vietnam's Ministry of Agriculture and Rural Development, Chinese investment projects are mostly in the industrial, manufacturing, and construction sectors.

United States and China Compete More Often with Other Countries in Goods Exports to Vietnam and Win Government Contracts in Different Sectors

Data on U.S. and Chinese goods exports to Vietnam indicate that since 2008, U.S. exports of goods to Vietnam have been more similar to Japanese and EU exports than to Chinese exports, suggesting that the United States is more likely to compete directly with Japan and EU countries than with China.[67] Figure 9 presents a commonly used index for assessing the similarity of the United States' goods exports to Vietnam to those of China and other countries.[68]

Data from Commerce's Advocacy Center, the World Bank, and the ADB provide some information about Vietnamese government contracts that U.S. and Chinese firms competed for or won. Although these data represent a small share of U.S. and Chinese economic activity in Vietnam, they offer insights into the degree of competition between U.S. and Chinese firms for the projects represented. These data indicate that U.S. firms in Vietnam have competed more often with firms from other countries than with Chinese firms and have tended to win contracts in different sectors.

- **Commerce's Advocacy Center.** Data from Commerce's Advocacy Center show that U.S. firms that the center supported in fiscal years 2009 through 2014 competed for Vietnamese government contracts more often, and for higher total contract value, with firms from Japan, South Korea, and several other countries than with Chinese firms (see table 3).[69] According to the center's data, Chinese firms competed with U.S. firms for 3 of 29 contracts, in the areas of energy and power, infrastructure, and services. These 3 contracts' total value was $92 million—3 percent of the $28.8 billion in total contract value for which the U.S. firms competed. In contrast, Japanese and South Korean firms competed against U.S. firms for 10 and 6 contracts, respectively, with a combined value of more than $11 billion for each country.
- **World Bank.** From 2000 through 2014, U.S. and Chinese firms generally won World Bank-financed contracts in Vietnam in different sectors.[70] Vietnamese firms received about $4.3 billion (70 percent) of the $6.1 billion in total contract value. Among firms from other countries, Chinese firms won the highest total contract value—$531 million—almost 9 percent of the total World Bank-financed contract value. The United States won $133 million, about 2 percent of the total World Bank-financed contract value. Most of the contract dollars won by Chinese firms were for civil works (71 percent) and goods (28 percent). In contrast, most of the contract dollars won by U.S. firms—$118 million (89 percent)—were for consultant services. Electrical equipment was the only category of procurement in which both U.S. and Chinese firms won more than $2 million in contract value. Chinese firms won $140 million, and U.S. firms won $14 million, in

contract value for electrical equipment for World Bank projects in Vietnam.

- **ADB.** U.S. firms won one ADB contract in Vietnam in 2013 and 2014—a $130,000 contract for consulting services related to water conservation. During this period, Chinese firms won 15 contracts valued at more than $250 million. The Chinese firms' contracts included about $207 million for the construction of roads and a hydropower plant, with the remainder for goods for electricity transmission, distribution, and renewable energy.

Table 3. Nationalities of Firms That Competed with U.S. Firms Supported by the Department of Commerce's Advocacy Center for Vietnamese Government Contracts, Fiscal Years 2009-2014

	Contracts competed	
Nationalities of firms competing with U.S. firms	**Total value (millions)**	**Number**
Japan	$11,753	10
South Korea	11,032	6
Russia	10,736	2
Switzerland	10,289	6
Sweden	8,663	5
Bulgaria	8,610	1
France	5,754	11
U.K.	2,116	3
Germany	1,942	7
China[a]	92	3
All contracts for which U.S. firms competed	**28,751**	**29**

Source: U.S. Department of Commerce Advocacy Center. | GAO-16-186.

Note: The value and number of contracts do not sum to the total for "all contracts for which U.S. firms competed" because multiple countries' firms competed for some contracts. The number and value of these contracts are included in each bidding country's total.

[a]Firms from five additional countries competed against U.S. companies for more contract dollars than did Chinese firms.

U.S. Firms Face a Challenging Business Environment in Vietnam

U.S. agencies and private sector representatives have articulated multiple challenges to trading and investing in Vietnam.

- **Restrictive regulatory environment.** A lack of transparency in the Vietnamese government's policies and decisions and slowness of government action are creating challenges for U.S. firms, according to State and Commerce. In addition, one U.S. business owner we spoke with in Vietnam described the regulatory environment he dealt with as "arcane, corrupt, and labyrinthine." According to a State and Commerce report, Vietnam has established regulations that limit the operations of foreign companies in the Vietnamese market.[71] For example, unless a foreign company has an investment license permitting it to directly distribute goods in Vietnam, the company must appoint a local authorized agent or distributor. USTR also reports that Vietnamese government restrictions on certain types of imports, such as used consumer goods, machinery and parts, and some agricultural commodities, affect U.S. firms' ability to operate in Vietnam.[72] The World Bank's 2015 Ease of Doing Business Index ranked Vietnam at 78 of 189 economies, where a ranking of 1 indicates the most business-friendly regulations relative to those of other countries in the index.[73] The 2015 index ranked Vietnam most favorably on *dealing with construction permits* (22) and least favorably on *paying taxes* (173). In 2015, according to the World Bank, Vietnam implemented reforms that made paying taxes less costly for companies and improved its credit information system.
- **Corruption.** Reports by USTR, Commerce, and State cite corruption as a significant barrier faced by U.S. and other foreign firms in Vietnam.[74] In addition, the owner of one small U.S. enterprise whom we spoke with in Vietnam said that onerous audit requirements and paperwork, such as the thick dossier required for obtaining an investment license, created barriers to trading and investing in Vietnam as well as opportunities for corruption. Transparency International's 2014 Corruption Perceptions Index ranked Vietnam at 119 of 175 countries and territories, where a ranking of 1 indicates the lowest perceived level of public sector corruption relative to other countries in the index.[75]

- **Weak infrastructure.** State and Commerce reports cite poorly developed infrastructure, such as electrical and Internet infrastructure, as a challenge for U.S. firms doing business in Vietnam.[76] In 2015, State reported that Vietnam needs an estimated $170 billion in additional infrastructure development in areas such as power generation, roads, railways, and water treatment to meet growing economic demand. According to a representative of one U.S. firm whom we spoke with in Vietnam, the capacity of Haiphong Harbor, a port near Hanoi, was so poor that the firm chose to ship goods to other Vietnamese ports and reload them onto smaller coastal vessels at an increased cost to avoid Haiphong. In addition, a representative of a U.S. clothing manufacturer in Vietnam noted that the capacity of Vietnam's electrical grid is weak. As a result, the Vietnamese government occasionally institutes controlled brownouts—generally on days when the garment manufacturing plants are not operating—to try to alleviate strain on the electrical grid. According to the clothing manufacturer's representative, any expansion of the garment industry could be limited without additional electrical capacity.
- **Violations of intellectual property rights.** In 2015, USTR reported that Vietnam remained designated as a Watch List country because of concerns about intellectual property rights violations and theft.[77] According to USTR, online piracy and sales of counterfeit goods are common; in addition, Vietnamese firms manufacture counterfeit goods. Moreover, Vietnam's capacity to enforce criminal penalties against counterfeiters is limited. Commerce similarly cited ineffective protection of intellectual property as a significant challenge. In addition, a representative of a technology company whom we spoke with in Vietnam stated that only 1 in 20 users of the company's software were paying for its use and that Vietnamese consumers knowingly purchase counterfeits.
- **Predominance of state-owned enterprises.** According to a Commerce and State report about Vietnam's business environment, state-owned enterprises dominate some sectors of the Vietnamese economy and receive some trade advantages over foreign firms.[78] For example, according to the report, state-owned enterprises dominate the oil and gas, electricity, mining, and banking sectors, among others. The top three telecommunications companies in Vietnam are also state-owned enterprises and control nearly 95 percent of the Vietnam telecommunications market. Similarly, a private sector representative

we spoke with in Vietnam stated that the Vietnamese government controls approximately 80 percent of Vietnam's insurance market. Moreover, according to a 2015 USTR *National Trade Estimates Report on Foreign Trade Barriers*, Vietnam's state-owned trading enterprises have been given the exclusive right to import certain products, including tobacco products; crude oil; newspapers, journals, and periodicals; and recorded media.[79] In addition, since U.S. and other foreign firms are restricted from majority ownership in some sectors, including telecommunications and banking, they must partner with a domestic firm—generally a state-owned enterprise—to conduct business in these sectors. However, Commerce and State have reported that few Vietnamese firms, including state-owned enterprises, are audited against international standards and, as a result, U.S. firms have difficulty verifying the financial information of prospective partners.[80]

- **Shortages of skilled labor.** Commerce and State reporting cited shortages of skilled labor as constraints to U.S. firms. In addition, a representative of one firm whom we interviewed in Vietnam noted that a lack of skilled labor in engineering limited the firm's ability to support the modernization of factory equipment.

U.S. and China Are Engaging Economically with Vietnam in Similar Ways, but Chinese Financing Has Exceeded U.S. Financing

The United States has no FTA with Vietnam but both are participants in the proposed regional TPP agreement, along with other countries. In contrast, China has free trade and investment agreements with Vietnam through its agreements with ASEAN countries and is negotiating the proposed RCEP agreement with Vietnam and other countries. Both countries support their domestic firms in Vietnam through financing and other means, but U.S. agencies estimate that China has provided a larger amount of financing than the United States. In addition, the United States and China have each supported economic development in Vietnam, with U.S. efforts focused on capacity building to improve Vietnam's economic governance and Chinese efforts focused on improving physical infrastructure and connectivity.

Unlike the United States, China Has Free Trade and Investment Agreements with Vietnam

While the United States does not have an FTA with Vietnam, the two countries have a bilateral trade agreement (BTA) to facilitate their trade relations. The United States–Vietnam BTA, which the United States signed in 2000, enabled the establishment of normal trade relations with Vietnam—significantly reducing tariffs for many Vietnamese exports—and incorporated elements modeled on WTO agreements.[81] As a result of the BTA, according to a 2014 study,[82] the average U.S. tariff for Vietnamese manufacturing exports, such as textiles, fell from 33.8 percent to 3.4 percent. According to the U.S.-Vietnam Trade Council, under the BTA, Vietnam agreed to reduce tariffs, typically by one-third to one-half, on a broad range of products of interest to U.S. businesses, including toiletries, film, mobile phones, tomatoes, and grapes. USTR officials stated that the BTA remains in effect and contains some provisions beyond those required by the WTO. Since Vietnam joined the WTO, the majority of U.S. exports of manufactured and agricultural goods have faced Vietnamese tariffs of 15 percent of less, according to a USTR Trade Fact Sheet. However, according to a report by Commerce and State, U.S. businesses have noted that eliminating high tariffs on certain agricultural and manufactured goods, including fresh food, fresh and frozen meats, and materials and machinery, would create significant new opportunities.[83]

In contrast, China has free trade and investment agreements with Vietnam through the ASEAN-China Comprehensive Economic Cooperation Agreement. The China-ASEAN Framework Agreement on Comprehensive Economic Cooperation comprises a series of agreements, on trade in goods, trade in services, and investment, to expand China's and ASEAN countries' access to each other's markets.[84]

- The China-ASEAN Trade in Goods Agreement, which entered into force in 2005, is intended to give China and Vietnam, as well as other ASEAN countries, tariff-free access to each other's markets for many goods and will reduce most duties for Vietnam's trade in goods with China to zero by 2018. According to a study by the ADB, the average tariff on ASEAN countries' exports to China was 0.1 percent in 2010, and 90 percent of Chinese exports are expected to face no tariffs in Vietnam by 2015.[85] In January 2015, Vietnam's Ministry of Finance stated that it had implemented the commitments it had made in the agreement to reduce tariffs.

- The China-ASEAN Trade in Services Agreement, which entered into force in 2007, is intended to provide market access in agreed-on sectors of China and Vietnam, as well as other ASEAN countries, to foreign companies and firms located in participant countries that is equivalent to domestic service providers' market access in their own countries.
- The China-ASEAN Investment Agreement, which entered into force in 2010, is intended to commit China and Vietnam, as well as other ASEAN countries, to treat each other's investors as equal to domestic investors.

Selected studies have projected that the China-ASEAN Trade in Goods Agreement generally increases trade for China and Vietnam.[86] All but two of these studies also estimated that the agreement improves the economies of both China and Vietnam.[87] In addition, one study estimated that the agreement increases investment in China and Vietnam.[88] In August 2014, China and Vietnam, as well as the other ASEAN countries, announced discussions to upgrade these agreements. The second round of discussions, held in February 2015, focused on investment, economic cooperation, and other areas. In August 2015, China's Commerce Minister announced that China and ASEAN had agreed to the goal of finalizing negotiations on the upgrade by the end of 2015.

United States and China Are Engaging Vietnam through Separate Regional Trade Agreement Negotiations

The United States and Vietnam are participants in the proposed TPP, while China and Vietnam are participants in the ongoing RCEP negotiations.

- **TPP.** The United States, Vietnam, and 10 other countries have negotiated the TPP, with an agreement announced in October 2015.[89] TPP negotiating parties agreed in 2011 that the TPP would address ensuring a competitive business environment and protecting the environment, labor rights, and intellectual property rights, among other issues. China is not a party to the TPP negotiations.[90]
- **RCEP.** China, Vietnam, and 14 other countries are parties to the RCEP negotiations, which negotiating partners have said they hope to complete in 2015.[91] Vietnam's trade with the other countries negotiating RCEP, including China, represented 58

> percent of its total trade in goods for 2013. RCEP negotiating parties seek to expand access to trade and investment among the parties by combining their existing FTAs into a single comprehensive agreement. The United States is not a party to the RCEP negotiations.

Vietnam has embraced TPP as part of its overall efforts to increase trade and access to foreign markets, particularly in the United States, according to State officials. State officials noted that Vietnam will need to overcome several challenges to meeting TPP requirements. In addition, according to State officials, TPP's labor and alternative dispute resolution requirements may be challenging for Vietnam to implement. However, State officials noted that Vietnam has shown a commitment to improving its economic governance.

According to U.S. officials, the dispute between Vietnam and China over China's placement of an oil rig near the disputed Paracel Islands in May through July 2014 briefly disrupted Chinese and Vietnamese trade. The officials noted that the incident also highlighted for Vietnamese officials the importance of their economic relationship with China and the need to diversify Vietnam's trade. According to State officials, China responded to Vietnamese riots and attacks on Chinese firms and individuals by slowing customs procedures and tightening controls at the typically porous China-Vietnam border.

According to U.S. officials, after the riots, Vietnam reviewed its economic relationship with China but found that it could not afford to reduce its reliance on China. For example, according to the U.S. officials, Vietnamese officials had not known exactly how intertwined Vietnam's economy was with China's because of the amount of undocumented cross-border trade. According to testimony before the U.S.-China Economic and Security Review Commission in May 2015, Vietnam relies on China for a number of intermediate goods as inputs for its exports; therefore, any disruptions to trade flows could spread throughout the Vietnamese economy.[92]

U.S. Agencies Have Provided Less Financing in Vietnam Than Chinese Agencies

Our analysis of U.S. agency data showed that in fiscal years 2009 through 2014, Ex-Im and OPIC provided approximately $205 million in financing for exports to, and investment in, Vietnam (see table 4). Although China does not publish data on its financing in Vietnam, our analysis of State-reported data found that China has financed at least $4.5 billion in investment projects in Vietnam since 2008.

Table 4. Ex-Im Authorizations and OPIC Commitments in Vietnam, Fiscal Years 2009-2014

Nominal U.S. dollars in millions			
Fiscal year	Ex-Im authorizations[a]	OPIC commitments	Total
2009	$1.9	$5.6	$7.5
2010	0.7	0	$0.7
2011	1.1	0	$1.1
2012	127.8	0	$127.8
2013	17.1	0	$17.1
2014	0.5	50.0	$50.5
Total[b]	$148.9	$55.6	$204.5

Legend: Ex-Im = Export-Import Bank of the United States; OPIC = Overseas Private Investment Corporation.

Source: GAO analysis of Ex-Im annual reports and data and OPIC data. | GAO-16-186.

[a]Ex-Im generally provides financing to businesses when private financing is unavailable; therefore, fluctuations in its financing activity may reflect changes in the business and banking environment rather than Ex-Im's initiative. Ex-Im authorizations shown do not sum to the total because of rounding.

[b]These data do not include Ex-Im multibuyer insurance, which may include multiple countries, or OPIC funds recorded as provided to the Asia and the Pacific Region, some of which may be used in Vietnam.

Our analysis of Ex-Im and OPIC information for fiscal years 2009 through 2014 found the following.

- Ex-Im authorized about $148.9 million in loans, loan guarantees, and insurance to support U.S. exports in Vietnam.[93] In fiscal year 2012, Ex-Im's largest authorization in Vietnam consisted of a $118 million direct loan to the government of Vietnam to purchase a telecommunications satellite. In fiscal year 2013, Ex-Im authorized $16.7 million for a long-term loan to Vietnam's National Power Transmission Corporation to purchase electricity transmission equipment.
- OPIC committed about $55.6 million in financing to U.S. investment projects in Vietnam.[94] In 2014, OPIC committed to provide an investment guarantee of up to $50 million for the Mekong Renewable

Resources Fund, which will invest in the environmental services and infrastructure sector, the renewable energy sector, and the energy efficiency sector in Vietnam, Cambodia, and Laos.

China does not publish data on its financing for exports, imports, and investment in Vietnam by private and state-owned enterprises. However, according to information provided by the U.S. Embassy in Hanoi, China made available approximately $4.5 billion in financing from 2008 to 2013 for coal-fired power plants and for part of the Hanoi rail transit system, all constructed by Chinese firms. China's Export-Import Bank has also published brief summaries of major projects for some countries, such as Vietnam. One such summary indicates that the bank provided a concessional loan in 2013 to support the construction of a chemical plant in Vietnam to manufacture fertilizer.

In addition, China provides financing and labor in support of projects in Vietnam. According to State officials, Vietnam's importation of Chinese labor for technical positions enhances China's role in the Vietnam economy because the Vietnamese labor market lacks the capacity to fill midlevel technical positions. However, according to testimony before the U.S.-China Security Review Commission in May 2015, local Vietnamese have sometimes resented the importation of Chinese labor.[95] According to State officials, such resentment contributed to the riots and violence in Vietnam after China placed the oil rig in the disputed Paracel waters.

United States and China Provide a Variety of Services to U.S. and Chinese Firms in Vietnam

State, Commerce, and USDA maintain staff in Vietnam to provide export promotion services and policy advocacy for U.S. firms operating in Vietnam.[96] For example:

- **State.** State's Economic Section at the U.S. Embassy in Hanoi advocates for U.S. investors and for trade and investment policies favored by the United States, according to a senior State official. The official said that the section also supports the negotiation of U.S. trade agreements, such as TPP, and other types of economic agreements, including a United States–Vietnam agreement related to taxation.
- **Commerce.** According to Commerce officials in Vietnam, Commerce personnel based in the country assist U.S. firms by, among other things, matching them with local partners, organizing trade missions,

and providing advocacy.[97] For example, the Commerce officials said that they organized a trade mission and provided advocacy for U.S. civil nuclear firms. Another Commerce official told us that Commerce officials had worked with the Vietnamese government to remove an illegal duty on goods that a U.S. company was importing into Vietnam.

- **USDA.** USDA personnel help address market access and development issues in Vietnam for U.S. agricultural products, according to a USDA official in Vietnam. For example, according to the official, USDA personnel track Vietnamese government regulations that would affect U.S. agricultural products and provide comments to the Vietnamese government as needed. The official noted that USDA personnel also work directly with the Vietnamese government to help U.S. firms retrieve stranded cargo, particularly perishable goods, from Vietnamese customs. For instance, one firm's product was delayed in customs because it lacked a plant quarantine certificate that is not required in the United States.

The Chinese government has also acted to support Chinese firms that do business in Vietnam. For example, according China's Ministry of Foreign Affairs, China and Vietnam have established two economic cooperation zones in Vietnam, near Ho Chi Minh City and in Haiphong City, to facilitate trade and investment by offering tax and other advantages for Chinese firms that invest in the zone.

United States and China Are Fostering Different Aspects of Vietnam's Economic Development

U.S. agencies have assisted Vietnam in increasing economic openness and integration and improving economic governance. In fiscal years 2009 through 2013, the U.S. agencies provided a total of $32 million in trade capacity building assistance—that is, development assistance intended to improve a country's ability to benefit from international trade—to Vietnam.[98] U.S. trade capacity building assistance to Vietnam has supported initiatives aimed at, among other things, modernizing Vietnam's commercial laws and legal system, providing assistance to Vietnam relevant to its trade agreement commitments, improving the country's customs and border control, and supporting potential U.S. investment opportunities. The majority of U.S. trade capacity building assistance to Vietnam during this period—about 64 percent—was provided by the U.S. Agency for International Development

(USAID) to, for example, improve Vietnam's regulatory environment to support economic growth and a better business and trade environment. For more information about U.S. trade capacity building assistance to Vietnam, see appendix IV.

China has assisted Vietnam's economic development through infrastructure construction as well as efforts to develop connectivity between China and Southeast Asian countries. According to the U.S. Embassy in Hanoi, China provided about $4.5 billion of approximately $10.8 billion in large infrastructure construction projects awarded to Chinese firms in Vietnam from 2008 to 2014. These infrastructure projects included power plants, processing plants, and a railway (see fig. 10). The report noted that the remaining funding for infrastructure construction was provided by Australia, ADB, and the World Bank and through joint ventures. In addition, according to the U.S. Embassy in Hanoi, as of 2014, Chinese firms had won contracts to build 15 of 24 new thermal power plants in Vietnam. In late 2013, China and Vietnam agreed to the implementation of the Shenzhen-Haiphong trade corridor to link the Vietnamese port city of Haiphong to Shenzhen in China. According to testimony before the U.S.-China Security Review Commission in May 2015, China has also announced that it will help upgrade the Haiphong port to accommodate large container ships.

Source: GAO. | GAO-16-186.

Figure 10. Chinese-Financed Infrastructure for the Hanoi Rail Transit System.

In addition, through the ADB-supported Greater Mekong Subregion (GMS) Economic Cooperation program, Vietnam and China are participating in a plan to connect Vietnam and other mainland Southeast Asian countries with each other and with China through a series of economic corridors that include improving transportation infrastructure. ADB's GMS Strategic Framework identifies corridors, including an eastern corridor running north-to-south and connecting China and Vietnam; an east-west corridor connecting Burma, Thailand, Laos, and central Vietnam; and a southern corridor connecting Burma, Thailand, Cambodia, and southern Vietnam.[99] For example, according to Chinese government reporting, the $952 million Hanoi to Lao Cai freeway, which a Chinese contractor is building, is part of the GMS strategic framework.

Similarly, the Master Plan on ASEAN Connectivity envisions a rail link through Vietnam connecting the interior of China with Singapore and connecting the capital cities in Vietnam, Cambodia, and Thailand with a spur line to the capital of Laos. This rail link would complement the various transport corridors under the GMS and other existing transport networks, with the aim of creating an integrated transport network throughout Southeast Asia and Asia as a whole. The railway running from China to Ho Chi Minh City in the south of Vietnam is already complete. The Master Plan on ASEAN Connectivity also calls for a network of highways meeting certain quality standards and connecting Vietnam with all of its neighbors, including China. Vietnam has constructed its portions of the highway network.

Vietnam is one of 57 prospective founding members of China's proposed Asian Infrastructure Investment Bank, an international institution to finance infrastructure projects throughout the Asia-Pacific region.[100] Under the bank's initial agreement, the bank's authorized capital is $100 billion, of which China has pledged $29.8 billion and Vietnam has pledged $663 million.[101] Bank documents indicate that the bank anticipates beginning operations before the end of 2015.

Agency Comments

We provided a draft of this report for review and comment to the Departments of Agriculture, Commerce, State, and the Treasury and to MCC, OPIC, USAID, Ex-Im, the U.S. Trade and Development Agency, and USTR. We received technical comments from Commerce, State, Treasury, MCC, OPIC, Ex-Im, USTR, which we incorporated as appropriate.

David B. Gootnick
Director
International Affairs and Trade

APPENDIX I: OBJECTIVES, SCOPE, AND METHODOLOGY

We examined available information about U.S. and Chinese trade and investment, competition, and actions to further economic engagement in Indonesia and Vietnam. This report is a public version of a sensitive but unclassified report that we are issuing concurrently. This report addresses the same objectives, and employs the same methodology, as the sensitive report.

We conducted fieldwork in Jakarta, Indonesia, and in Hanoi and Ho Chi Minh City, Vietnam. We based our selection of these two countries, among the 10 members of the Association of Southeast Asian Nations (ASEAN),[1] on the amounts of U.S. and Chinese exports to, and imports from, each country; foreign direct investment (FDI) in each country; and development assistance in each country. We also considered whether (1) a country participated in U.S. and Chinese trade agreements or was a negotiating partner in the Trans-Pacific Partnership, (2) any regional institutions were located in the country, (3) the country was an emerging partner based on gross domestic product, and (4) the country was a South China Sea claimant.[2]

U.S. and Chinese Trade and Investment in Indonesia and Vietnam

To describe U.S. and Chinese trade and investment in Indonesia and Vietnam, we analyzed data on U.S. and Chinese trade in goods, trade in services, and FDI. To assess the reliability of these data, we crosschecked the data on trade in goods and FDI for internal consistency, and consulted with U.S. officials on the data on trade in goods and the U.S. data on trade in services and FDI. Because of the limited availability of data and the differing contexts for the data sets we report, the time period for each of these data sets varied. We determined that the data were sufficiently reliable for the purposes of our report and have noted caveats, where appropriate, to indicate limitations in the data.

To obtain data on U.S. and Chinese trade in goods from 1994 through 2014, we accessed the United Nations' Commodity Trade Statistics (UN

Comtrade) database through the U.S. Department of Commerce's (Commerce) Trade Policy Information System. The UN Comtrade database provides data for comparable categories of exports and imports of goods for the United States and China. Because, according to a Commerce official, the goods exports data that China reports to the UN Comtrade database do not distinguish total exports from re-exports (i.e., goods that are first imported and then exported in substantially the same condition), we used data on total goods exports, which include re-exports, to ensure the comparability of U.S. and Chinese data on goods exports. The data on goods exports from the UN Comtrade database show the free-on-board prices of the goods, which exclude transportation and insurance charges. For imports, we used data on general imports, which include goods that clear customs as well as goods that enter bonded warehouses or foreign trade zones. The data on goods imports show the prices paid for the goods, including the cost of freight and insurance. We determined that the UN Comtrade data on trade in goods for the United States and China were generally reliable for comparing trends over time and the composition of trade.

To categorize the goods traded by the United States and China, we assigned each good recorded in the UN Comtrade database to one of the UN's three Broad Economic Categories—capital, intermediate, or consumer. For goods that the UN does not classify as capital, intermediate, or consumer, we created an unclassified category. For example, the UN does not classify passenger motorcars as capital or consumer goods.

To examine each country's trade in goods with its trading partners over time, we analyzed data from the ASEANstats database for 2003, 2008, and 2013 for Indonesia and 2004, 2008, and 2013 for Vietnam.[3] Because some of Indonesia's and Vietnam's trading partners do not report data to the UN Comtrade database, we used data from the ASEANstats database as a comprehensive set of data on trade in goods for all of Indonesia's and Vietnam's trading partners. We compared trade data from the ASEANstats and the UN Comtrade databases and found some differences in values of bilateral trade between Indonesia and Vietnam and their trading partners. Reasons for the differences include differences in the valuation of goods, differences in data quality, and the omission of some Indonesia and Vietnam trading partners from UN Comtrade data.

We determined that the data from the ASEANstats database for Indonesia and Vietnam were generally reliable for comparing each country's trade in goods with its trading partners over time. We determined that the data from the

ASEANstats database for Indonesia and Vietnam were generally reliable for comparing each country's trade in goods with its trading partners over time.

To illustrate the importance of accounting of a country's exports that originate in other countries, we analyzed data from the Organisation for Economic Co-operation and Development (OECD) and the World Trade Organization (WTO) on trade in value-added goods and services.

For U.S. trade in services with Indonesia, we used publicly available data from Commerce's Bureau of Economic Analysis (BEA). BEA's data on trade in services with Vietnam for several categories—travel and passenger fares, transportation, education, and "other" private services— are based on data from various sources. According to BEA, its survey data are from mandatory surveys of primarily U.S. businesses with services trade that exceeds certain thresholds. BEA does not survey a random sample of U.S. businesses and therefore does not report the data with margins of error. We calculated the value of U.S. trade in services with Vietnam for 2012 based on tabulations prepared for us by BEA and other sources, including the U.S. Census Bureau. Our estimates of U.S. trade in services with Vietnam represent broad estimates rather than precise values. We extrapolated values for certain services at the country level from broader data (e.g., we calculated values for travel services by multiplying the number of travelers for Vietnam by the average traveler expenditure for the region). We calculated values for other services (e.g., business, professional, and technical services) from a range of estimates based on survey data. When the volume of trade for a service was presented as a range, we used the midpoint value to estimate the volume of trade for that service. When the volume of trade for a service was presented as a range and described by BEA as trending upward, we used the lowest value for the earlier years and the highest value for the later years.

For data on U.S. firms' investments in Indonesia and Vietnam from 2007 through 2012, we used data that we obtained directly from BEA. For Chinese firms' investments, we used data from the UN Conference on Trade and Development as reported by China's Ministry of Commerce. To identify patterns in, and to compare, U.S. and Chinese FDI, we used U.S. and Chinese data on FDI and noted in our report the following limitations.

- As we have previously reported, both U.S. and Chinese FDI may be underreported, and experts have expressed particular concern regarding China's data.[4] U.S. and Chinese firms set up subsidiaries in places such as the Netherlands and the British Virgin Islands, which can be used to make investments that are not captured by U.S. and

Chinese data on FDI. Experts state that this could be a significant source of underreporting of China's FDI. According to BEA, data on U.S. FDI are based on quarterly, annual, and benchmark surveys. BEA's benchmark survey is the most comprehensive survey of such investment and covers the universe of U.S. FDI. BEA notes that its quarterly and annual surveys cover samples of businesses with FDI that exceed certain thresholds. Because BEA does not survey a random sample of businesses, and therefore does not report the data with margins of error, our report does not include margins of error for BEA data.

- China does not provide a definition of FDI when reporting FDI data. However, the types of data included in Chinese FDI data (e.g., equity investment data and reinvested earnings data) appear similar to data reported for U.S. FDI, for which the United States uses OECD's definition.

Despite the limitations of China's FDI data, various reports, including those published by international organizations such as the International Monetary Fund (IMF), government agencies, academic experts, and other research institutions, use China's reported investment data to describe China's FDI activities. In addition, despite some potential underreporting of FDI data, we determined that the FDI data were reliable for reporting general patterns when limitations are noted.

Because of challenges in determining appropriate deflators for some data, we used nominal rather than inflation-adjusted values for U.S. and Chinese trade and investments in Indonesia and Vietnam. However, we first tested the impact of deflating these values and found a limited impact for descriptions of the overall trends. For example, using the U.S. gross domestic product deflator to remove inflation in the goods trade values included in this report would cause total Chinese trade in goods with Indonesia to surpass total U.S. trade in goods in 2005, similar to trends shown for nominal trade values. U.S. total trade in goods in Indonesia increased by a factor of 2.8 from 1994 through 2014 if not adjusted for inflation and by a factor of 1.9 if adjusted for inflation. Over the same period, Chinese total trade in goods increased by a factor of 24.1 in Indonesia if not adjusted for inflation and by a factor of 16.3 if adjusted for inflation.

U.S. and Chinese Competition in Indonesia and Vietnam

To assess the extent of competition between exporters from the United States, China, and other countries, we calculated an export similarity index to compare U.S., Chinese, and other countries' exports to Indonesia and Vietnam in 2006 through 2014.[5] The export similarity index is a measure of the similarity of exports from two countries to a third country. For example, to calculate the index for U.S. and Chinese exports to Indonesia and Vietnam, we first calculated, for each type of good that the United States and China exports, the share of that good in the United States' and China's total exports to Indonesia and Vietnam. We then took the minimum of the United States' and China's shares. The index is the sum of the minimum shares for all types of goods that the United States and China export to Indonesia and Vietnam. We used data on goods exports from the UN Commodity Trade database at the four-digit level and calculated each country's export of a particular good as a share of that country's total exports to Indonesia and Vietnam.

We also analyzed data from Commerce's Advocacy Center on host-government contracts and data for contracts funded by the Asian Development Bank (ADB) and World Bank. Although these data represent a small share of activity in Indonesia and Vietnam, they provide insights into the degree of competition between U.S. and Chinese firms for the projects represented.

- Commerce's Advocacy Center data comprised cases where U.S. firms requested the agency's assistance in bidding for host-government contracts in either Indonesia or Vietnam from 2009 through 2014. Because these data included the nationality of other firms bidding on a host-government contract, we used this information to determine the extent to which Chinese firms or firms of other nations were competing with U.S. firms for these contracts. We counted the numbers of contracts and summed the value of contracts for which each foreign country's firms competed against U.S. firms. For Vietnam, we excluded five contracts for which the nationalities of competitors were not identified. In cases where foreign competitors comprised a consortium of firms from different countries, we counted the whole value of the contract in each competing nationality's total. We also used the Advocacy Center's classification of contracts by sector to determine the sectors in which Chinese firms competed for the highest proportion of contracts. To determine the reliability of these data, we manually checked the data for missing values and also reviewed information about the data's collection. In addition, we interviewed Advocacy Center staff about the data. Advocacy Center staff told us that data from before 2010, when the center began using a new database, may be incomplete because data for some contracts that were closed before 2010 may not have been transferred to the new database. Overall, we found the Advocacy Center data to be reliable for reporting on competition between U.S. and other firms, including Chinese firms, in Indonesia and Vietnam.

- The World Bank publishes data on the value, sector, and suppliers of its contracts in Indonesia and Vietnam. We used the World Bank's classification of contracts into procurement categories (goods, civil works, consultant services, and nonconsultant services) to compare the value and types of contracts that U.S. and Chinese firms won from 2001 through 2014. However, we combined the consultant services and nonconsultant services categories into one category, "consultant and other services." The World Bank data include contracts that were reviewed by World Bank staff before they were awarded. To determine the reliability of these data, we electronically checked the data for missing values and possible errors. We also contacted World Bank personnel to learn how the data were collected and identify any limitations of the data. We found that the data for contracts funded by the World Bank were generally reliable for the purpose of demonstrating U.S. and Chinese competition in Indonesia and Vietnam over time.
- We used ADB's published data on the value, sector, and recipient of its contracts for consulting services, goods, and civil works provided as technical assistance or funded by loans and grants to Indonesia and Vietnam in 2013 and 2014 to compare the value and types of contracts won by U.S. and Chinese firms. ADB only publishes data for consulting contracts over $0.1 million in value and other contracts over $1.0 million, so our analysis of ADB contracts does not include some smaller ADB contracts. In addition, a portion of the ADB data did not have the contracts classified according to the nature of the contract (construction, consulting services, goods, turnkey, and others). Therefore, we classified contracts won by U.S. and Chinese firms that were missing these categories according to those used in the rest of the data. To determine the reliability of these data, we checked the data for missing values and other types of discrepancies. We found that the ADB data were generally reliable for our purpose of

reporting on U.S. and Chinese competition in Indonesia and Vietnam in 2013 and 2014.

To identify the challenges that U.S. firms face when conducting business in Indonesia and Vietnam, we reviewed the Office of the United States Trade Representative's (USTR) 2014 and 2015 *National Trade Estimate Reports on Foreign Trade Barriers* and its *2015 Special 301 Report* on intellectual property rights protections. We reviewed the U.S. Department of Agriculture's (USDA) country strategies for Indonesia and Vietnam, Department of State (State) cables, and Commerce and State's 2014 reports on doing business in Indonesia and Vietnam. We also interviewed representatives of 12 U.S. firms in Indonesia and Vietnam, in sectors such as agriculture and manufacturing, as well as representatives of five private sector and research organizations, such as the American Chamber of Commerce-Vietnam and the Center for Strategic and International Studies. The views expressed in these interviews are not generalizable.

U.S. and Chinese Actions to Further Economic Engagement in Indonesia and Vietnam

To examine the actions that the U.S. and Chinese governments have taken to further economic engagement in Indonesia and Vietnam, we reviewed regional and country studies and U.S. and Chinese agency documents and interviewed U.S. and third-country officials, officials from private sector business associations, and experts from research institutes. We tried to arrange visits with Chinese government officials in Indonesia and Vietnam and in Washington, D.C.; however, they were unable to accommodate our requests for a meeting. U.S. agencies included in the scope of our study were USDA, Commerce, State, the Department of the Treasury, USTR, the Millennium Challenge Corporation, the U.S. Agency for International Development (USAID), the Export-Import Bank of the United States (Ex-Im), the Overseas Private Investment Corporation (OPIC), and the U.S. Trade and Development Agency.

- To obtain information about U.S. and Chinese trade agreements with Indonesia and Vietnam, we reviewed the trade agreements; U.S. and Chinese government documents; studies from research institutions;

prior GAO reports; and documents from multilateral organizations, such as WTO. We identified studies assessing the effect of the China-ASEAN free trade agreement on China's, Indonesia's, and Vietnam's economies by searching the ProQuest database (which includes the EconLit database) and the studies of international organizations such as ADB, and we selected and reviewed studies that estimated the impact of the agreement on these three economies.[6] We also interviewed U.S. officials in Indonesia and Vietnam, officials from private sector business associations, and experts from research institutes.

- To calculate the percentage of Indonesia's and Vietnam's total goods trade represented by their trade with the participants in the Regional Comprehensive Economic Partnership Agreement, we used data on trade in goods from the ASEANstats database. To determine the reliability of these data, we compared trade data from the ASEANstats and the UN Comtrade databases and found some differences in values of bilateral trade between ASEAN countries and their trading partners. Reasons for the differences include differences in the valuation of goods, differences in data quality, and the omission of some ASEAN trading partners from UN Comtrade data. We determined that the data from the ASEANstats database for Indonesia and Vietnam were generally reliable for comparing each country's trade in goods with its trading partners.
- To obtain information about U.S. financing in Indonesia and Vietnam, we compiled Ex-Im and OPIC data from these agencies' annual reports and congressional budget justifications and interviewed agency officials to provide additional context and to clarify elements of the data. Where relevant, we note that additional Ex-Im insurance may include Indonesia and Vietnam but do not include these data in our totals. To determine the reliability of these data, we interviewed agency officials and checked their published annual reports against agency-provided summary data to determine any limitations or discrepancies in the data. We determined that data from Ex-Im and OPIC were generally reliable for presenting trends and aggregate amounts by year.
- To document U.S. efforts to provide export promotion services in Indonesia and Vietnam, we reviewed information on State's Economic Sections at the U.S. Embassy in Indonesia and Vietnam

and interviewed State, Commerce, and USDA officials in Washington, D.C., and in Vietnam and Indonesia.

- To describe Chinese financing in Indonesia and Vietnam, we used information reported by State and China's Export-Import Bank. We also interviewed private sector and research institute representatives. To document Chinese support for firms in Indonesia and Vietnam, we used publicly available information from a variety of sources, including Chinese embassy websites; the Bank of Indonesia's website; China's Ministry of Commerce; and Xinhua, China's state press agency.
- To document U.S. support for economic development and integration in Indonesia and Vietnam, we used the USAID trade capacity building database to capture U.S. development assistance efforts related to trade in Indonesia and Vietnam. USAID collects data to identify and quantify the U.S. government's trade capacity building activities in developing countries through an annual survey of agencies on behalf of USTR. We also reviewed agency project summaries and interviewed agency officials in Washington, D.C., and in Indonesia and Vietnam. To determine the reliability of these data, we interviewed agency officials regarding their methods for compiling and reviewing the data. We determined that data from USAID's trade capacity building database were sufficiently reliable for our purposes.
- To describe China's support for regional integration in Indonesia, we assessed public statements from Chinese and Indonesian officials and information reported by U.S. agencies, including State, and we interviewed U.S. and Indonesian officials. To describe China's support for regional integration in Vietnam, we assessed information reported by U.S. agencies, including State and USAID, and interviewed U.S. and Vietnamese officials. We also reviewed publicly available information on the Asian Infrastructure Investment Bank's website.

We conducted this performance audit from April 2014 to October 2015 in accordance with generally accepted government auditing standards. Those standards require that we plan and perform the audit to obtain sufficient, appropriate evidence to provide a reasonable basis for our findings and conclusions based on our audit objectives. We believe that the evidence obtained provides a reasonable basis for our findings and conclusions based on our audit objectives.

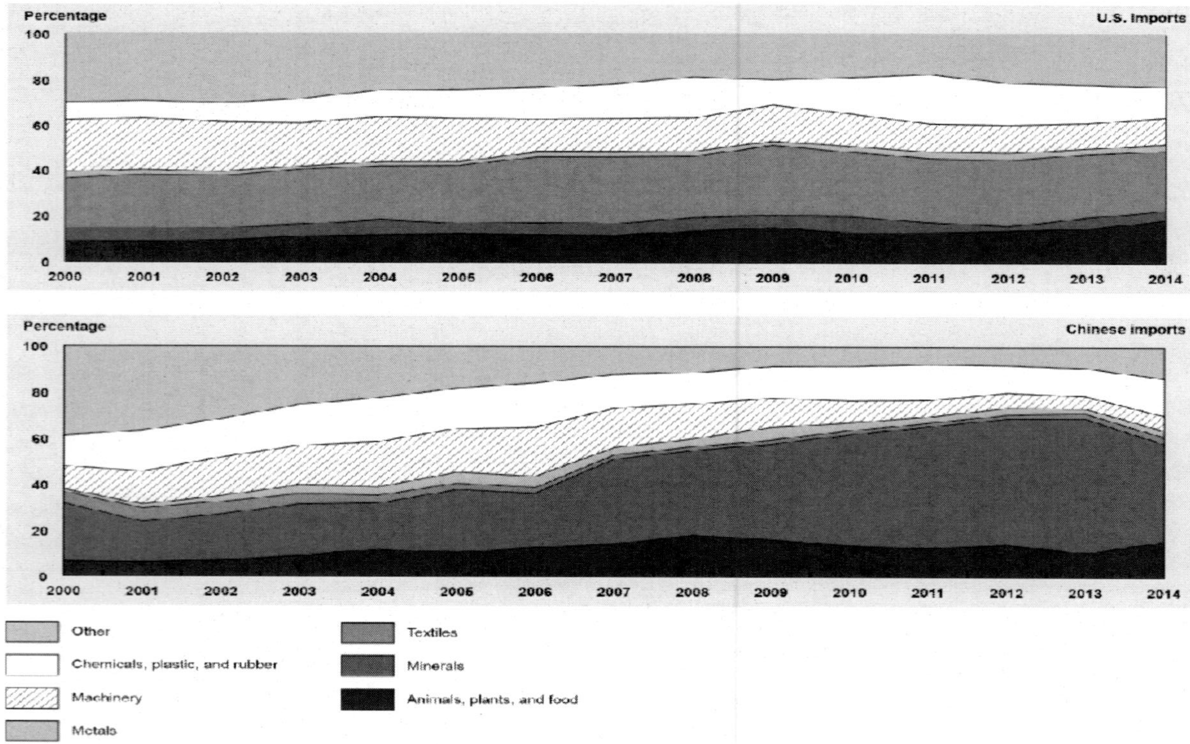

Source: GAO analysis of U.S. and Chinese data from the United Nations Commodity Trade database. | GAO-16-186.

Figure 11. U.S. and Chinese Imports of Goods from Indonesia in 2000-2014, by Type.

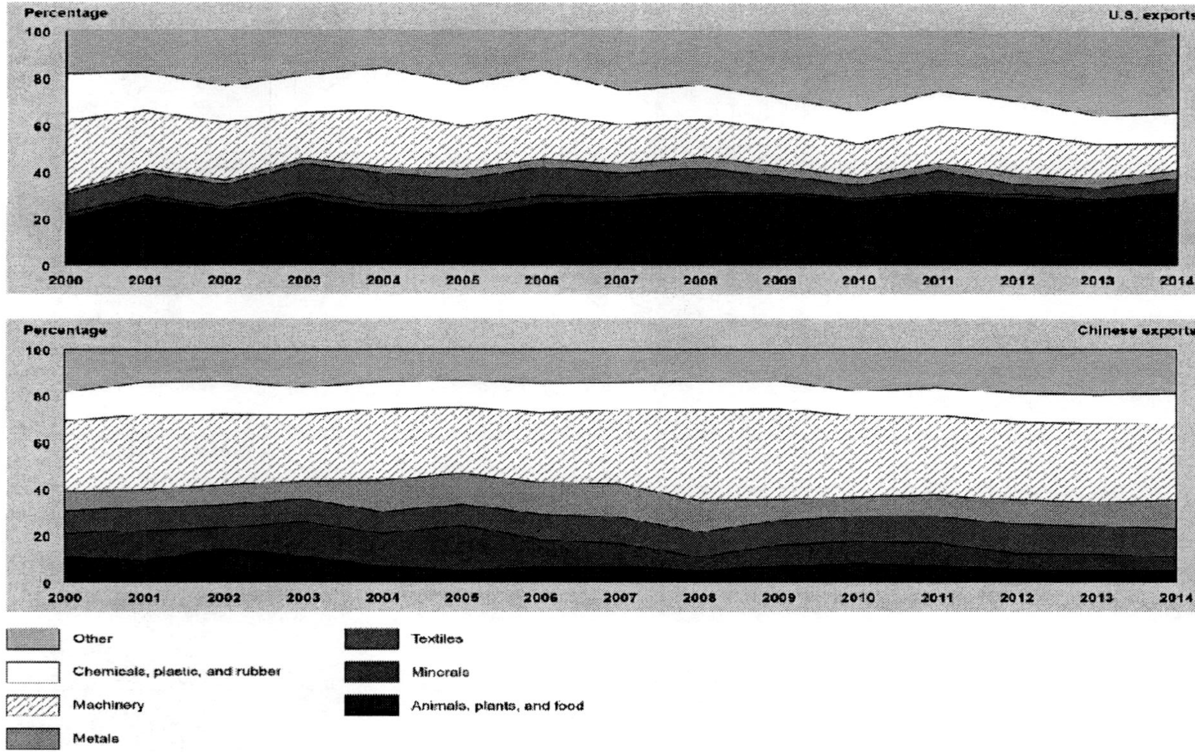

Source: GAO analysis of U.S. and Chinese data from the United Nations Commodity Trade database. | GAO-16-186.

Figure 12. U.S. and Chinese Exports of Goods to Indonesia in 2000-2014, by Type.

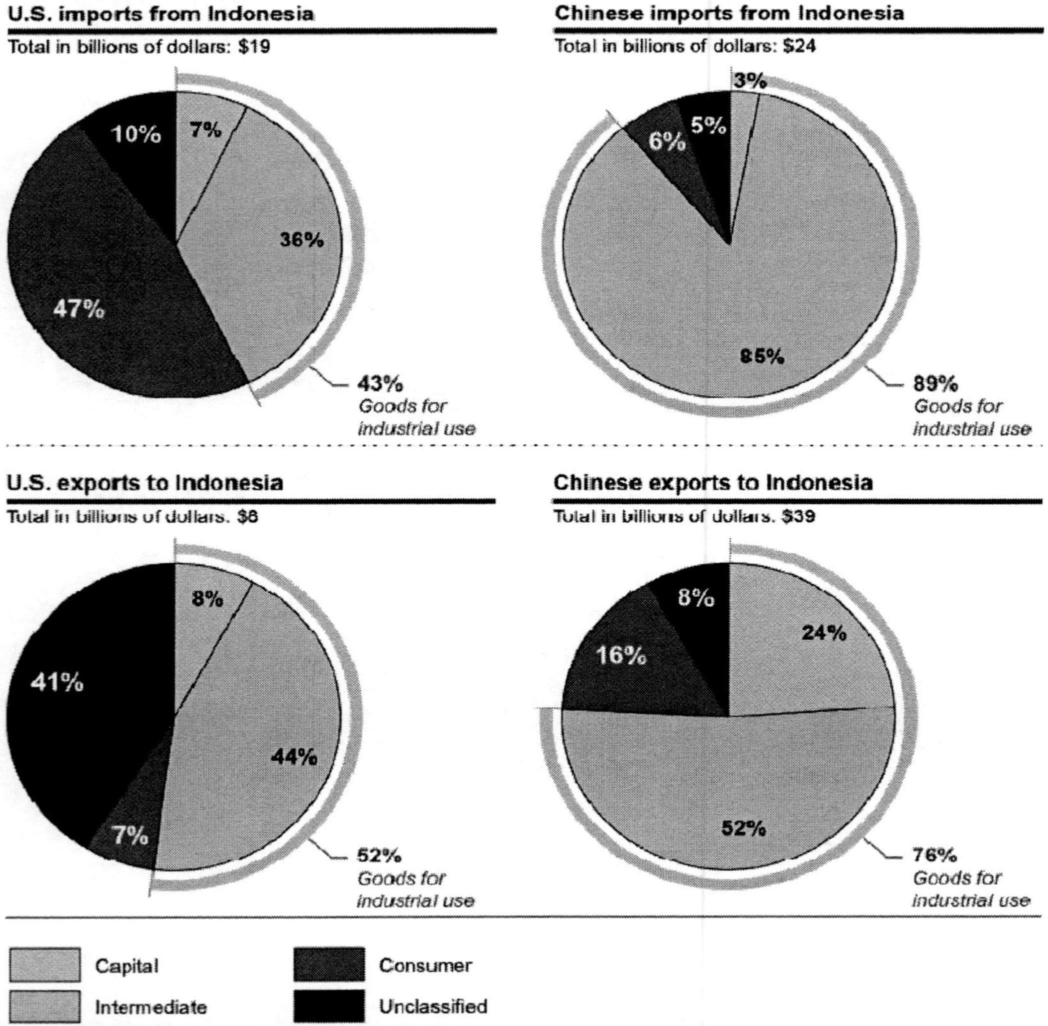
U.S. imports from Indonesia
Total in billions of dollars: $19
10%
7%
36%
47%
43%
Goods for industrial use
Chinese imports from Indonesia
Total in billions of dollars: $24
3%
5%
6%
85%
89%
Goods for industrial use
U.S. exports to Indonesia
Total in billions of dollars: $8
8%
41%
44%
7%
52%
Goods for industrial use
Chinese exports to Indonesia
Total in billions of dollars: $39
8%
24%
16%
52%
76%
Goods for industrial use
Capital
Intermediate
Consumer
Unclassified

Source: GAO analysis of U.S. and Chinese data from the United Nations Commodity Trade database. | GAO-16-186.

Notes: We used the United Nations Statistics Division's Broad Economic Categories to classify U.S. and Chinese total trade in goods into these categories. We defined goods for industrial use as including both capital and intermediate goods. According to the Organisation for Economic Cooperation and Development, an intermediate good is an input to the production process that has itself been produced and, unlike capital, is used up in production. Unclassified goods are those that are not classified as capital, intermediate, or consumer goods.

In 2014, the top overall U.S. export to Indonesia was civilian aircraft, aircraft engines, and aircraft parts, which represents 23 percent of U.S. exports to Indonesia and includes capital, intermediate, and consumer goods. The U.S. Census Bureau suppresses data that further disaggregate this export.

Percentages shown may not sum to 100 percent for each chart because of rounding.

Figure 13. U.S. and Chinese Imports and Exports of Goods to Indonesia in 2014, by Use.

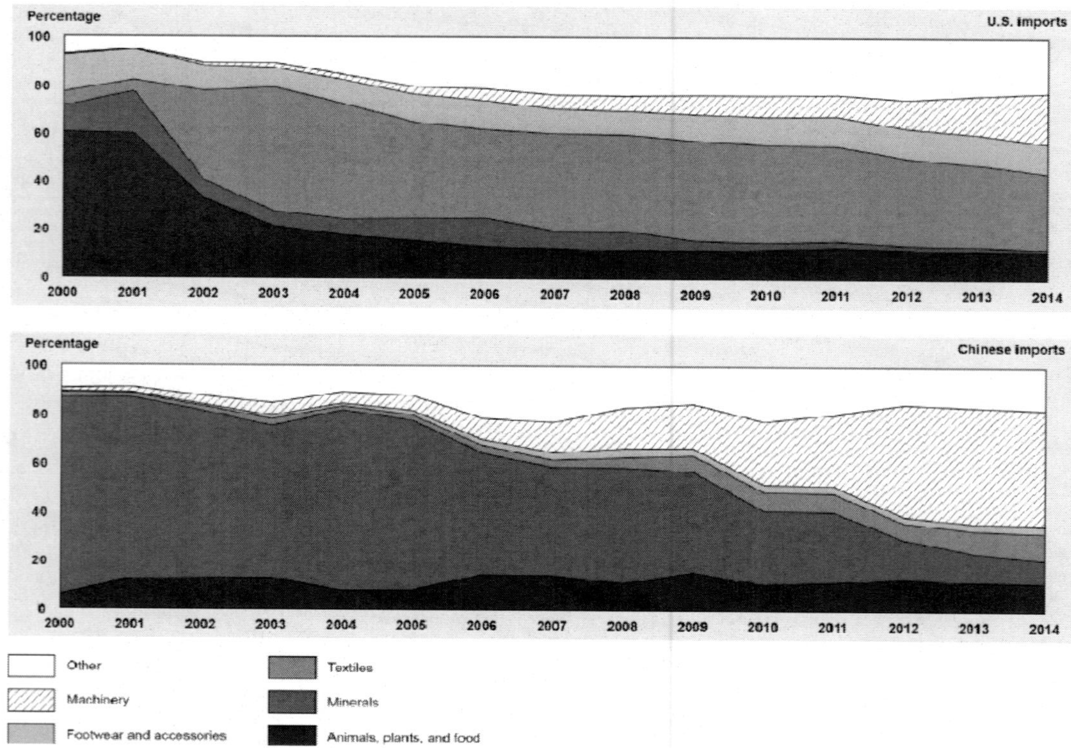

Source: GAO analysis of U.S. and Chinese data from the United Nations Commodity Trade database. | GAO-16-186.

Figure 14. U.S. and Chinese Imports of Goods from Vietnam in 2000-2014, by Type.

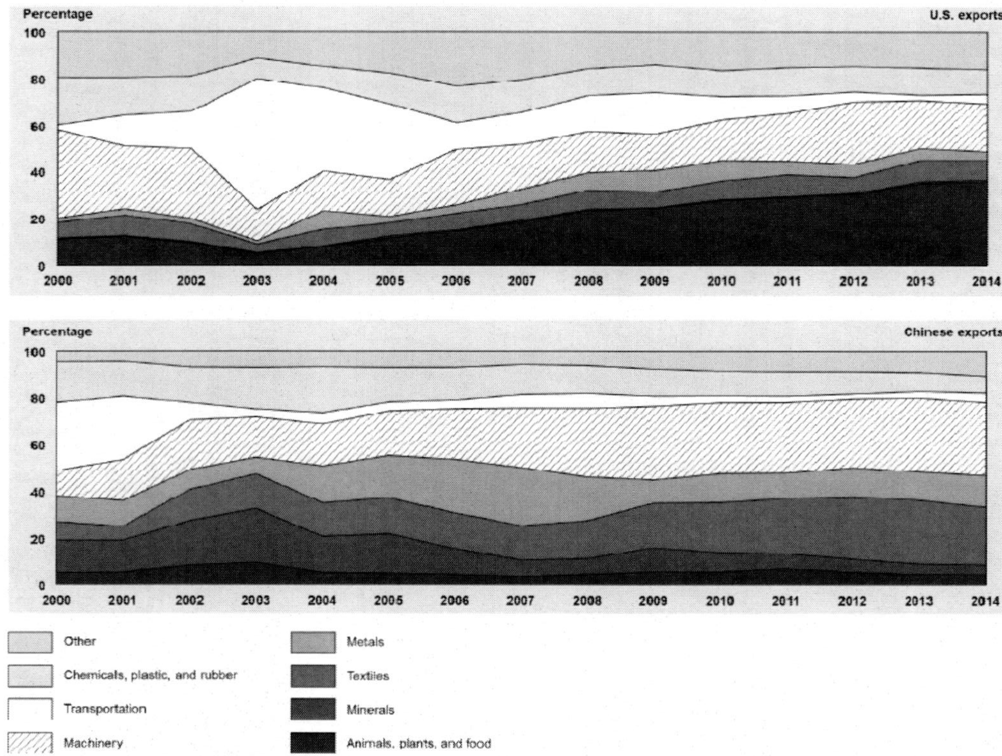

Source: GAO analysis of U.S. and Chinese data from the United Nations Commodity Trade database. | GAO-16-186.

Figure 15. U.S. and Chinese Exports of Goods to Vietnam in 2000-2014, by Type.

Appendix II: Composition and Use of U.S. and Chinese Trade in Goods with Indonesia

From 2000 through 2014, the composition of U.S. and Chinese trade in goods with Indonesia, in terms of value, remained relatively stable except for a significant increase in China's mineral imports (see figs. 11 and 12). Textiles represented the largest share of U.S. imports from Indonesia since 2005. China's mineral imports increased from 25 percent of its total imports from Indonesia in 2000 to a peak of 58 percent in 2013 before declining to 42 percent in 2014. Animals, plants, and food generally represented the largest share of U.S. exports to Indonesia from 2005 through 2014, and machinery represented the largest share of Chinese exports to Indonesia from 2000 through 2014.

In 2014, almost half of the United States' and most of China's goods trade with Indonesia consisted of goods for industrial use, most of which are intermediate goods (see fig. 13).[1] Among the industrial goods that the United States traded with Indonesia, rubber was the top U.S. industrial import and cotton was the top U.S. industrial export in 2014. Among the industrial goods that China traded with Indonesia in 2014, coal was the top Chinese industrial import and phones for cellular and other networks were the top Chinese industrial export. In 2014, the United States exported $1.9 billion of civilian aircraft, aircraft engines, and aircraft parts—the overall top U.S. export to Indonesia, which represents 23 percent of U.S. exports to Indonesia and includes capital, intermediate, and consumer goods.[2]

Appendix III: Composition and Use of U.S. and Chinese Trade in Goods with Vietnam

From 2000 through 2014, the composition of U.S. and Chinese trade in goods with Vietnam generally shifted, in terms of value, from predominantly raw commodities to manufactured goods (see figs. 14 and 15). In 2000, the largest share of U.S. imports from Vietnam consisted of animals, plants, and food, while the largest share of Chinese imports from Vietnam consisted of minerals. However, by 2014, the largest share of U.S. imports from Vietnam consisted of textiles, which rose from 6 percent of U.S. imports in 2000 to 31 percent in 2014, while the largest share of Chinese imports consisted of machinery, which rose from 1 percent in 2000 to 47 percent in 2014. From 2000 through 2014, animals, plants, and food grew to represent the largest share of U.S. exports to Vietnam, while machinery grew to represent the largest share of Chinese exports to Vietnam.[1]

In 2014, the majority of U.S. imports from Vietnam consisted of goods for consumer use, while the majority of U.S. exports to Vietnam—as well as Chinese imports from, and exports to, Vietnam—consisted of goods for industrial use (see fig. 16). Among the consumer goods that the United States and China traded with Vietnam, wooden bedroom furniture was the top U.S. import and nuts were the top U.S. export, while cameras were the top Chinese import and women's and girl's cotton jackets and blazers were the top Chinese export. Among the industrial goods that the United States and China traded with Vietnam, portable digital automatic data processing machines were the top U.S. import and cotton was the top U.S. export, while microchips were the top Chinese import and phone-set parts were the top Chinese export.

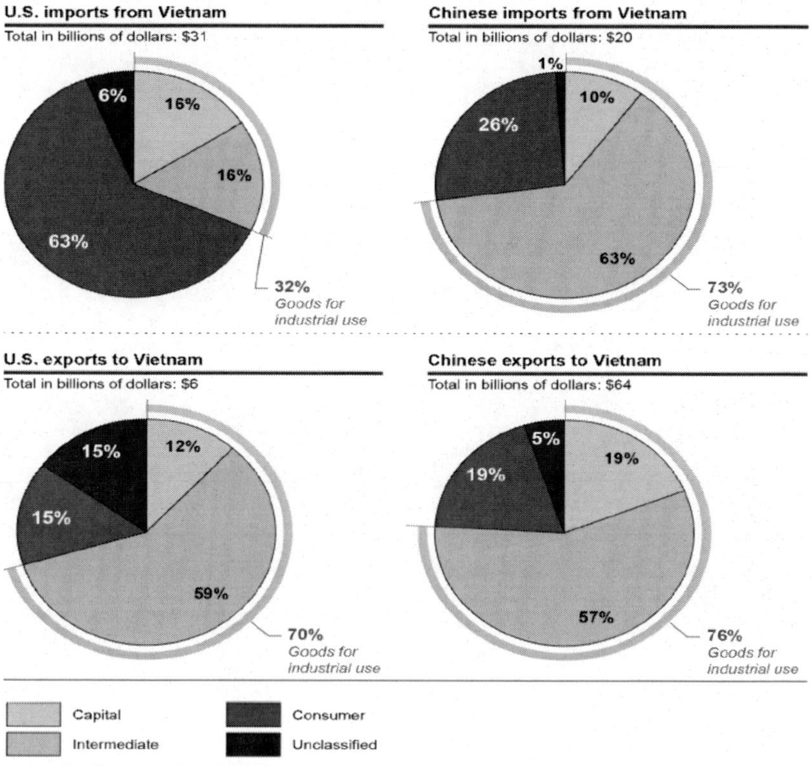

Source: GAO analysis of U.S. and Chinese data from the United Nations Commodity Trade database. | GAO-16-186.

Figure 16. (Continued).

Notes: We used the United Nations Statistics Division's Broad Economic Categories to classify U.S. and Chinese total trade in goods into the four categories shown. We defined goods for industrial use as including both capital and intermediate goods. According to the Organisation for Economic Co-operation and Development, an intermediate good is an input to the production process that has itself been produced and, unlike capital, is used up in production. Unclassified goods are goods that are not classified as capital, intermediate, or consumer goods. Percentages shown may not sum to 100 percent for each chart because of rounding.

Figure 16. U.S. and Chinese Imports and Exports of Goods to Vietnam in 2014, by Use.

APPENDIX IV: U.S. TRADE CAPACITY BUILDING ASSISTANCE TO INDONESIA AND VIETNAM

U.S. agencies have identified certain official development assistance to Indonesia and Vietnam as trade capacity building assistance. This assistance addresses, for example, the countries' regulatory environment for business, trade, and investment; constraints such as low capacity for production and entrepreneurship; and inadequate physical infrastructure, such as poor transport and storage facilities.

Table 5. Funding Provided by U.S. Agencies for Trade Capacity Building to Indonesia, Fiscal Years 2009-2013

U.S. dollars in millions	
U.S. agency	**Funding**
Millennium Challenge Corporation	$332.5[b]
U.S. Agency for International Development	19.1
Department of Labor	11.4
Department of State	4.0
Department of the Treasury	3.4
Other agencies[a]	2.7
Total	**$373.1**

Source: U.S. Agency for International Development Trade Capacity Building Database. | GAO-16-186.

[a]Other agencies include the Departments of Agriculture, Commerce, Health and Human Services, and the Interior; the Federal Trade Commission; and the U.S. Trade and Development Agency.

[b]In technical comments on a draft of this report, MCC stated that it revised its reported trade capacity building amount to Indonesia from $332.5 million to $378.2 million as of September 2014.

Indonesia

In fiscal years 2009 through 2013, U.S. agencies provided about $373 million in trade capacity building assistance to Indonesia (see table 5).

As table 5 shows, three agencies—the Millennium Challenge Corporation (MCC), the U.S. Agency for International Development (USAID), and the Department of Labor (Labor)—provided the largest amounts of U.S. trade capacity building assistance to Indonesia in fiscal years 2009 through 2013.

- **MCC** provided about $333 million—about 90 percent of U.S. trade capacity building assistance to Indonesia during this period—as part of a 5-year, $600 million compact with Indonesia.[1] One of the compact's three projects, the Green Prosperity Project, provides technical and financial assistance for projects in renewable energy and natural resource management to help raise rural household incomes. A second project, the Procurement Modernization Project, is designed to help the government of Indonesia develop a more efficient and effective process for the procurement of goods and services.[2] MCC obligates compact funds when a compact enters into force, disbursing the funds over the 5 years of the compact. As of March 2015, MCC had expended $2.3 million of its $333 million commitment for the Green Prosperity Project and $6 million of its $50 million commitment for the Procurement Modernization Project.
- **USAID** provided about $19 million in trade capacity building assistance, among other things, to provide economic policy advisory services to the Indonesian government; strengthen key trade and investment institutions by contributing to a World Bank Fund; and strengthen the Indonesian Ministry of Trade's capacity to analyze, negotiate, and implement bilateral and multilateral trade agreements. In addition, USAID officials told us that they are working to build and sustain a culture of accountability in Indonesia at the national and subnational levels by, for example, working with the U.S. Department of Justice to train investigators to support Indonesia's Corruption Eradication Commission. However, according to agency officials, after consultations with Indonesian officials and others knowledgeable about the Indonesian economy, USAID stopped providing direct support for economic and trade policy issues. USAID officials also

said that the Indonesian government did not view the support as a priority.

- **Labor** provided about $11 million in trade capacity building assistance to improve Indonesia's compliance with labor standards and its competitiveness in global supply chains, to combat child labor, and to build the capacity of domestic labor organizations.

Vietnam

In fiscal years 2009 through 2013, U.S. agencies provided about $32 million in trade capacity building assistance to Vietnam (see table 6).

Table 6. Funding Provided by U.S. Agencies for Trade Capacity Building to Vietnam, Fiscal Years 2009-2013

Nominal U.S. dollars in millions	
Agency	**Funding**
U.S. Agency for International Development	$20.4
Department of the Treasury	5.9
Department of State	2.6
U.S. Trade and Development Agency	2.1
Other agencies[a]	0.9
Total	**$31.9**

Source: U.S. Agency for International Development Trade Capacity Building Database. I GAO-16-186.

[a]Other agencies include the Departments of Commerce, Health and Human Services, Labor, and the Interior and the Federal Trade Commission.

As table 6 shows, four agencies—USAID, the Departments of the Treasury (Treasury) and State (State), and the U.S. Trade and Development Agency (USTDA)—provided the majority of U.S. trade capacity building assistance to Vietnam in fiscal year 2009 through 2013.

- **USAID** provided approximately $20.4 million—about 64 percent of U.S. trade capacity building assistance to Vietnam during this period—to enhance the country's economic governance. From 2001 through 2010, USAID's Support for Trade Acceleration projects sought to modernize Vietnam's commercial laws and legal system to help the country meet its bilateral trade agreement commitments and prepare it to join the World Trade Organization. In addition, the Vietnam Competitiveness Initiative, which began in 2003 and ended in 2013, sought to strengthen Vietnam's regulatory system and regulatory framework and models for infrastructure development. The Provincial Competitiveness Index, which began in 2013 and is scheduled to end in 2016, assesses and reports on barriers to economic development and doing business in Vietnam. Moreover, USAID's Governance for Inclusive Growth project—which began in 2013 and is scheduled to end in 2018—seeks to provide assistance relevant to Vietnam's Trans-Pacific Partnership commitments, among other things. Finally, the Lower Mekong Initiative, encompassing Thailand, Cambodia, Laos, Burma, and Vietnam, supports, among many development efforts, reduction of the development gap between the more economically developed Association of Southeast Asian Nations countries and less developed countries, such as Vietnam, and also supports regional efforts toward economic integration.

- **Treasury** provided, through its Office of Technical Assistance, about $5.9 million in trade capacity assistance for several projects to improve Vietnam's government operations. For example, OTA is currently assisting Vietnam with implementation of International Public Sector Accounting Standards. Previously, OTA provided assistance in the areas of banking supervision, strengthening of tax administration, and debt management.[3]
- **State** provided about $2.6 million in trade capacity assistance, primarily for improving Vietnam's customs and border control. State's Export and Border Security Assistance program promotes border security and customs operations by providing training, equipment, vehicles, spare parts, infrastructure, travel to workshops and conferences, translations of key documents such as control lists, and other exchanges. State has provided equipment and training to Vietnamese officials in support of these efforts.
- **USTDA** provided about $2 million in U.S. trade capacity building assistance for projects to support potential U.S. investment opportunities. In 2014, USTDA provided $900,000 for a feasibility study—the largest USTDA-funded project in Vietnam that year—for an integrated telecommunications control center for the Ho Chi Minh City urban rail system. In August 2014, Vietnam became the second country to sign a memorandum of understanding with USTDA, under which USTDA will provide training and technical assistance to public

procurement officials to implement Vietnam's revised procurement law. In July 2015, USTDA signed two additional grant agreements with Vietnam for (1) technical assistance and training in support of Vietnam's efforts to meet civil aviation safety standards and (2) a feasibility study to support the efforts of a Vietnamese private firm to develop an offshore wind power project.

End Notes

[1] The 10 members of ASEAN are Brunei Darussalam (Brunei), Burma (Myanmar), Cambodia, Indonesia, Laos, Malaysia, the Philippines, Singapore, Thailand, and Vietnam. In August 2015, we reported that China had surpassed the United States in goods trade, and traded a similar amount of services, with the 10 ASEAN countries but that U.S. investment had exceeded reported Chinese investment. We also found that the United States and China were furthering economic engagement in these countries through trade agreements, support for firms, and support for regional integration. See GAO, *Southeast Asia: Trends in U.S. and Chinese Economic Engagement*, GAO-15-724 (Washington, D.C.: Aug. 13, 2015).

[2] The World Bank's World Development Indicators does not include data on Burma's (Myanmar) GDP in constant 2005 U.S. dollars.

[3] The $1.25 per day is in terms of purchasing power parity. According to the World Bank, for the purpose of comparing levels of poverty across countries, the World Bank uses estimates of consumption converted to U.S. dollars using purchasing power parity rates.

[4] See GAO-15-724, app. II, for information about the roles and responsibilities of U.S. and Chinese entities in Southeast Asian countries.

[5] U.S. law authorizes the imposition of antidumping duties on products exported to the United States at unfairly low prices (i.e., dumped). The designation "nonmarket economy" allows for the use of an alternative dumping calculation methodology to that which is used for market economies for the purpose of antidumping enforcement.

[6] U.S. dollar amounts cited in this report are in nominal terms unless otherwise specified.

[7] According to the Organisation for Economic Co-operation and Development (OECD), FDI is the ownership by a foreign person or business of 10 percent or more of the voting equity of a firm located in the host country. Data on FDI flows provide information about FDI activity in a given period of time, while data on FDI stock indicate the level of FDI at a given point in time. FDI flows represent outflows (e.g., when a U.S. or Chinese parent company establishes an affiliate in Indonesia) minus inflows (e.g., when a U.S. or Chinese parent company sells or reduces its stake in its affiliate in Indonesia). We used data on FDI flows to Indonesia instead of data on FDI stock in Indonesia, which, according to the U.S. Bureau of Economic Analysis, are available only by historical cost and do not reflect changes in the FDI's market value.

[8] After joining the World Trade Organization in 2001, China's total trade in goods increased worldwide.

[9] See International Monetary Fund, "2014 Article IV Consultation—Staff Report; Press Release; and Statement by the Executive Director for Indonesia," *IMF Country Report*, No. 15/74 (March 2015).

[10] When Indonesia implemented the ban on mineral ore exports in early 2014, it levied taxes of 20 to 25 percent on exports from mining companies seeking a temporary waiver from the ban. The ban's biggest impact was on exports of copper concentrate. According to the Office of the U.S. Trade Representative, the taxes applied only to a subset of 7 mineral ores and not to the more than 200 other banned mineral ores. In addition, the tax increases every 6 months until January 1, 2017, when the ban is scheduled to extend to the subset of 7 mineral ores. In mid-2014, the Indonesian government agreed to allow copper exports to resume while it granted tax concessions until new process plants are built in Indonesia.

[11] To calculate the value of Indonesian trade in goods by trading partner, we used data from the ASEANstats database, which vary from data on Indonesian trade in goods that the United States and China report to the United Nations (UN) Commodity Trade database. Because some of ASEAN's trading partners do not report data to the UN Commodity Trade database, we used data from the ASEANstats database as a comprehensive set of data on trade in goods for all of ASEAN's trading partners. Reasons for the variation in trade values between the ASEANstats database and the UN Commodity Trade Database include differences in the valuation of goods, differences in data quality, and the omission of some ASEAN trading partners' data from the UN Commodity Trade Database. The most recent goods trade data available from the ASEANstats database are for 2013, while the most recent data available from the UN Commodity Trade Database are for 2014. According to the OECD, intermediate goods, such as electronic components used in the manufacture of computers, are inputs to the production process that have themselves been produced and used up or transformed in production.

[12] See Organisation for Economic Co-operation and Development and World Trade Organization, *Trade in Value-Added: Concepts, Methodologies and Challenges*, Joint OECD-WTO Note (2012).

[13] We do not compare the United States' and China's exports of services in 2011, because data on China's trade in services with Indonesia are unavailable. However, data from the U.S. Bureau of Economic Analysis show that the United States exported around $1.9 billion in services to Indonesia in 2011.

[14] In 2005, we found that BEA had experienced challenges in identifying all U.S. services importers and obtaining high-quality survey data from importers. However, since 2005, BEA has implemented methods to better identify all U.S. services importers. In addition, BEA's data on trade in services may differ from other countries' data, including China's, because of differences in definitions, coverage, and methods used to measure services. For example, we found that BEA's data on trade in services differed from data collected by India because of differences in the methodologies used to define and collect the data. See GAO, *International Trade: U.S. and India Data on Offshoring Show Significant Differences*, GAO-06-116 (Washington, D.C.: Oct. 27, 2005). According to BEA, its survey data are from mandatory surveys of U.S. businesses with services trade that exceeds certain thresholds. BEA does not survey a random sample of U.S. businesses and therefore does not report the data with margins of error.

[15] "Trade in services" refers to the buying and selling of intangible products and activities; examples of services include tourism, financial services, and telecommunications. Contracted activities, such as construction and consulting services, are also examples of services.

[16] Business services include professional and management consulting, architectural and engineering, and research and development services.

[17] A holding company typically does not itself produce goods or services but exists to own assets of other companies, which may be located in countries other than that of the holding company.

[18] According to the IMF, the United States' highest export similarity index with a selected group of 28 countries in 2008 was 0.587, with Germany, and its lowest was 0.312, with Hong Kong. The IMF calculated the export similarity index using six-digit product categories, whereas we calculated the export similarity index using four-digit product categories. Higher-digit product categories tend to result in lower export similarity index values. See International Monetary Fund, *Changing Patterns of Global Trade* (June 15, 2011).

[19] The creation of an export similarity index is described in J. M. Finger and M. E. Kreinin, "A Measure of 'Export Similarity' and Its Possible Uses," *The Economic Journal*, vol. 89, no. 356 (1979), 905-912. The World Bank includes the export similarity index as an indicator to describe export trends. The IMF has stated that the index is a common indicator for gauging export competitiveness; see International Monetary Fund, *Changing Patterns of Global Trade*. Other academic studies have also used the index to compare the similarity between exports. For example, see Marcus Noland, "Has Asian Export Performance Been Unique?," *Journal of International Economics*, vol. 43 (1997), 79-101, and Peter K. Schott, "The Relative Similarity of China's Exports to the United States *vis a vis* Other U.S. Trading Partners" (July 2004). See app. I for a brief description of our methodology in calculating the export similarity index.

[20] The Advocacy Center is responsible for coordinating the U.S. government's advocacy efforts on behalf of U.S. exporters bidding on public sector contracts overseas. Advocacy Center data reflect public sector contracts for which the center received applications by U.S. firms for commercial advocacy.

[21] According to the World Bank, the data include only major contract awards reviewed by World Bank staff prior to award—approximately one-fifth of all contracts. The data show the nationality of a firm as the country where the firm is registered, although the firm's parent may be headquartered in another country. In addition, though subcontractors may perform a majority of the awarded contract, the data reflect the nationality of only the prime contractor.

[22] U.S. firms won 46 Work Bank contracts in Indonesia, exceeding the number of contracts won by firms from other countries outside Indonesia during this period.

[23] Office of the U.S. Trade Representative, *2014 National Trade Estimate Report on Foreign Trade Barriers* (March 2014); *2015 National Trade Estimate Report on Foreign Trade Barriers* (March 2015).

[24] According to the U.S. Department of Agriculture, in response to the WTO case, Indonesia has made some revisions to its import licensing requirements; however, the United States believes the requirements continue to breach WTO rules and restrict U.S. agriculture exports. In May 2015, the WTO established a panel to adjudicate this dispute.

[25] World Bank, *Doing Business 2015: Going Beyond Efficiency* (Washington, D.C.: 2014). The report uses 10 indicators to track and measure the ease of doing business, trade, or exchange in each country. These indicators measure the ease of starting a business, dealing with construction permits, getting electricity, registering property, getting credit, paying taxes, trading across borders, enforcing contracts, and resolving insolvency. The last indicator measures the strength of protections for minority investors.

[26] Office of the U.S. Trade Representative, *2015 National Trade Estimate Report on Foreign Trade Barriers*.

[27] U.S. companies are subject to the Foreign Corrupt Practices Act of 1977, which outlaws payments to foreign government officials to assist in securing business opportunities (Pub. L. No. 95-213, as amended (codified at 15 U.S.C. §§78dd-1 et seq.)). Further, as a member of the OECD, the United States is bound by its Convention on Combating Bribery of Foreign Public Officials in International Business Transactions.

[28] Transparency International, *Corruption Perceptions Index 2014* (Berlin: 2014). Transparency International is a global organization that publishes a corruption perceptions index based on expert opinion from around the world.

[29] U.S. Department of Commerce and U.S. Department of State, *Doing Business in Indonesia: 2014 Country Commercial Guide for U.S. Companies.*

[30] Office of the U.S. Trade Representative, *2015 Special 301 Report* (April 2015). Each year, USTR reports to the President regarding the state of intellectual property rights protection and enforcement for U.S. trading partners around the world. Indonesia has been included on USTR's Priority Watch List every year since the report's inception more than 25 years ago. USTR assembles the Priority Watch List with substantial input from interested persons and in consultation with U.S. agencies.

[31] According to USTR, Indonesia's Economic Policy Package focuses on deregulation as a means of improving Indonesia's business climate and competiveness.

[32] See Congressional Research Service, *Generalized System of Preferences: Background and Renewal Debate* (Jan. 8, 2015).

[33] See GAO-15-724 for more information about these agreements.

[34] See Yu Sheng, Hsiao Chink Tang, and Xinpeng Xu, "The Impact of ACFTA on People's Republic of China-ASEAN Trade: Estimates Based on an Extended Gravity Model for Component Trade," *Asian Development Bank Working Paper Series on Regional Integration*, No. 99 (July 2012), 1-38.

[35] We identified 12 studies assessing the effect of the China-ASEAN trade and investment agreements on China's and Indonesia's economies. See app. I for a list of the studies as well as information about our methodology for identifying them. A 2011 study did not show an increase in trade for Indonesia. See Tavi Supriana, "Indonesia Trade Under China Free Trade Area," *Economic Journal of Emerging Markets,* Vol. 3, No. 2 (August 2011), 139-151.

[36] A 2008 study projected that the China-ASEAN Trade in Goods Agreement will fail to benefit China's economy; see Donghyun Park, Innwon Park, and Gemma Esther B. Estrada, "Prospects of an ASEAN-People's Republic of China Free Trade Area: A Qualitative and Quantitative Analysis," *Asian Development Bank Economic Working Paper Series*, No. 130 (October 2008), 1-17.

[37] See Csilla Lakatos and Terrie Walmsley, "Investment Creation and Diversion Effects of the ASEAN-China Free Trade Agreement," *Economic Modelling*, vol. 29 (2012), 766-779.

[38] On October 26, 2015, Indonesia's President announced that Indonesia intends to join the TPP. As of August 2015, Indonesia had expressed no formal interest in joining the TPP negotiations, according to USTR officials. These officials said that the direction of Indonesia's trade and investment policies made it unlikely that Indonesia would be able to undertake the reforms needed to join the TPP.

[39] Although the potential impacts of TPP and RCEP are uncertain, U.S. officials cited a recent study that estimated that in 2025, TPP could cause U.S. GDP to increase by 0.4 percent and could cause Indonesia's and China's GDP to decrease by 0.1 percent and 0.2 percent, respectively, compared with each country's GDP without TPP. The study also estimated that in 2025, RCEP would cause no change in U.S. GDP and could cause Indonesia's and

China's GDP to increase by 1.1 percent and 1.4 percent, respectively, compared with their GDP without RCEP. The study was based on a projection of TPP's and RCEP's impacts on current trade flows. See Peter A. Petri and Ali Abdul-Raheem, "Can RCEP and the TPP Be Pathways to FTAAP?," *State of the Region, 2014-2015* (Singapore: Pacific Economic Cooperation Council, 2014), 31-43.

[40] The RCEP negotiating parties are China, Indonesia and the nine other ASEAN members, Australia, India, Japan, South Korea, and New Zealand.

[41] Ex-Im is the United States' official export credit agency. Ex-Im makes fixed-rate loans directly to international buyers of goods and services and also guarantees loans by private lenders to international buyers of goods or services, promising to pay the lenders if the buyers default. Export credit insurance products protect the exporter from the risk of nonpayment by foreign buyers for commercial and political reasons.

[42] OPIC is the United States' development financing institution. OPIC supports U.S. investment projects in overseas countries by providing direct loans, loan guarantees, political risk insurance, and support for private equity investment funds to U.S. private sector investors.

[43] According to State and Indonesian government officials, China's planned investments are often not realized. For example, Indonesian officials representing an Indonesian agency responsible for promoting and approving domestic and foreign direct investment in Indonesia stated that China has provided only a small percentage of funds for planned Chinese investments in Indonesia that the agency has approved.

[44] China's Development Bank and Export-Import Bank generally offer this financing as extended joint ventures, sometimes referred to as cooperation pacts, between a Chinese state-owned enterprise and an Indonesian government body or a state-owned enterprise. For more information about the roles and responsibilities of China's Development and Export Banks, see GAO-15-724, app. II.

[45] In addition, other federal entities, such as USTR, support U.S. business and investment in Indonesia through the development of U.S. trade and investment policy.

[46] Some of these services are fee-based services and can include finding and arranging appointments with potential business partners; providing logistical and administrative support while U.S. company representatives are on international travel; helping to organize promotional events in Jakarta, such as seminars; and providing market intelligence.

[47] Trade missions may include one-to-one meetings with foreign industry executives and government officials, networking events with local industry representatives, briefings and roundtables on local business practices and opportunities, and site visits to local facilities where U.S. firms' technologies or services may be applied. Commerce officials in Indonesia said they have also supported trade missions that are organized by states and private sector organizations, such as the U.S.-ASEAN Business Council or the American Chamber of Commerce.

[48] China had established one economic cooperation zone in Bitung, North Sulawesi, and announced the establishment of another in Bekasi, near Jakarta.

[49] At the June 1, 2015 exchange rate of 6,199 Chinese yuan per U.S. dollar, China's currency swap arrangement with Indonesia totaled $16.1 billion.

[50] The exchange of currencies by the central banks of two countries is known as a currency swap. Currency swap agreements allow countries to exchange local currency for foreign currency through another country's central bank or monetary authority's currency reserves. Currency swap agreements are generally designed for short-term support, with the exchange to be reversed at a future date. The United States does not have a currency swap agreement with Indonesia.

[51] China and Indonesia are also each party to a $240 billion multilateral currency swap agreement, the Chiang Mai Initiative Multilateralisation, with the nine other ASEAN countries, Japan, and South Korea. The Chiang Mai initiative provides for liquidity among participant economies experiencing short-term liquidity difficulties.

[52] Since at least 2001, the United States has committed to providing trade capacity building assistance to developing countries to help them participate in, and benefit from, global trade. The U.S. Agency for International Development (USAID) maintains a database to track this assistance. For more information about U.S. trade capacity building assistance, see GAO, *Foreign Assistance: USAID Should Update Its Trade Capacity Building Strategy*, GAO-14-602 (Washington, D.C.: Aug. 11, 2014). Our analysis of trade capacity building assistance does not include support provided by multilateral institutions to which the United States contributes funds, such as the World Bank.

[53] MCC is a U.S. government corporation that seeks to reduce global poverty through economic growth.

[54] Through the 2012 U.S.-Asia Pacific Comprehensive Energy Partnership, State and the U.S. Trade and Development Agency have supported renewable power in Indonesia. For example, according to State, the agency has supported three feasibility studies to develop an estimated $2 billion worth of 600-megawatt geothermal projects.

[55] Chinese officials have said that all countries are welcome to join the Asian Infrastructure Investment Bank. However, as of August 2015, the United States and Japan had declined to join the bank. U.S. Department of the Treasury officials have stated that the United States welcomes the creation of new development institutions but have also expressed concerns about the new bank's governance and standards.

[56] The Chinese government stated that it was willing to subscribe up to 50 percent of the Asian Infrastructure Investment Bank's capital, but prospective members have since agreed to determine share allocation primarily by GDP.

[57] U.S. dollar amounts in this report are in nominal terms unless otherwise specified.

[58] According to USDA, some U.S. food and agricultural exports to Vietnam may be destined for neighboring countries. For example, USDA reports that some U.S. exports of beef and tree nuts are transshipped through Vietnam into China under preferential trade agreements and border trade provisions.

[59] To calculate the value of Vietnamese trade in goods by trading partner, we used data from the ASEANstats database, which vary from the data on Vietnamese trade in goods that the United States and China report to the UN Commodity Trade database. Because some of ASEAN's trading partners do not report data to the UN Commodity Trade database, we used data from the ASEANstats database as a comprehensive set of data on trade in goods for all of ASEAN's trading partners. Reasons for the variation in trade values between the ASEANstats database and the UN Commodity Trade Database include differences in the valuation of goods, differences in data quality, and the omission of some ASEAN trading partners' data from the UN Commodity Trade Database. The most recent goods trade data available from the ASEANstats database are for 2013, while the most recent data available from the UN Commodity Trade Database are for 2014. According to the OECD, intermediate goods, such as electronic components used in the manufacture of computers and textiles, are inputs to the production process that have themselves been produced and used up or transformed in production.

[60] Although the United States does not have diplomatic relations with Taiwan, we have listed Taiwan as a separate country, because whenever the laws of the United States refer or relate

to foreign countries, nations, states, governments, or similar entities, such terms shall include and shall apply to Taiwan.

[61] See Organisation for Economic Co-operation and Development and World Trade Organization, *Trade in Value-Added: Concepts, Methodologies and Challenges*.

[62] We do not compare the United States' and China's exports of services in 2011, because data on China's trade in services with Vietnam are unavailable. However, our analysis of data on U.S. trade in services with Vietnam, based on data from BEA and other sources, shows that in 2011 the United States exported $1.3 billion in services to Vietnam.

[63] In 2005, we found that BEA had experienced challenges in identifying all U.S. service importers and in obtaining high-quality survey data from importers. However, since 2005, BEA has implemented methods to better identify all U.S. service importers. In addition, BEA's data on trade in services may differ from other countries' data, including China's, because of differences in definitions, coverage, and methods used to measure services. For example, we found that BEA's data on trade in services differed from data collected by India because of differences in the methodologies used to define and collect the data. See GAO, *International Trade: U.S. and India Data on Offshoring Show Significant Differences*, GAO-06-116 (Washington, D.C.: Oct. 27, 2005). According to BEA, its survey data are from mandatory surveys of U.S. businesses with services trade that exceeds certain thresholds. BEA does not survey a random sample of U.S. businesses and therefore does not report the data with margins of error.

[64] "Trade in services" refers to the buying and selling of intangible products and activities, such as tourism, financial services, and telecommunications, and of contracted activities, such as construction and consulting services.

[65] BEA has not released data on U.S. trade in services for Vietnam because of confidentiality concerns and data limitations. BEA identified ways to estimate the value of U.S. trade in services with Vietnam that required us to make various assumptions. Data for 2013 were not available. See app. I for details of our methodology.

[66] According to the OECD, FDI is the ownership by a foreign person or business of 10 percent or more of the voting equity of a firm located in the host country. Data on FDI flows provide information about FDI activity in a given period of time, while data on FDI stock indicate the level of foreign direct investment at a given point in time. FDI flows are outflows (e.g., when the U.S. or Chinese parent company establishes an affiliate in Vietnam) minus inflows (e.g., when the U.S. or Chinese parent company sells or reduces its stake in its affiliate in Vietnam). According to BEA, data on FDI stock in Vietnam are available only by historical cost and do not reflect changes in the market value of FDI. When using a U.S. GDP deflator to deflate the nominal data, we calculated that cumulative U.S. and Chinese FDI flows for 2007 through 2012 were $460 million and $1.2 billion 2009 dollars.

[67] According to the IMF, among a selected group of countries, the United States' highest export similarity index in 2008 was 0.587, with Germany, and its lowest was 0.312, with Hong Kong. The authors calculated the export similarity index using six-digit product categories, whereas we calculated the export similarity index using four-digit product categories. Higher digit product categories tend to result in lower export similarity index values. See International Monetary Fund, *Changing Patterns of Global Trade*.

[68] The creation of an export similarity index is described in Finger and Kreinin, "A Measure of 'Export Similarity' and Its Possible Uses." The World Bank includes the export similarity index as an indicator to describe export trends. The IMF has stated that the index is a common indicator for gauging export competitiveness; see International Monetary Fund, *Changing Patterns of Global Trade*. Other academic studies have also used the index to

compare the similarity between exports. For example, see Noland, "Has Asian Export Performance Been Unique?," and Schott, "The Relative Similarity of China's Exports to the United States *vis a vis* Other U.S. Trading Partners." For a brief description of our methodology for calculating the export similarity index, see app. I.

[69] The Advocacy Center is responsible for coordinating the U.S. government's advocacy efforts on behalf of U.S. exporters bidding on public sector contracts overseas. Advocacy Center data reflect public sector contracts for which the center received applications from U.S. firms for commercial advocacy.

[70] According to the World Bank, the data include only major contract awards reviewed by World Bank staff prior to award—approximately one-fifth of all contracts. The data show the nationality of a firm as the country where it is registered, although the firm's parent may be headquartered in another country. In addition, though subcontractors may perform a majority of the awarded contract, the data reflect the nationality of only the prime contractor.

[71] U.S. Department of Commerce and U.S. Department of State, *Doing Business in Vietnam: 2014 Country Commercial Guide for U.S. Companies* (2014).

[72] According to a U.S. health care provider operating in Vietnam, Vietnam's restriction on imports of used equipment has limited the ability of health care providers in Vietnam to import serviceable medical equipment. According to U.S. officials, Vietnam has blocked the import of used electronic goods, but the United States exports reconditioned electronics, such as magnetic resonance imagers, that are still usable and are less expensive than new equipment.

[73] World Bank, *Doing Business 2015: Going Beyond Efficiency*. The report uses 10 indicators to track and measure the ease of doing business, trade, or exchange in each country. These indicators include the ease of starting a business, dealing with construction permits, getting electricity, registering property, getting credit, paying taxes, trading across borders, enforcing contracts, and resolving insolvency. The last indicator measures the strength of protections for minority investors.

[74] U.S. Department of State, *2015 Investment Climate Statement for Vietnam* (May 2015); U.S. Department of Commerce and U.S. Department of State, *Doing Business in Vietnam: 2014 Country Commercial Guide for U.S. Companies* (2014); and Office of the U.S. Trade Representative, *National Trade Estimates Report on Foreign Trade Barriers*.

[75] Transparency International, *Corruption Perceptions Index 2014*. Transparency International is a global organization that publishes a corruption perceptions index based on expert opinion from around the world.

[76] U.S. State Department, *2015 Investment Climate Statement for Vietnam* (May 2015); and U.S. Department of Commerce and U.S. Department of State, *Doing Business in Vietnam: 2014 Country Commercial Guide for U.S. Companies*.

[77] Office of the U.S. Trade Representative, *2015 Special 301 Report* (April 2015). According to the report, designating a country as a Watch List or a Priority Watch List country means that particular problems exist in that country with respect to intellectual property rights protection, enforcement, or market access for persons relying on these rights. USTR identifies these countries with substantial input from interested persons and in consultation with U.S. agencies.

[78] U.S. Department of Commerce and U.S. Department of State, *Doing Business in Vietnam: 2014 Country Commercial Guide for U.S. Companies*.

[79] Office of the U.S. Trade Representative, *National Trade Estimates Report on Foreign Trade Barriers*.

[80] U.S. Department of Commerce and U.S. Department of State, *Doing Business in Vietnam: 2014 Country Commercial Guide for U.S. Companies*.

[81] The United States also signed a TIFA with Vietnam in 2007. TIFAs, in contrast to FTAs, are short agreements that provide principles and structure for dialogue on trade and investment issues. According to USTR officials, efforts under the United States–Vietnam TIFA have largely been subsumed by TPP negotiations. Therefore, according to the officials, the United States and Vietnam have not held any formal meetings under the TIFA since 2011.

[82] Brian McCaig and Nina Pavcnik. "Export Markets and Labor Allocation in a Low-Income Country," *NBER Working Paper Series* (September 2014).

[83] U.S. Department of Commerce and U.S. Department of State, *Doing Business in Vietnam: 2014 Country Commercial Guide for U.S. Companies*.

[84] See GAO-15-724 for more information about these agreements.

[85] See Yu Sheng, Hsiao Chink Tang, and Xinpeng Xu, "The Impact of the ACFTA on People's Republic of China-ASEAN Trade: Estimates Based on an Extended Gravity Model for Component Trade," *Asian Development Bank Working Paper Series on Regional Economic Integration*, No. 99 (July 2012).

[86] We identified 9 studies assessing the effect of the China-ASEAN trade and investment agreements on China's and Vietnam's economies. See app. I for a list of the studies and information on our methodology for identifying them. A 2004 study showed the China-ASEAN Trade in Goods Agreement increased total exports but decreased total imports for Vietnam. See Chia Siow Yue, "ASEAN-China Free Trade Area," Paper for presentation at the AEP Conference (April 12-13, 2004).

[87] A 2008 study projected that the China-ASEAN Trade in Goods Agreement will fail to benefit China's economy; see Park, Park, and Estrada, "Prospects of an ASEAN-People's Republic of China Free Trade Area: A Qualitative and Quantitative Analysis." In addition, a 2012 study showed that the agreements will harm Vietnam's economy; see Lakatos and Walmsley, "Investment Creation and Diversion Effects of the ASEAN-China Free Trade Agreement," *Economic Modelling*, vol. 29 (2012), 766-779. A 2004 study showed the China-ASEAN Trade in Goods Agreement decreased total exports for Vietnam; see Chia Siow Yue, "ASEAN-China Free Trade Area."

[88] See Lakatos and Walmsley, "Investment Creation and Diversion Effects of the ASEAN-China Free Trade Agreement." 766-779.

[89] The 10 other participants of TPP are Australia, Brunei, Canada, Chile, Japan, Malaysia, Mexico, New Zealand, Peru, and Singapore.

[90] Although the potential impacts of TPP and RCEP are uncertain, U.S. officials have cited a recent study that estimated that in 2025, TPP could cause U.S. and Vietnam GDP to increase by 0.4 percent and 10.5 percent, respectively, and China's GDP to decrease by 0.2 percent compared with each country's GDP without TPP. The study also estimated that in 2025, RCEP would cause no change in U.S. GDP and could cause Vietnam's and China's GDP to increase by 5.1 percent and 1.4 percent, respectively, compared with their GDP without RCEP. The study was based on a projection of TPP's and RCEP's impacts on current trade flows. See Peter A. Petri and Ali Abdul-Raheem, "Can RCEP and the TPP Be Pathways to FTAAP?," *State of the Region, 2014-2015*, eds. Pacific Economic Cooperation Council (Singapore: Pacific Economic Cooperation Council, 2014), 31-43.

[91] The RCEP negotiating parties are China, Vietnam, the nine other ASEAN members, Australia, India, Japan, South Korea, and New Zealand.

[92] U.S.-China Economic and Security Review Commission hearing, "China's Relations with Southeast Asia," May 13, 2015. The commission was created by Congress to report on the

national security implications of the bilateral trade and economic relationship between the United States and the People's Republic of China.

[93] Ex-Im is the United States' official export credit agency. Ex-Im makes fixed-rate loans directly to international buyers of goods and services and also guarantees loans made by private lenders to international buyers of goods or services, promising to pay the lenders if the buyers default. Export credit insurance products protect the exporter from the risk of nonpayment by foreign buyers for commercial and political reasons.

[94] OPIC is the United States' development financing institution. OPIC supports U.S. investment projects in overseas countries by providing U.S. private sector investors with direct loans, loan guarantees, political risk insurance, and support for private equity investment funds.

[95] U.S.-China Economic and Security Review Commission hearing, "China's Relations with Southeast Asia," May 13, 2015.

[96] In addition, other federal entities, such as USTR, support U.S. business and investment in Vietnam through the development of U.S. trade and investment policy.

[97] Some of these services are fee-based services and can include arranging appointments with potential business partners; providing logistical and administrative support while U.S. company representatives are visiting Vietnam; and providing market intelligence.

[98] Since at least 2001, the United States has committed to providing trade capacity building assistance to developing countries to help them participate in, and benefit from, global trade. USAID maintains a database to track this assistance. For more information about U.S. trade capacity building assistance, see GAO-14-602. Our analysis of trade capacity building assistance does not include any support provided by multilateral institutions to which the United States contributes funds, such as the World Bank.

[99] Asian Development Bank, *The Greater Mekong Subregion Economic Cooperation Program Strategic Framework 2012-2022* (Mandaluyong City, Philippines: 2011).

[100] Chinese officials have said that all countries are welcome to join the Asian Infrastructure Investment Bank. However, as of August 2015, the United States and Japan had declined to join the bank. U.S. Treasury officials have stated that the United States welcomes the creation of new development institutions but have also expressed concerns about the governance and standards of the new bank.

[101] The Chinese government stated that it was willing to subscribe up to 50 percent of the Asian Infrastructure Investment Bank's capital. Prospective members subsequently agreed to determine share allocation primarily by GDP.

End Notes for Appendix I

[1] The 10 countries of ASEAN are Brunei Darussalam (Brunei), Burma (Myanmar), Cambodia, Indonesia, Laos, Malaysia, the Philippines, Singapore, Thailand, and Vietnam.

[2] The information we provide about foreign law is not a product of our original analysis but is derived from interviews and secondary sources.

[3] Data from the ASEANstats database on Vietnam's trade in goods were not available for 2003.

[4] GAO, *Sub-Saharan Africa: Trends in U.S. and Chinese Economic Engagement*, GAO-13-199 (Washington, D.C.: Feb. 7, 2013).

[5] The export similarity index is described in J. M. Finger and M. E. Kreinin, "A Measure of 'Export Similarity' and Its Possible Uses," *The Economic Journal*, vol. 89, no. 356 (1979): 905-912. The World Bank includes the export similarity index as an indicator to describe

export trends. An IMF study stated that the index is a common indicator for gauging export competitiveness. See International Monetary Fund, *Changing Patterns of Global Trade* (June 15, 2011). Other academic studies have also used the index to compare the similarity of exports. For example, see Marcus Noland, "Has Asian Export Performance Been Unique?," *Journal of International Economics*, 43 (1997), 79-101, and Peter K. Schott, "The Relative Similarity of China's Exports to the United States *vis a vis* Other U.S. Trading Partners," (July 2004).

[6] See Danupon Ariyasajjakorn, James P. Gander, Somchai Ratanakomut, and Stephen Reynolds, "ASEAN FTA, Distribution of Income, and Globalization," *Journal of Asian Economics*, vol. 20 (2009), 327-335; Suthiphand Chirathivat, "ASEAN-China Free Trade Area: Background, Implications and Future Development," *Journal of Asian Economics*, No. 13 (2002), 671-686; Toh Mun Heng and Vasudevan Gayathri, "Impact of Regional Trade Liberalization on Emerging Economies: The Case of Vietnam," *ASEAN Economic Bulletin* vol. 21, no.2 (August 2004), 167-182; Ibrahim, Meily Ika Permata, and Wahyu Ari Wibowo, "The Impact of ACFTA Implementation on International Trade of Indonesia," Bank of Indonesia *Bulletin of Monetary Economics and Banking* vol. 13, no. 1 (July 2010), 23-74; Csilla Lakatos and Terrie Walmsley, "Investment Creation and Diversion Effects of the ASEAN-China Free Trade Agreement," *Economic Modelling*, No. 29 (2012), 766-779; Donghyun Park, Innwon Park, and Gemma Esther B. Estrada, "Prospects of an ASEAN-People's Republic of China Free Trade Area: A Qualitative and Quantitative Analysis," *Asian Development Bank Economic Working Paper Series*, No. 130 (October 2008), 1-17; Yu Sheng, Hsiao Chink Tang, and Xinpeng Xu, "The Impact of the ACFTA on People's Republic of China-ASEAN Trade: Estimates Based on an Extended Gravity Model for Component Trade," *Asian Development Bank Working Paper Series on Regional Integration*, No. 99 (July 2012), 1-38; Sasatra Sudsawasd and Prasopchoke Mongsawad, "Go with the Gang, ASEAN!," *ASEAN Economic Bulletin vol.* 24, no. 3 (December 2007), 339-56; Tavi Supriana, "Indonesia Trade Under China Free Trade Area," *Economic Journal of Emerging Markets,* vol. 3, no. 2 (August 2011), 139-151; Marinos Tsigas and Zhi Wang, "A General Equilibrium Analysis of the China-ASEAN Free Trade Agreement," submitted for presentation at the 13th Annual Conference on Global Economic Analysis (June 2010), 1-12; Jun Yang and Chunlai Chen, "The Economic Impact of the ASEAN-China Free Trade Area: A Computational Analysis with Special Emphasis on Agriculture," from *Agriculture and Food Security in China: What Effect WTO Accession and Regional Trade Agreements?* (Canberra: 2008), 372-407; Chia Siow Yue, "ASEAN-China Free Trade Area," Paper for presentation at the AEP Conference (April 12-13, 2004); Longyue Zhao, Mariem Malouche, and Richard Newfarmer, "China's Emerging Regional Trade Policy," *Journal of Chinese Economic and Foreign Trade Studies* vol. 1, no. 1 (2008), 21- 35.

End Notes for Appendix II

[1] In this report, "goods for industrial use" refers to goods used in producing other goods and includes capital and intermediate goods. We used the United Nations Statistics Division's Broad Economic Categories to classify U.S. and Chinese total trade in goods as "capital," "intermediate," "consumer," or "unclassified." According to the Organisation for Economic Co-operation and Development (OECD), an intermediate good is an input to the production process that has itself been produced and, unlike capital, is used up in production.

According to the OECD, an intermediate good is an input to the production process that has itself been produced and, unlike capital, is used up or transformed in production. Examples of intermediate goods include electronic components used in manufacturing computers. Capital goods include, for example, construction or mining equipment. Consumer goods are goods used without further transformation for the satisfaction of needs or wants. Some goods, such as passenger motorcars, may be used for production or as consumer goods, and we have therefore categorized them as "unclassified."

[2] The U.S. Census Bureau suppresses data that further disaggregate this export.

End Note for Appendix III

[1] From 2003 through 2005, transportation became the largest share of U.S. exports to Vietnam mostly because of exports related to the sale of aircraft.

End Notes for Appendix IV

[1] MCC is a U.S. government corporation that seeks to reduce global poverty through economic growth. MCC's compact with Indonesia entered into force in April 2013.

[2] Specifically, the project is intended to help the government of Indonesia achieve significant government expenditure savings on procured goods and services, while assuring their quality satisfies the public need, and to achieve the delivery of public services as planned. The compact's third project, the Community-Based Health and Nutrition to Reduce Stunting Project, is designed to, among other things, reduce and prevent low birth weight, childhood stunting and malnourishment, and increase household income through cost savings, productivity growth, and higher lifetime earnings.

[3] The Secretaries of Treasury, State, and Education also serve, along with four members of Congress and presidential appointees, on the board of the Vietnam Education Foundation. The Foundation is an independent agency created by the Congress with an annual budget of $5 million until 2018. The Foundation provides opportunities for Vietnamese nationals to pursue graduate and post-graduate studies in science, technology, engineering, mathematics, and medicine in the United States, and for American citizens to teach in the same fields of study in Vietnam.

INDEX

C

E

F

J

K

L

M

N

O

P

Q

R

S

T

U